ACKNOWLEDGEMENTS

It has been an absolute pleasure to work with Michael Nolan (again!) and his team at Peachpit. Margaret Anderson probably read this manuscript more times than I did. Thank you to Gretchen Dykstra, Mimi Heft, Becky Winter, Danielle Foster, Jackie Hill, Jack Lewis, and Glenn Bisignani.

I am grateful for my supportive colleagues in the Department of Communications at California State University, Fullerton. A special thank you must be expressed toward those students who used this book in draft format as we worked the kinks out of exercises that appear in each chapter. Savannah Leigh Steele reviewed nearly all of the exercises and was a lifesaver during the writing process.

Thank you, always, to Christopher James at The Art Institute of Boston at Lesley University for showing me what a passion for photography and visual communication looks like.

This book includes a lot of images of works of art that could easily result in a great amount of permissions expenses. Nearly all of the images in the text were donated. (I paid a grand total of $50 in image permissions for the entire book.) Dear artist and designer contributors, I am forever grateful for your willingness to have your works printed without the fees that often accompany image permissions.

Finally, I have much gratitude for the ongoing support that my friends and family provide: Emily Erickson, Laurie Cella, Lucy HG Solomon, Crystal Adams, Lauren Thompson, Sasha Papovich, Henry Puente, and, of course, mom and dad. Paul Lester, you continue to teach me with an open mind and an open heart. Thank you.

CONTENTS

£34.99

FOUNDATIONS of
DIGITAL ART and DESIGN

with ADOBE® CREATIVE CLOUD

xtine burrough

New
Riders

VOICES THAT MATTER™

*For Parker and Martin, born 2/22/13 when this manuscript was
one chapter shy of completion*

FOUNDATIONS OF DIGITAL ART AND DESIGN WITH ADOBE® CREATIVE CLOUD
xtine burrough

New Riders
www.newriders.com

To report errors, please send a note to errata@peachpit.com

New Riders is an imprint of Peachpit, a division of Pearson Education.

Copyright © 2014 by xtine burrough

Project Editor: Michael J. Nolan
Development Editor: Margaret S. Anderson/Stellarvisions
Production Editor: Rebecca Winter
Copyeditor: Gretchen Dykstra
Indexer: Jack Lewis
Proofreader: Marta Justak
Cover Designer: Mimi Heft
Interior Designer: Mimi Heft
Compositor: Danielle Foster

ISBN 13: 978-0-321-90637-3
ISBN 10:   0-321-90637-3

9 8 7 6 5 4 3 2 1

Printed and bound in the United States of America

**BONUS CHAPTERS AVAILABLE IN DIGITAL BOOKS AND ONLINE FROM
WWW.DIGITALART-DESIGN.COM OR PEACHPIT.COM**

INTRODUCTION

WHAT ARE THE FOUNDATIONS OF DIGITAL ART AND DESIGN?

I teach in a university communications department. Most of my students have little time in their schedules for classes that would heighten their understanding of visual communication: foundations of two-dimensional design, typography, drawing, and so on. Instead, they enroll in a survey course, Visual Communication, which seats more than 200. Some of them sign up for an elective "skills" course to learn how to use the Adobe Creative Suite (or at least part of it). Obviously, mastery doesn't happen in a single course. At best, the skills course creates awareness of the concepts and techniques that someone entering the creative professional industries should master. (Of course, I advise students to follow up with related coursework to deepen their knowledge of the craft.)

First developed to serve these students, this book is now used by readers and educators in two-year and four-year fine arts and applied arts programs, college-level communications and media departments, and U.S. high schools. With all of this in mind, the aim of this book is to offer the most information at the confluence of media design (principles, histories, and theories) and software (namely, Adobe) for a wide variety of readers, educators, and practitioners. My goal is to be thorough enough for university students and clear enough for high school students.

The majority of my students are interested in practicing the exercises and mastering the software, because they're anxious to jump in and create. However, the majority of educators I know are interested in teaching art and design, because they're passionate not about software, but about media art or graphic design, digital video, and so on.

My approach to mediating this clash of interests is to write (or lecture) about and show as many ideas and examples of art and design history and principles as I can *while* demonstrating the use of the tools. For example, instead of showing students how to remove red-eye from a photograph (there are loads of videos on YouTube for such a specific endeavor), I demonstrate making a conscious design choice in regard to scale, proximity, the rule of thirds, or other principles while using the same tools. I've tried to keep the exercises short, while also showing the fundamental tools in many of the Adobe programs. Most of the tools have changed very little since the first time I used Photoshop in 1992 (with the major exception of the development of layers in 1994, but I digress).

Since my students don't typically take a course in two-dimensional design, I start in Section 1, *Bits, Pixels, Vectors, and Design*, with material that's been presented by the authors and artists on whose shoulders I'm crouching: Donis A. Dondis (*A Primer of Visual Literacy*), Johannes Itten (*Design and Form: The Basic Course at the Bauhaus and Later*), David A. Lauer and Stephen Pentak (*Design Basics*), Wucius Wong (*Principles of Form and Design*), and others. It is this understanding of the language of design that I consider foundational. I also include examples of each principle or basic element drawn from contemporary works of digital art. While this book may be assigned in a graphic design program, it's often read within the broader context of digital art. Though I'm an education advisor on the AIGA Orange County board, my personal identity as a digital artist is also part of this equation.

Two-dimensional design is followed by Section 2, *Digital Photography*. In the classroom, I find it easier to present basic vector graphics before introducing the pixel-loaded arena of digital imaging—Illustrator is often a much more forgiving application than Photoshop due to the insignificance at such a basic level of file resolution. In this text, photography is primarily considered to be another vehicle through which the basic elements of design can be understood.

Since photo manipulation is nearly as old as the medium itself, the natural follow-up to photography is Section 3, *Digital Manipulation and ~~Free~~ Fair Use*—where better to talk about contrast through juxtaposition?

Section 4, *Typography,* teaches students to honor and manipulate type. This is essential, as most visual communication comprises type and image, and occasionally time. I studied photography in my undergraduate days at the Art Institute of Boston; typography is an art that I learned during my professional life as a web designer in the 1990s and since then as an instructor. It helped that I lived with one of the best typographic educators in Southern California in the early 2000s. I've talked with many educators who are strong in one area—photography, typography, web design, or something else—but feel a deficit in another. As such I provide resources for additional materials throughout the book, both for students and educators who might be using this text in a classroom.

The Coda, at the end of the book, explains the important concept of revision. A student may assume that she has an experiential understanding of design principles after simply following the steps in a software application. Students and readers must remember that reading a book on learning to play the guitar is not the same as mastering the instrument. Practice, and of course revision, is the best way to learn the craft and become more efficient. I've included revision stories from artists and design professionals alike.

In addition, you'll find two bonus sections online or in the electronic version of this book:

Section 5, *The Web,* touches just the tip of the interactive iceberg. I rarely reach this section of the text in my own foundations class, but I've received feedback from educators who used my prior coauthored publication (*Digital Foundations)* that the chapters are helpful in a variety of courses. I dropped the Flash chapters because the advent of HTML5 and the lack of support for the Flash player on touchpad devices has cornered the program into more of a niche than fits the foundation-level aim of this text.

Automation is key to working efficiently, so one chapter in Section 6, *Effective Work Habits,* available online is dedicated to it. The other chapter addresses the question, "How do you suggest I make a portfolio I can send someone?" There's no one perfect answer, as each student has different talents and different needs. But learning pagination in InDesign can help students who want to create their own books—a handy thing for soon-to-be graduates or those applying for internships. Lastly, I would like to offer an update of Dondis's scale that registers the differences (or similarities) among specific artistic media on a continuum of "fine" and "applied" art in **FIGURE I.1**. To demonstrate that the Bauhaus "would group any and all of the fine and applied arts on one central point in the continuum" [1], Dondis placed the media of the time grouped around a central point on the horizontal axis (Figure I.1). All forms of visual

REFERENCE [1] Donis A. Dondis, *Primer of Visual Literacy* (Cambridge, MA: MIT Press, 1973). pg. 4.

FIGURE I.1 Donis A. Dondis developed the original illustration in reference to the perceived intellectual divide between the two purposes, outcomes, or beliefs about art making. (The image is essentially the same, where the labels would have been the text that appears here with a strike through it.)

message-making are influenced and analyzed by an understanding of the basic elements of design, on the screen, in print, as a hologram, or however else they may come to us on future platforms. Whether you intend to be a web designer, a social media entrepreneur, a digital installation artist, or a digitally inspired printmaker, the design foundations offered in this book—coupled with the exercises in each of the software applications—will help you achieve your goals.

Since all students or readers will have different hardware, software, and needs, you'll learn to use this book in the most fitting way for your setup in the following exercises.

OPERATING SYSTEMS

When the Mac was released in 1984, it included a graphical user interface and a mouse, two visual user-oriented components that were missing from other personal computers (**FIGURE I.2**). Artists and designers developed a strong loyalty to Apple over time as their needs and concerns were often met first on the Apple platform. For a while, there was no question about which platform was best suited to making art on the computer: Mac. Universities now have Mac labs dedicated to art and design programs. And in these industries, Mac is still the standard platform. However, multimedia and web designers often work on Windows machines because they need to see what their work will look like in the environment common to most of their users.

Today, it really doesn't matter if you use a Mac or a PC. Your files will transfer easily from one machine to the other. (Be sure to include the file extensions in the name of your file—something you'll learn more about in Chapter 1, *The Dot, the Path, and the Pixel*). If you're creating multimedia art or designs, you'll want to view the work on both platforms. However, this should not dictate where you conceive and develop the project.

Since most schools, colleges, and universities offer digital art and design classes on the Mac platform, I've written this book for the Mac operating system. The screenshots were made on my MacBook Pro. If you're using a PC, you'll simply need to translate the following keys as you follow the exercises in this book:

FIGURE I.2 The first Mac computer sold commercially in 1984. It included a mouse and a graphical user interface instead of the ever-intimidating command line.

- On a PC, the Control key is used where the Command key (⌘) is indicated for Mac users.

- On a PC, the Alt key is used where the Option key is indicated for Mac users.

That's it. The rest is more or less the same.

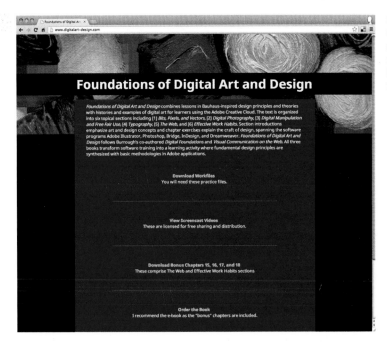

FIGURE I.3 A screenshot of the companion website, www.digitalart-design.com. You can download any necessary work files from this site before beginning exercises in most of the chapters.

DOWNLOADING WORK FILES

Some of the exercises in this book will require you to download a work file or a set of files before you begin. All of the files are on the companion website I've created for readers of *Foundations of Digital Art and Design*, www.digitalart-design.com (**FIGURE I.3**). I've also posted a link to the work files on my personal website (www.missconceptions.net), and there's a Facebook page for *Foundations of Digital Art and Design* where I'll post updates and answer reader questions (www.facebook.com/ FoundationsOfDigitalArtAndDesign).

CREATIVE COMMONS

Many of the images in this book were donated by artists and designers. Some were available for me to use in a commercial publication because the copyright had expired, or because the work was part of a government archive, which usually puts it into the public domain, or because the artist(s) who created the work used a Creative Commons (CC) license in lieu of a traditional copyright. To those who donated or published with CC licenses: thank you!

You'll learn more about the copyleft movement and creative licensing techniques in the introduction to Section 3, *Digital Manipulation and ~~Free~~ Fair Use.*

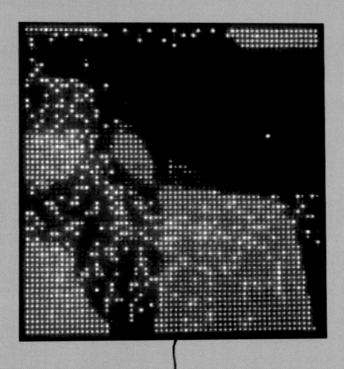

FIGURE S1-01 Leo Villareal often incorporates LEDs, custom circuitry, and a microcontroller in his light installations (http://youtu.be/Jxjhki-s3V8).

SECTION 1

BITS, PIXELS, VECTORS, AND DESIGN

IN 1995, Nicholas Negroponte wrote *Being Digital*, a book that would become a classic among digital art, media, and lifestyle enthusiasts. While resurrecting a text as seemingly outdated as Negroponte's digital hit may seem like the equivalent of starting this book with pictures of cave drawings, reflecting on the work from a vantage point of more than 15 years reveals Negroponte to be a true visionary. He wrote the manuscript long before iTunes, Napster, MySpace, Facebook, eBay, cell phones (at least in the United States), and other common digital phenomena. Yet his predictions included developments similar to the iPhone's Siri, holographic imaging like that found in augmented reality, "high touch computing" where the interface common to the iPad was once considered the "dark horse in graphic input" [1], videocassette rental stores going out of business by 2010, streaming video on the web (hello, YouTube, Vimeo, Netflix, Hulu, and others), the end of getting lost thanks to what we commonly refer to as GPS (global positioning systems), and more.

REFERENCE [1] Nicholas Negroponte, *Being Digital* (New York: Vintage, 1996). pg. 131.

REFERENCE [2] *Ibid.,* pg. 229.

Being digital, Negroponte wrote, "has four very powerful qualities that will result in its ultimate triumph: decentralizing, globalizing, harmonizing, and empowering" [2]. These qualities are present in many of the works of art and design presented in this book. We'll investigate the decentralized nature of the internet in Section 5, *The Web*, and the globalized economy and automated processes inherent to digital applications in Section 6, *Effective Work Habits*. You'll learn about harmony as a design strategy, but see it applied in many examples that utilize social media or require participation. Completing the exercises in this book will give you the knowledge of digital tools necessary to communicate effectively in a networked mediascape.

Digital technologies let us participate in realities beyond the physical world: virtual reality, augmented reality, screen spaces such as video games and the internet, and so on. However, our understanding of these digital spaces is predicated on human perception, which is in turn guided by visual cues. While a digital artist might create media to develop an augmented reality educational game such as *Oyster City* (FIGURES S1.2 AND S1.3), a graphic designer might create media to communicate a concept in the physical world. Both artists and designers rely on their knowledge of human perception to develop effective visual messages.

Visual images created on a computer are developed either as a sampled set of pixels or as vector coordinates. The pixel, developed at Xerox's PARC in the mid-1960s, was initially:

REFERENCE [3] *Ibid.,* pg. 105.

a shape-oriented approach to computer graphics in which amorphous areas were handled and textured by storing and displaying images as a massive collection of dots [3].

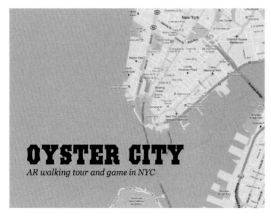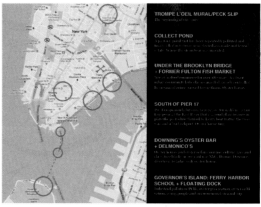

FIGURE S1.2 Title slide and overview of sites in *Oyster City*, an augmented reality game and walking tour by Meredith Drum, Rachel Stevens, and Phoenix Toews (oystercity.org).

FIGURE S1.3 Panoramic view (top), East River view (lower left), and user interaction (lower right) in *Oyster City*.

The dot is the most primary visual element. It is the simplest way to point to the existence of something. A dot is either present or not. Place a single black dot in a field of white, and you'll be quick to judge which is the figure (or the positive space) and which is the ground (or the negative space), as in Leo Villareal's light installations (see **FIGURE S1.1** at the beginning of this section). It's no wonder that the dot was the go-to method of image creation in the earliest computer graphics. In the Huffington Post, Villareal wrote, "I am interested in lowest common denominators such as pixels or the zeros and ones in binary code" [4].

Coincidentally, the dot has been used as a primary method of mark making throughout the history of art. Leo Villareal's digital work references pointillism seen in neoimpressionist paintings of the 1880s by Georges Seurat, Paul Signac, and others (**FIGURE S1.4**). The digital halftone also makes use of the illusory effects of placing small dots of color near enough to one another to express a photorealistic image.

REFERENCE [4] See www.huffingtonpost.com/leo-villareal/the-essence-of-light-thir_b_720351.html#141416

Listen to (or read) "One Dot at a Time, Lichtenstein Made Art Pop," Susan Stamberg's excellent review of Roy Lichtenstein's retrospective at the National Gallery of Art in Washington, DC, on NPR.org (www.npr.org/2012/10/15/162807890/one-dot-at-a-time-lichtenstein-made-art-pop).

FIGURE S1.4 This detail of Georges Seurat's *La Parade* (1889) demonstrates the painter's pointillist technique. Seurat created the work by dabbing dots onto the canvas in close proximity.

In the exercises for Chapter 1, you'll develop a figure/ground study with black dots on a white background. Your digital composition will reference late nineteenth century pointillist paintings and the expression of digital technologies in code as "on" or "off" (ones or zeroes, true or false, present or missing, and so on).

REFERENCE [5] *Sketchpad* is discussed in Negroponte's book on page 103. To see a demonstration of *Sketchpad*, visit http://youtu.be/mOZqRJzE8xg.

In 1963, before the invention of the pixel, Ivan Sutherland developed Sketchpad [5]. Users could draw lines with a "light pen," but the challenge of real-time computation and photorealistic rendering hindered Sutherland and other programmers from further developing his concept. The pixel (a term derived from the words *picture* and *element*) is to Sketchpad what the dot is to the line. Why compute an entire line when two dots could be used to establish its starting and ending points?

In the exercises for Chapter 2, you'll learn to "see" the lines in a photograph. You'll trace the lines in the image to convert a detailed, photographic picture into a line drawing with a similar composition.

Of course, lines have visual qualities in addition to a beginning and an end. A line has a defined weight or thickness (also called a *stroke* in Adobe applications). It may be drawn tightly (a perfectly straight line, achieved in Adobe applications by holding the Shift key as you draw) or loosely and expressively to suggest a hand-drawn artifact.

A basic unit of computing is a bit, or as Negroponte refers to it, "the smallest atomic element in the DNA of information. It is the state of being: on or off, true or false, up or down, in or out, black or white." Bits combine together to form a signal (visual, auditory, tactile, and so on). In the realm of design, lines are often viewed as contoured edges that surround shapes. An infinite number of forms can be made by combining any or all of the three basic shapes: the circle, the square, and the triangle. These shapes can be understood, to use Negroponte's metaphor, as the smallest element in the DNA of image construction [6].

REFERENCE [6] Negroponte, pg. 14.

DRAWING, LITERALLY, WITH A MOUSE

Joseph DeLappe's *The Artist's Mouse* (**FIGURE S1.5**) cleverly—and literally—traces mouse movements while "the artist" uses the contraption. DeLappe's project is an analog response to one of the earliest digital interface challenges: how to track the cursor's position on the screen.

By completing the exercises in Chapter 3, you'll learn to combine the basic shapes—the circle, the triangle, and the square—into complex icons. This activity provides a lesson in design and abstraction, as well as a way to understand computing processes. When simple elements are combined, the new combination can be exponentially more complex.

FIGURE S1.5 *The Artist's Mouse* (1998) by Joseph DeLappe.

In the first three chapters of this book, you'll work with the foundational elements of design—the dot, the line, and the three basic shapes—and you'll be encouraged to think about the relationship between these design elements and computing technologies. The dot is analogous to the bit, the vector line is created in Adobe Illustrator as a path between two dots, and basic shapes can be combined to form an infinite number of complex forms. Negroponte understood that "computing is not about computers anymore. It is about living" [7]. Artists and designers are essentially developers of the way we live—somewhere between the analog and virtual worlds, and the way we create meaning for such a visual landscape.

REFERENCE [7] *Ibid.,* pg. 6.

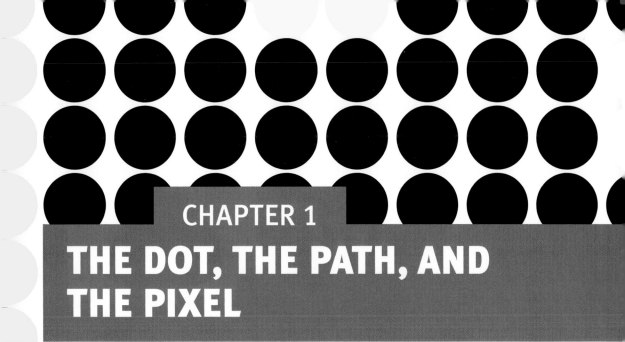

CHAPTER 1
THE DOT, THE PATH, AND THE PIXEL

THE EXERCISES IN this chapter show you how to create and manipulate dots and make meaning with basic design elements. Remember the observation we made in the introduction: when you place a single black dot in a field of white, you can quickly judge which is the figure (or the positive space) and which is the ground (or the negative space). A group of same-shaped circles creates a repeated pattern of dots. You read this pattern as one giant shape that dominates the composition. The pattern of black dots that you create becomes the foreground while the white space is understood as the background (**FIGURE 1.1**).

The division between the foreground and background or the figure and ground is a visual tool that can be used to manipulate a viewer's perception. When it's difficult to distinguish between the figure and the ground, a viewer may have trouble deciphering the message. Messages may imply unintended meanings due to an unexpected shift of the figure and ground. Gestalt psychology, which studies human perception, has provided artists and designers with a set of laws and properties that are incredibly useful for predicting how a viewer

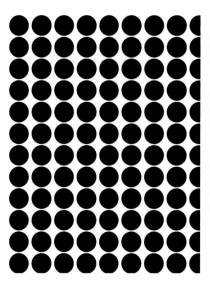

FIGURE 1.1 A pattern created by repetitive black dots is read as the foreground on a white background in this composition.

FIGURE 1.2 Rubin's vase was developed in 1915 by Danish psychologist Edgar Rubin to demonstrate the instability of a figure and ground relationship. Images such as this are often used as examples of the property of instability in Gestalt psychology.

will interact with or perceive a visual work. *Multistability* is a Gestalt property that accounts for the shifting nature of figure and ground elements. Rubin's vase, developed by psychologist Edgar Rubin in 1915, is often used in the classroom as a visual demonstration of multistability (**FIGURE 1.2**), where the viewers can possibly see two dominant images at once if they are able to inverse the relationship between the figure and ground.

Once a pattern of dots is placed on a contrasting background, a new focal point can be made within the pattern by deleting a selection of dots. Those that are dismissed reveal the ground, which becomes dominant—if its shape is recognizable. While the following exercises may seem abstract and elementary, you'll begin to notice that these basic techniques are commonly in play in digital art and design. For instance, Leo Villareal's light installations (see the introduction to this section) are visually translated as a series of repetitions of the activity: "create the dot pattern, then remove some dots." Roe, a fish marketplace and restaurant in Long Beach, California, sports a simple logo featuring the letter "r" missing from a pattern of various sized dots (in orange, representing the hard roe you might see atop an order of sushi) set in a circular pattern (**FIGURE 1.3**). In *Gyre II* (2011), Chris Jordan re-creates Vincent van Gogh's *The Starry Night* (1889) using 50,000 cigarette lighters, equal to the estimated number of pieces of floating plastic found in every square mile in the world's oceans (**FIGURE 1.4**).

The exercises in this chapter will show you how to use the Ellipse tool in Adobe Illustrator to create a series of dots that form a pattern. Then you'll experiment with removing dots to invert the figure/ground relationship. Before we begin, it's important to understand how the software interprets your commands.

FIGURE 1.3 Logo design for Roe, a restaurant in Long Beach, California.

FIGURE 1.4 In *Gyre II* (2011), Chris Jordan re-creates Vincent van Gogh's *The Starry Night* (1889) using 50,000 cigarette lighters, equal to the estimated number of pieces of floating plastic found in every square mile in the world's oceans. © Chris Jordan, 44 by 56 inches and 60 by 76 inches.

PATHS AND VECTOR GRAPHICS

Illustrator is primarily a vector graphic application. When you draw a circle with the Ellipse tool, you're instructing Illustrator to create an anchor point on each of the four "sides" of the circle: think of a circle as the face of a clock, with anchor points at the hours of 12, 3, 6, and 9. These anchor points hold mathematical coordinates that have a relationship to one another (FIGURE 1.5). When you scale the circle, you're simply multiplying the coordinates by a common factor. Vector graphics are smooth, scalable, and plotted by anchor points.

PIXELS AND BITMAP GRAPHICS

In contrast, Adobe Photoshop is primarily a bitmap application. When you draw a circle or even paint a dot with the Brush tool, you're instructing Photoshop to create pixels. Each pixel contains one unit of color. If you zoom in close enough, you can actually see the pixels that make up a bitmap image (FIGURE 1.6). Pixels are finite. They can't be scaled by a common factor, so file size and resolution are extremely important. (You'll learn more about these topics in Chapter 5, *Resolution and Value*.)

FIGURE 1.5 Anchor points are visible in the edges, or contours, of this circle. The blue square at 3 o'clock (where the mouse is pointing) is a selected anchor, while the white squares at the 12, 6, and 9 o'clock positions are unselected.

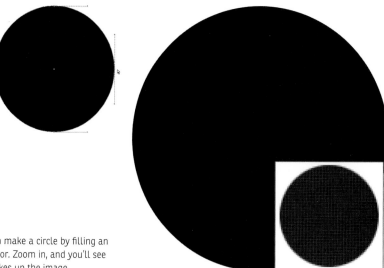

FIGURE 1.6 In Photoshop, you can make a circle by filling an elliptical selection with black color. Zoom in, and you'll see each black, square pixel that makes up the image.

WHAT YOU'LL NEED

You don't need to download files to complete the exercises in this chapter. You'll simply use your ability to see, think, and perceive.

WHAT YOU'LL MAKE

In the exercises for Chapter 1, you'll develop a figure/ground study with black dots on a white background (FIGURE 1.7). Your digital composition will reference late nineteenth century pointillist paintings (look back to the section opening, FIGURE S1.4) and the expression of digital technologies in code as "on" or "off" (ones or zeroes, true or false, present or missing, and so on).

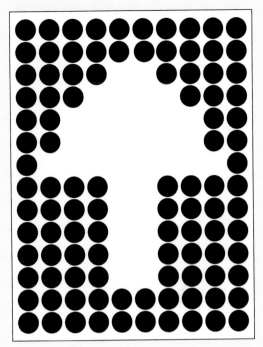

FIGURE 1.7 You'll choose which black dots to remove to make your final composition. Here, the selection of missing dots might represent an arrow.

EXERCISE 1 FILE PRESETS IN ILLUSTRATOR

1. Open Adobe Illustrator. Choose the Window menu > Workspace > Essentials. You can set or reset the workspace at anytime. Reset the workspace by choosing the Window menu > Workspace > Reset (whichever workspace is active). You'll want your workspace to look like mine so the screenshots reflect more closely what is in front of you.

    You'll see a note regarding the workspace used in the remaining chapters at the start of the first exercise.

2. Choose the File menu > New or press **Command(⌘)-N** to create a new document.

3. The Profile menu helps you make decisions about the format of your file. You can change the format, depending on how you want to display the work. Notice that the list of profiles includes print, web, devices, video and film, basic RGB, and Flash builder. Output settings for file resolution, pixel area (width and height), color mode, and more will change for each of those digital (or paper) environments. From the Profile pull-down menu, choose Print to make a sharp print of the file when you're finished (FIGURE 1.8).

    If you notice it, change the units of measurement from points to inches while you're creating the new document. You can always change the units of measurement once you're in the document, too.

FIGURE 1.8 Choose a profile in the New Document dialog window.

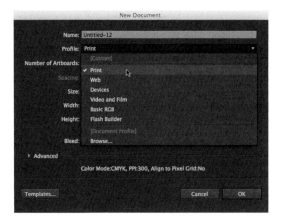

You can also keep media in the gray area to the left or right of the artboard. This comes in handy when there are questionable design elements that you want to keep nearby but aren't yet ready to place on the artboard.

4. The new document appears as a blank white page. In Illustrator, the page is called the *artboard*. Anything you place on the artboard—typography, graphics, or photographs—will print or be exported to a published file.

5. This is as good a time as any to begin saving the file. Choose File > Save As and name the file **chapter01.ai**. Notice that "Adobe Illustrator (ai)" is the first option in the Format pull-down menu. For now, we'll save in this format.

EXERCISE 2 SHAPES, FILLS, AND STROKES

1. Choose the Ellipse tool from the Tools panel on the left side of the application window (**FIGURE 1.9**).

2. Click from tool to tool and notice that whenever you choose a new tool, the Control panel at the top of the application frame displays options specific to that tool (**FIGURE 1.10**). The Ellipse tool is one of several shape tools. It is used to draw a shape. As you'll see in the next step, shapes are made of a fill color and an outline, called a *stroke*. The Ellipse tool options include pull-down menus for fill and stroke colors, the weight of the stroke, and more.

FIGURE 1.9 Load the Ellipse tool from the Tools panel. Notice that this tool "hides" or is packaged behind the Rectangle tool.

FIGURE 1.10 Set the Stroke or other tool options in the Control panel at the top of the application window.

3. Click and drag with the Ellipse tool on the artboard. As you drag the mouse away from the starting point (where you clicked), the ellipse grows. As you drag the mouse back toward where you initially clicked, the ellipse shrinks. Do this a few times to master the movement of drawing an ellipse on the artboard. After you've practiced making several ellipses, you'll delete all of them. Choose the Selection tool—the first arrow in the Tools panel (**FIGURE 1.11**).

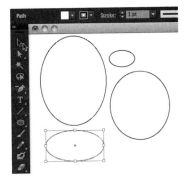

FIGURE 1.11 Four ellipses were drawn. The object remains selected when you let go of the mouse, until you take further action. Clicking anywhere outside of it on the artboard will deselect the shape.

4. The Selection tool is used to choose objects for the purpose of copying, moving, rotating, scaling, deleting, applying effects, and so on. Click on one of the ellipses to select it; then press the Delete key on your keypad. To select all the ellipses (so you can delete all of them at once), click anywhere outside one of the ellipses that's outside the group (**FIGURE 1.12**) and drag the Selection tool over all the shapes (**FIGURE 1.13**). This is called *marqueeing*. When you're finished, all the ellipses will be selected, made visible by a blue path around each shape and identifiable anchor points (**FIGURE 1.14**). If you didn't quite pick up every shape, click anywhere on the artboard to deselect and marquee over all the shapes again. Press the Delete key to remove all the shapes.

WATCH OUT! The default stroke and fill values are black and white, but if you're working in a shared computer lab, you never know what those settings might include. If you made ellipses that have no assigned fill color, you'll be able to select the shapes only by clicking directly on their contours (or outlines).

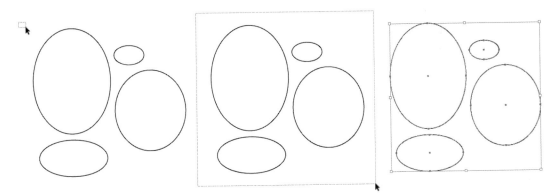

FIGURES 1.12, 1.13, AND 1.14 To *marquee* over a group of paths, first load the Selection tool. Click and drag it from the empty artboard to make a box around all the items you intend to select. Release the mouse and notice whether all elements are selected. If they're not, click on an empty area of the artboard to deselect and try it again.

Why use Shift? The Shift key is commonly used in Adobe applications to constrain the proportions of shapes and images, or to constrain mouse m□ovements. You'll often use the Shift key while using Illustrator shape tools, Photoshop marquee tools, and Photoshop Free Transform, among others. In key combinations, ⇧ stands for the Shift key.

5. Choose the Ellipse tool again. This time hold the Shift key while you draw a new shape to constrain its proportions. Instead of drawing an ellipse, draw a circle (**FIGURE 1.15**).

6. Click back on the Selection tool. With the circle selected, you can now change its properties. The circle is defined in Illustrator as a *path*. The path is governed by a set of anchor points. These anchor points define the edges of the path, which are the stroke surrounding the circumference of the circle and the area inside the shape, or the fill. The stroke and the fill each contain information such as transparency or opacity, hue, saturation and brightness, and weight (or the value of the stroke). With the circle selected, look at the bottom of the Tools panel, and you'll see an icon for the fill and stroke. In my document (**FIGURE 1.16**), the stroke is on top, and the fill is on the bottom.

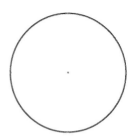

FIGURE 1.15 Draw a circle with the Ellipse tool by holding the Shift key while dragging the mouse. The Shift key will keep the proportions constrained—this key command can be used with the Rectangle tool, for instance, to draw a square.

You'll find yourself toggling between different tools and the Selection tool as you work in Illustrator. This toggling is so common that you can use the Command key on a Mac (or the Control key on a PC) to activate the Selection tool from any of the Shape tools.

7. Click on the Fill or Stroke icon to move it to the front. Don't click the curvy arrow above the two icons. (Doing this will swap the fill and stroke values, which can be confusing when you're learning to master this area of the Tools panel.) With the stroke in front and the circle still selected, choose the button with a red slash to set the stroke to none, or turn off the outline (**FIGURE 1.17**).

FIGURE 1.16 The Fill and Stroke icons are near the bottom of the Tools panel. In this screen capture, the Stroke icon is on top of the Fill icon. You can click directly on the Fill icon to swap its position with the Stroke icon.

FIGURE 1.17 Beneath the Fill and Stroke icons are three buttons directly related to fill and stroke. The first applies a color in a selected path's fill or stroke (whichever is on top in the Tools panel), the second applies a gradient, and the third sets the fill or stroke value to none. This essentially renders the fill or stroke invisible.

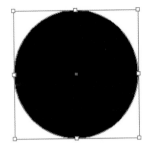

FIGURE 1.18 Open the Color panel from the set of icons in the panel bar on the right side of the application window.

FIGURE 1.19 Fill a path with black using the quick button in the Color panel.

8. While the circle is still selected, click the Fill icon to bring it to the front. The Color panel will probably expand on the right side of the application window if it isn't already showing. If you don't see it, you can press the Color panel button (FIGURE 1.18) or choose Window > Color. Click on the black color chip in the Color panel to fill the circle with black (FIGURE 1.19).

EXERCISE 3 FIGURE AND GROUND WITH REPEATED DOTS

There are various techniques for creating a pattern of black dots (or circles) on the artboard in Illustrator. For instance, you can copy, paste, and move a single dot repeatedly to create a line of dots and then copy that line and paste it repeatedly. Or, you can define a brush with the dot as a pattern and "paint" the line of dots. There are probably other methods as well. Your way of creating digital media will be different from anyone else's, which is one of the reasons the applications are so robust and can be overwhelming to learn. In this exercise, you'll copy, paste, and move a single dot, because it's essential that you feel comfortable performing this action. Copy, paste, and move are three common commands; they are performed similarly in most Adobe applications.

1. Choose the Selection tool and click on the circle to select or activate it. Press and hold the Option key while you click and drag the circle to another position on the artboard, being sure to release the mouse before you release the Option key with your non-mouse hand. This is the swiftest way to make a copy of a path. Delete the new circle, as you'll perform this activity again with an additional key. (See Step 4 in Exercise 2 for a refresher on selecting and deleting.) Once again, press and hold the Option key *and* press and hold the Shift key (that's two keys with your non-mouse hand); then click and drag the circle to a new position on the artboard (FIGURE 1.20). Release the mouse before you release the keys. You'll notice that your movement is constricted to a 45- or 90-degree increment.

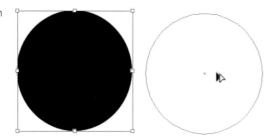

FIGURE 1.20 Hold the Option key while clicking and dragging on a path with the Selection tool to create a copy of it. If you also hold the Shift key **Select tool-Option-⇧**, the copy will move in 45-degree increments.

2. To make a straight line of dots, **Shift-Option-drag** the circle repeatedly across the top of the artboard (**FIGURE 1.21**). Don't worry about the distance between the circles or at the margins. You'll attend to that in the next steps.

When you combine key commands with mouse actions, remember to release the mouse before you release key commands. For instance, when pressing the Shift key to constrict a mouse movement, you should always complete the task, release the mouse first, and then release the Shift key.

3. How many dots did you make? Depending on the size of your original circle, you may have any number of repeated dots (figures) on the white space (ground) of the page. Consider the page of dots as a set of rows and columns. Your goal is to create a grid of 10 columns (the number of horizontal dots) and 14 rows (the number of vertical dots). You'll probably need to scale your dots in order to fit 10 going across the top of the page. The work file documented here has six dots, so you'll need to decrease their scale to fit four more on the page. Whether you need to increase or decrease the size of your dots, follow these same directions: Marquee over all the circles with the Selection tool (Step 4 in Exercise 2). You'll see a box with anchor points surrounding all the circles. Click on one of the four anchors at the corner and hold down the Shift key while moving your mouse toward the circles (to scale down) or away from the circles (to scale up) (**FIGURE 1.22**). You'll have to judge visually how small the circles need to be to fit more or less of them on the page.

4. Use the Selection tool to deselect the group of circles by clicking on an empty part of the artboard. Select the number of circles you need to reach a count of 10 by marqueeing over that number of circles.

   or

FIGURE 1.21 Multiple copies of the dot on the artboard.

FIGURE 1.22 Scale all the dots at once by selecting all of them and then scaling the group using the Selection tool.

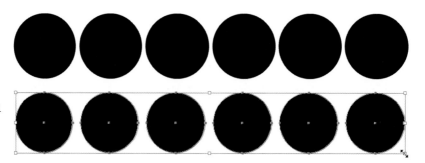

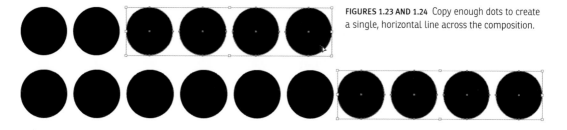

FIGURES 1.23 AND 1.24 Copy enough dots to create a single, horizontal line across the composition.

Click on one circle and press the Shift key while clicking on each of the others (this is called *shift-clicking*). Press the Option and Shift keys again, or ⇧-**Option-click** (FIGURE 1.23), and drag to copy and move the remaining circles on a straight line, filling the space of the page in your first row (FIGURE 1.24).

SCREENCAST 1-1 THE PATTERN BRUSH

See a video demonstrating how to define and apply a pattern brush to the composition. This method is probably easier than what you labored through in Exercise 3, but it's a less essential skill. The repetition you did in Exercise 3 will help you to remember your new skills.

All screencasts are available on the companion website, www.digitalart-design.com or on the YouTube playlist, www.youtube.com/playlist?list=PLAy6P5IoEjy2v3kZKCt8spqJ50nLb2XQI.

 EXERCISE 4

GROUPING AND ALIGNMENT

1. Press ⌘-**A** (**Control-A** on a PC) to select all the dots on the artboard.

2. The dots are probably aligned, since you used the Shift key while copying and moving them. If they're not, press the Vertical Align Top button in the alignment area of the Control panel (FIGURE 1.25). Actually, since all the dots are the same size, you can use any of the vertical alignment buttons (Top, Center, or Bottom). If your circles are like those in Figure 1.25, no changes will take place on the artboard.

TOOL TIPS The Align and Distribute button icons can be difficult to read when you're first learning Illustrator. Hover the cursor over the button to see the Tool Tip, which labels each button. If Tool Tips are not enabled, check the Tool Tips box in General Preferences by choosing Illustrator > General > Preferences (⌘-**K**). This can be useful for any tools you don't recognize.

FIGURE 1.25 Align multiple paths (in this case, dots) by pressing the Vertical Align Top button in the Control panel.

3. The distribution of the dots, that is, the spacing between each dot, is likely to be asynchronous (FIGURE 1.26). While all the circles are still selected, press the Horizontal Distribute Center button in the Control panel. (Use the Tool Tips to help you locate it.)

4. While the dots are selected, use the Left, Right, Up, and Down arrow keys on your keypad to nudge the group of dots into a position on the page where the top, left, and right margins appear to be equally distant from the group of dots (FIGURE 1.27).

5. Select all again (⌘-A), if all the dots aren't already selected, and Choose Object > Group (⌘-G) to group the row of dots. Now the Selection tool will treat all the dots as one unit.

6. **Option-⇧-click** and drag to copy the first row of dots to create a second row (FIGURE 1.28).

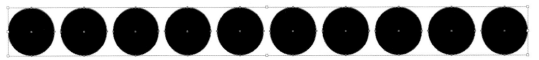

FIGURE 1.26 Notice the differences in the negative space between the selected dots. The negative space is not distributed evenly, which will be easily noticed in repetitive rows.

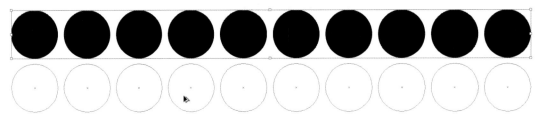

FIGURE 1.27 While all the dots are selected, use the arrow keys to nudge the group up, down, left, or right. Keep an eye on the margins of the page and aim to create equal negative space there.

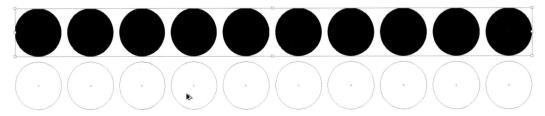

FIGURE 1.28 Use the Selection tool with the Option and Shift keys (**Option-⇧**) to create a copy of the first row of dots.

7. Repeat Step 6 until you have 14 rows of dots on the artboard (**FIGURE 1.29**).

8. Do you need to adjust the alignment or distribution of your grouped rows? If this portion of the Control panel doesn't appear, choose Window > Align. If you do need to redistribute the rows of dots, you'll probably want to use the Vertical Distribute Center button.

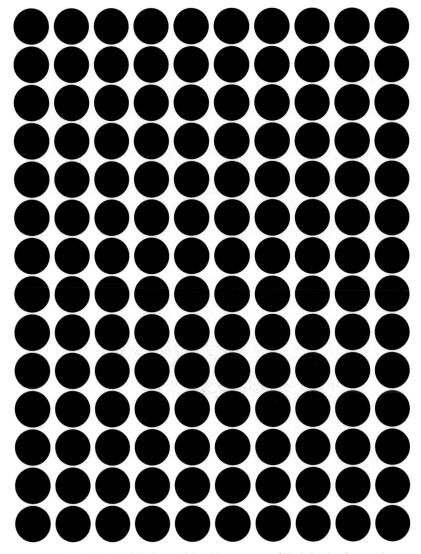

FIGURE 1.29 The artboard is full of rows of dots. Now a pattern of black dots has become the foreground of the compositional space. The background is white. You also might say that the black dots are the figure, and the white space is the ground.

FIGURE 1.30 Various figure/ground studies can be created by deleted black dots from the patterned composition. When the white space begins to look like a familiar graphic icon, the figure and ground relationship will be reversed: the white space becomes the figure, while the black dots are newly understood as the ground.

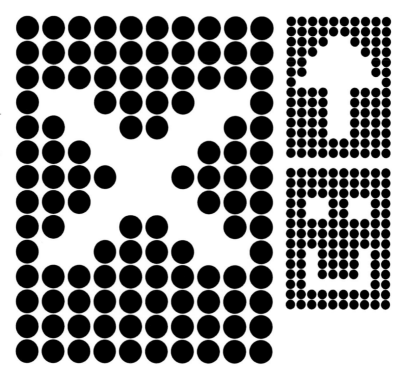

A FIGURE AND GROUND OR "ON" AND "OFF" STUDY

EXERCISE 5

In this exercise, you'll delete some of the dots to make a recognizable form appear in the sea of black dots. The white space (what was the ground) will become the figure as the black dots move to the background (ground). You'll do this with the Selection tool, although later you'll learn how to use the Direct Selection tool to modify parts of paths or just some paths within groups.

1. Press ⌘-**A** to select all.

2. Choose Object > Ungroup (⌘-⇧-**G**) to ungroup all the rows, freeing every dot on the page.

3. Use the Selection tool to select and delete one dot at a time as you create a white form within the pattern of black dots by "turning off" the dots. Try making a letterform, arrow, smiley face (**FIGURE 1.30**), or something else.

 **LAB CHALLENGE**

Express each letter in a word (using a typeface of your choice) with a repeated shape such as a circle, square, or image.

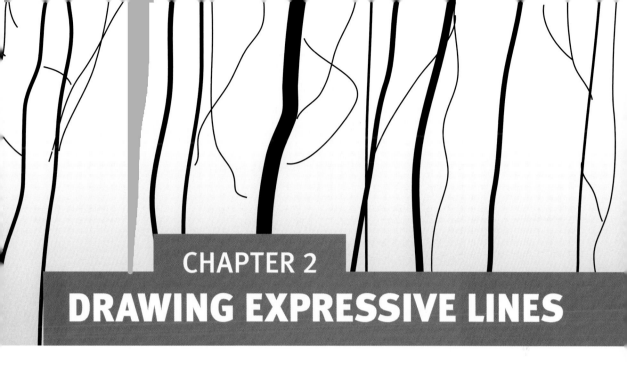

CHAPTER 2
DRAWING EXPRESSIVE LINES

THE EXERCISES IN this chapter encourage you to study line as a design element found in a landscape photograph of trees. The dark lines produced by the bark of the trees are read in stark contrast against a winter sky (FIGURE 2.1). You'll use the Pencil and Brush tools and explore the Gradient and Transparency panels in Adobe Illustrator.

A group of similar lines create a repeated pattern that is easy to read and understand when the weight (or thickness) of the lines is contrasting. Thicker lines will seem to push to the front of the composition, while thinner lines recede into the background. The same is true for dark and light values, respectively. In Chapter 1, *The Dot, the Path, and the Pixel*, we focused on the separation between the foreground and background of the composition space. In this chapter, lines will express the individuality of each tree in the landscape. While foreground and background are less likely to shift in this composition, you'll begin to see how the sizes and values of design elements affect human perception.

REFERENCE [1] Maggie Macnab, *Decoding Design* (Blue Ash, OH: HOW Books, 2008) pg. 62.

Since a line connects two dots, it makes sense to follow a chapter study on dots with one on lines. In her book *Decoding Design*, Maggie Macnab articulates the complexity of the line by referring to the anchor points at each end of the line as a pole. "The poles, while repulsed in their division, are attracted back to one another—the paradox of this principle" [1]. A line can be used to join two elements or to separate parts of a whole (FIGURE 2.2).

A line can be *tight* or *loose*, meaning it can be straight and mechanical or flowing and organic. The plans for an architectural space will be clean and organized. The "hands" of Alicia Eggert and Mike Fleming's *Eternity* clock form a composition of tight, black lines on a contrasting white background (FIGURE 2.3), while flowing water in Colleen Ludwig's *Cutaneous Habitats: Shiver* demonstrates free-form movement (FIGURE 2.4).

FIGURE 2.2 In this March 2007 photograph by Staff Sgt. D. Myles Cullen, members of a Chinese military honor guard march during a welcome ceremony for Chairman of the Joint Chiefs of Staff Marine Gen. Peter Pace at the Ministry of Defense in Beijing, China. Notice how each red flag and its pole divides the rows of marching men. The poles themselves stretch in opposite directions, from the earth toward the sky. At the same time, each row of marching men can be read as a set of vertical and diagonal (their front legs) lines.

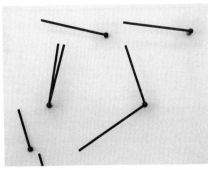

FIGURE 2.3 Alicia Eggert and Mike Fleming, *Eternity*, 78 x 96 x 3 inches, 2010. Electric clocks, acrylic, and power strips. *Eternity* uses the hour and minute hands of 30 electric clocks to spell the word "eternity" once every twelve hours. Photo credit: Mike Fleming.

FIGURE 2.4 Colleen Ludwig, *Shiver* from the series *Cutaneous Habitats*, interactive environment, 2012. *Shiver* integrates programming, electronics, and a recirculating water system into a prefabricated, architectural framework with water-resistant fabric walls. Images courtesy of the artist. Images ©Colleen Ludwig.

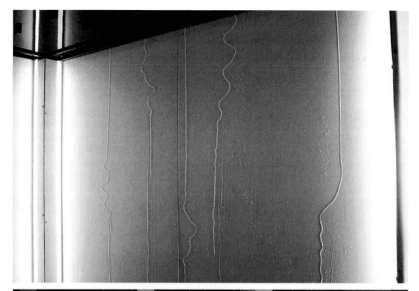

The exercises in this chapter will show you how to create a series of lines using the Pencil and Brush tools. You'll experiment with various strokes (line weights) and values to alter the perception of depth between the foreground and background elements.

SAVING AND SHARING FILES

When you save a file, you have many choices to make. How will you name the file? Are you collaborating with others? If so, will you all adhere to the same naming conventions? What type of file do you want to save? What do you plan to do with the file once it's saved? How you answer these questions will play a role in how you choose to name and save your files. What follows are a few general guidelines that will help you determine how to save and share your files.

File names should be concise, organized, and descriptive. If you're working on a series of files or collaborating with others (for instance, if you're a student submitting a file to an instructor who is in effect "collaborating" with you and all of your peers), you should consider naming all files for one project with a consistent naming convention. File names should not include spaces or foreign characters, and they should always include an extension (for example, .ai, .psd, .jpg, and so on). The file name "My BEST picture ever!!!!!!!" is sloppy—it includes spaces and exclamation points, mixes upper- and lowercase letters, lacks the file extension, and, worst of all, it doesn't describe the content of the image. In my classroom, I ask students to label all files with their first initial dash last name dot file extension, all in lowercase, for example, x-burrough.ai. I insist on file names with all lowercase letters as many of my foundations-level students later enroll in interactive media design classes where lowercase letters are the norm. (It saves time troubleshooting code if you know that the file names don't utilize uppercase letters.)

In addition to how you name your files, you have to consider the saved format. Best practices include always saving the file in its master or native format (for instance, always save an Illustrator file in .ai format). The master file can be edited at any time in the application in which the file was originally developed. In addition, you may want to save a separate file for sharing. The file formats JPG and PDF are often used for sharing photographic images or type and image layouts. These formats may compress the file (which means that some data may be lost), resulting in a smaller file size. Most importantly, viewers don't need Adobe applications in order to open these formats, as all computers can display JPG and PDF files via basic previewing applications, the freely downloadable Adobe Reader application, or even a web browser. It's common to save two versions of the same file: one in the master format (which can be especially useful for later revision) and one in a format conducive to sharing a finished work.

FILE NAMING If an image is saved in two different formats, the files will have different file extensions. Therefore, you can keep the same file name in place, resulting in something like: x-burrough.ai and x-burrough.pdf so it's clear they're the same image.

WHAT YOU'LL NEED

Download the following source materials to complete the exercises in this chapter:

✔ Aleš Jungmann's original photograph (trees.jpg) from the Chapter 2 downloads area on the companion website

You'll also benefit from the ability to see lines in all aspects of the original image.

WHAT YOU'LL MAKE

In the exercises in Chapter 2, you'll create a study of expressive lines by transforming a black-and-white photograph into an abstracted vector illustration (FIGURE 2.5). Your digital composition will consist of a set of loose, hand-drawn lines.

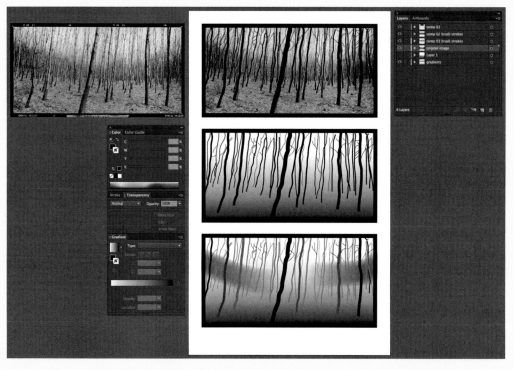

FIGURE 2.5 The final results file for exercises in Chapter 2 includes studies of lines in a black-and-white photograph. Aleš Jungmann's photograph appears courtesy of the artist. It can also be found on Wikimedia Commons, http://commons.wikimedia.org/wiki/File:Ales_jungmann_krajina_1994-1997_8.jpg.

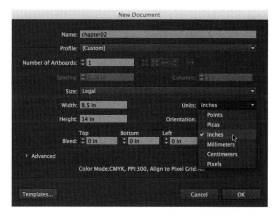

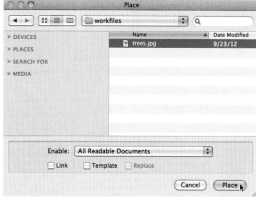

FIGURE 2.6 Start your new document by selecting a profile. When you modify a profile, its submenu is displayed as [Custom].

FIGURE 2.7 Browse for a file and add it to the artboard using File > Place.

 PLACE AND LOCK AN IMAGE

1. Download the original photograph by Aleš Jungmann, **trees.jpg**, and save it in a folder named **chapter02**.

2. Choose File > New and adjust the following settings: use the Print profile, set the paper size to Legal (8.5 by 14 inches), and choose Inches from the Units pull-down menu. Once you alter the profile, the profile will reset to [Custom]. Name the new file **chapter02** (FIGURE 2.6). Press OK.

3. Choose File > Place to add the photograph of trees to the artboard. Browse your computer for the file **trees.jpg** in the **chapter02** folder you created in Step 1 (FIGURE 2.7).

4. The photograph will appear small on the page. Since you'll eventually create your own vector abstraction based on the image, don't worry about file resolution for printing purposes. (This topic is thoroughly investigated in Chapter 5, *Resolution and Value*.) In this situation, it's safe to enlarge

WORKSPACE > ESSENTIALS
Open Illustrator and set the workspace to Essentials by selecting it from the pull-down list in the Application bar or by choosing the Window menu > Workspace > Essentials.

WORKSPACE You can set or reset the workspace at anytime. Reset the workspace by choosing the Window menu > Workspace > Reset (whichever workspace is active). You'll want your workspace to look like mine so the screenshots are more likely to reflect what's in front of you.

LINKS AND TEMPLATES

There are two buttons at the bottom of the Place dialog: Link and Template. If you link images to the Illustrator document, the size of the .ai file remains small because the images are referenced on the computer rather than embedded in the document. However, if you want to view or print the .ai file from another computer, remember to take the image files with you (and if they're not saved in the same relative position to the master file, you may need to relink them). I encourage new students to leave the Link button unchecked and embed images within the file. The Template button will automatically place the image on a locked layer at a reduced opacity.

the photographic image. Use the Selection tool to click on the image and then hold the Shift key while dragging any of the four corners out from the image. Click on the image and drag it to the top of the artboard while keeping an eye on the margin spacing—aim for equal margins on the top, left, and right sides of the image (FIGURE 2.8).

5. You'll be drawing lines on top of the image in the next exercise. If you don't lock the image, you may unintentionally select and move it while you're trying to work. With that in mind, lock the image now in anticipation of the next steps. This is easily accomplished with the Layers panel in Illustrator. Any paths you draw or images you place on the artboard will appear in the Layers panel. Press the Layers button in the Panel menu on the right side of the application window (FIGURE 2.9). The Layers panel will appear.

6. If it's not already expanded, press the sideways arrow next to **Layer 1** to flip it into a downward pointing arrow, revealing content saved on this layer (FIGURE 2.10). The image appears in **Layer 1** as **<Image>**. Press the unlabeled box to the left of **<Image>** to lock it inside **Layer 1** (FIGURE 2.11).

FIGURE 2.8 When the image is in position on the artboard, you'll see equal margin spacing on the top, left, and right sides. There should be plenty of room for you to work toward the bottom of the page.

FIGURE 2.9 The arrow in this image represents the mouse clicking on the button to access the Layers panel. (You can also choose the Window Menu > Layers.) The Layers panel displays paths and images added to the artboard.

FIGURE 2.10 By default, all media is stored in **Layer 1**. Expand and collapse layers by clicking on the arrow to the left of its icon.

FIGURE 2.11 Click on the unlabeled box to the left of a layer to lock it inside **Layer 1**.

Finding panels If the Layers panel button is not easily visible, you can always open it by choosing the Window menu > Layers.

EXERCISE 2   UNDERSTAND LAYERS

The Layers panel is a standard feature in many Adobe applications. Illustrator and Photoshop treat layers slightly differently because of the difference between how art is created in vector and bitmap applications.

In Illustrator, you'll begin with one layer. Each time you add content to the artboard, it's added as an element that's part of **Layer 1**. You can lock elements. You can lock layers. You can create and delete layers. You can rearrange what's referred to as the "stacking order" of layers to make content appear more in the foreground (or background) of the document, in front of or behind other elements. When you click where there are multiple elements, the topmost unlocked element will be selected. Much of this is also true in Photoshop, though you'll see in later chapters that it's safer to work with each element (graphic or text) on its own layer in bitmap applications.

One of the primary roles of layers is to help you organize your document. In the following exercises, you'll create new layers to make the content of separate compositions easy to find.

FIGURE 2.12 The Create New Layer icon appears at the bottom of the panel next to the Trash icon. (I always tell students that birth and death live next to each other.) The bottom of a panel is often the location for Create New and Trash icons in Adobe programs.

EXERCISE 3   CREATE LINES WITH THE PENCIL TOOL

1. Click on the Create New Layer button in the bottom row of the Layers panel (**FIGURE 2.12**). **Layer 2** will appear on top of **Layer 1**.

2. Double-click on the name **Layer 2** and type the new name **comp-01**; then press the Enter key on your keypad or click anywhere outside the text field to set the text (**FIGURE 2.13**). You'll draw all the new lines for the first composition on this layer.

3. Choose the Pencil tool from the Tools panel on the left side of the application window—it's the 10th tool in the panel when tools are listed in a single column. Notice that many of the tools have a small arrow on the bottom right side. If you click this arrow, you can expand the tool to see

FIGURE 2.13 Double-click on **Layer 2** and simply type on top of its name to rename it.

FIGURE 2.14 Clicking the small arrow in the lower right corner of a tool's icon reveals related tools that are bundled with the top tool.

FIGURE 2.15 Set the Pencil tool to a black stroke (the front icon seen here) and no fill (the back icon).

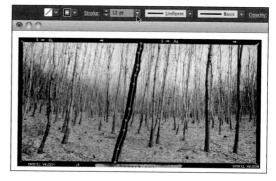

FIGURE 2.16 Modify the weight of a selected line by changing its stroke value in the Control bar.

related tools that are bundled with the top tool. The Pencil is the top tool, but it's good for you to see the other tools that are bundled with this tool (**FIGURE 2.14**).

4. The default fill and stroke values for the pencil are no fill and a black stroke. Check this area of the Tools panel and set it to no fill with a black stroke if the default settings have been modified (**FIGURE 2.15**).

5. Use the Pencil tool to draw a line along the contour of the tree that's most in the foreground (or the tree's outline—you can choose the side). When you finish drawing the line, it will remain selected. Modify the weight of the line by increasing its stroke value in the Control area at the top of the application window (**FIGURE 2.16**). I set mine to 12 points, resulting in a line that's nearly the same width as the trunk of the tree.

6. Repeat Step 3 to trace enough trees to create a recognizable abstract line drawing of the photograph. Change the weight of the line (the stroke value) as you develop lines that appear in the background (**FIGURE 2.17**).

FIGURE 2.17 Continue to trace trees. Watch out for intersecting lines. You will need to deselect the path before drawing a new line that intersects with the previous drawn line.

FIGURE 2.18 Use the Rectangle tool to create a border.

Watch out for areas where two lines seem to connect (for instance, in those tiny sideways branches in the background). When you draw a line with the Pencil tool, it's constructed by a series of anchor points. The line remains selected after it's drawn. If you draw another line on a new area of the artboard, the first line becomes deselected, and the second line is selected. If you try to draw a line that connects with the first line, instead of creating a new line, you'll end up modifying the first (selected) line. Inevitably, you'll do this when you don't intend to. You'll have to manually deselect the first line—use the Selection tool and click in any white space on the artboard—then draw the second line.

KEY COMMAND While you're using the Pencil tool, you can easily access the Selection tool by pressing the Command key on a Mac (or the Control key on a PC). Hold this key while you're using the converted Pencil to Selection tool. When you release the key, the tool returns to a Pencil.

7. Choose the Rectangle tool and draw a black border around the image, covering the film edges. Modify the stroke value to match the weight of this line at the edge of the photograph (**FIGURE 2.18**).

EXERCISE 4 DUPLICATE THE COMPOSITION

1. Rename **Layer 1** so that it better describes the content on the layer. I named mine **original-image**.

2. Toggle off the eyeball icon next to the **comp-01** layer so you can see the original image layer set behind it (**FIGURE 2.19**). The stacking order of the layers prevents you from seeing lower-level layers when top layers contain content that covers the same areas.

FIGURE 2.19 Toggle off the eyeball icon in the Layers panel to view the original layer.

FIGURE 2.20 Expand the **original-image** layer and press the lock icon to unlock the image.

FIGURE 2.21 Select the image within the Layers panel by pressing the box icon to the far right of the layer.

3. Expand the **original-image** layer and unlock the image (**FIGURE 2.20**).

4. Select the image within the Layers panel by clicking in the last column to its right (**FIGURE 2.21**), called the Selection Column. When you see a box (mine is blue, yours may be another color), you've selected a layer element. Look on your artboard to see that the image has been selected.

5. Choose the Selection tool. **Shift(⇧)-Option-drag** to create a copy of the image beneath the first original image. Repeat this process to make a second copy. Keep the spacing of the margins (the negative space) in mind as you position both images. You'll reference these when you create the next two compositions (**FIGURE 2.22**).

FIGURE 2.22 Choose the Selection tool and use **Shift-Option-drag** to copy the image. New images appear in the Layers panel.

EXERCISE 5

ADD A GRADIENT BACKGROUND

1. Toggle on the eyeball icon to make the **comp-01** layer visible. Don't expand the layer. Click in the Selection Column (**FIGURE 2.23**). This selects everything contained within the **comp-01** layer. Every pencil stroke you created is selected. Choose the Edit menu > Copy or press **Command(⌘)-C.**

FIGURE 2.23 Clicking in the Selection column of the collapsed layer selects everything stored within it.

2. Before pasting all those paths, create a new layer and title it **comp-02.**

3. While the **comp-02** layer is active, press ⌘-**V** or choose Edit > Paste. If yours is like mine, you'll end up with a pasted set of lines that are not aligned with the second original photograph (**FIGURE 2.24**). While the lines are selected, use the Arrow keys on your keypad to move the composition of lines into position. I used ⇧-→ to move my composition of lines to the left significantly faster than if I didn't use the Shift key.

FIGURE 2.24 Pasted items land on a new layer.

FIGURE 2.25 A layer can be moved to a new stacking order by dragging it into position in the Layers panel. The **gradients** layer is dragged into stacking position just above the **original-image** layer.

FIGURE 2.26 Use the Gradient tool to fill a rectangle in the **gradients** layer.

KEY COMMAND Press the Shift key and the appropriate arrow key to move items faster—they travel by ten units rather than one unit at a time.

4. Create a new layer to store gradient fills. Name the layer **gradients** and drag it to the stacking position just above the **original-image** layer (**FIGURE 2.25**).

5. Click the **gradients** layer in the Layers panel to make it active. Draw a rectangle (use the Rectangle tool) on the **gradients** layer that's the same size as the compositional space of the photographic image. Click once on the Fill to bring it to the front of the Stroke, if necessary, at the bottom of the Tools panel. Click once on the Gradient tool. The Fill has a default gradient applied, which you'll modify in the next step (**FIGURE 2.26**).

BE CAREFUL! If you followed the last few steps but didn't see a change on your artboard, you may have deselected the gradient fill before modifying the settings in the Gradient panel. Select the gradient fill on your artboard and then try those steps again.

6. You'll see the Gradient panel (if you don't see it, choose Window > Gradient) when you activate the Gradient tool. While the rectangle is still selected, modify the gradient settings in the Gradient panel. I chose a black-and-white gradient (the large pull-down box in the top-right corner) set to a linear (rather than radial) direction, or Type, at −90 degrees. At 90 degrees, the darker value was on top, where the sky should appear white (**FIGURE 2.27**).

7. You can modify the colors at the two ends of the gradient spectrum at any time. You can also add an additional "pit stop" of color or value by Option-dragging one of the color chip handles in the Gradient panel. Adjust the dark value so it's 80% black (dark gray) rather than true black. Double-click the black color chip near the bottom of the Gradient panel. This will open a Color panel specific to the Gradient settings. Change the 100% K (or black) value to 80% (**FIGURE 2.28**).

FIGURE 2.28 Double-click the black chip in the Gradient panel to open a Color panel controlling the Gradient settings.

BE CAREFUL! Value and Tonal Range 80% black is a value in the tonal range from white to black. Value and the tonal range of an image are explored in Chapter 5, *Resolution and Value*.

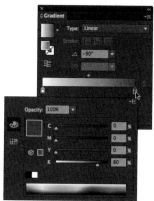

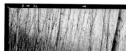

CREATE DEPTH WITH CONTRASTING VALUES

EXERCISE 6

In this third composition, you'll modify the value of some of the lines to make viewers of your version of the forest perceive even greater depth. Depth and space are alluded to in two-dimensional space by properties that appear in our three-dimensional reality. The size of the trees becomes smaller as the viewer perceives the depth of the forest (both in terms of their height and the line weight of their contours). The overlapping nature of trees also helps the viewer perceive depth. These two values (size and overlap) were translated from the original photograph in black and white. However, atmospheric perspective accounts for the depth that's achieved due to less visibility through contrast as items are farther from the viewer's plane of vision. In this case, you'll need to modify the values of the trees toward the background to allude to the atmospheric perspective.

You'll also add a final diffused line to the third composition to separate the horizon line from the ground. All aspects of the original image can be translated with one basic design element: line.

1. Repeat Steps 1, 2, and 3 from Exercise 4 to create a third composition. This time, copy **comp-02** and name the new layer **comp-03**. You'll also need to copy, paste, and position the gradient for the third composition on the **gradients** layer (**FIGURE 2.29**).

2. Leave the tree in the very front black (the one with the trunk that extends all the way to the bottom of the frame). Choose the Selection tool and click on one of the trees/lines near the foreground. In the Color panel, set the Stroke value to 90% black (**FIGURE 2.30**).

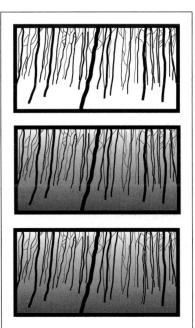

FIGURE 2.29 A view of the Layers panel with the new layer, **comp-03**.

PRINT PROFILE Since you used the Print profile when setting up your document, the Color panel will display with CMYK or cyan, magenta, yellow, and black values.

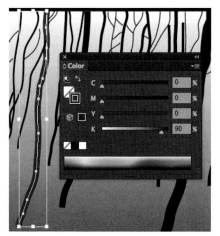

FIGURE 2.30 Use the Selection tool to select a line; then change its Stroke value in the Color panel.

FIGURE 2.31 Hold the Shift key and click to select multiple trees with the Selection tool. Use the Color panel to decrease the stroke values on all of the selected lines.

SCREENCAST 2-1 ADD THE "SWOOSH" AT THE HORIZON

I added an extra line at the horizon using the Brush tool with a gradient and the Feather filter (one of the Stylize options in the Filter menu). View the online screencast to see my process.

All screencasts are available on the companion website, www.digitalart-design.com, or on the YouTube playlist, www.youtube.com/playlist?list=PLAy6P5IoEjy2v3kZKCt8spqJ50nLb2XQI.

3. Select the next set of near-foreground trees together. You can select multiple lines by pressing the Shift key as you click each one. If you accidentally add a line to your multi-selection, Shift-click it again to remove it. Set the value to 80% black (FIGURE 2.31).

4. Repeat this process as you set another group of lines to 70% black, then 60%, and so forth as you move backward in the compositional space. You may leave some of the smaller twigs black as they overlap other tree branches. This contrast between black and mid-gray will help the viewer see the details in the forest.

USE MASTER FILES AND SHARED FILES

1. When the design is finished, save the master file—either press ⌘-S or choose File > Save As to rename or reposition the file on your hard drive. Save the file in master format, meaning .ai (Adobe Illustrator), the format that is specific to the Illustrator application. You can click OK through the Illustrator

If you're using a different version of the Adobe Creative Suite at home than you used to create this drawing (in a public computer lab, for instance), save the file using the correct version of the Creative Suite. Choose File > Save As, name the file, and save it in .ai format. The next dialog allows you to save with backward compatibility. For instance, if you're using CS5, you can choose that format from the Version pull-down menu (**FIGURE 2.32**).

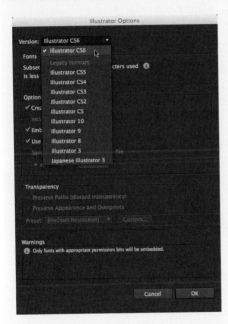

FIGURE 2.32 Choose File > Save As to save a native file. In the Illustrator Options window, select a version to save a master file compatible with your system settings.

Options dialog unless you'll need to open and edit the file in a prior version of Illustrator. (If so, see the following note on backward compatibility.)

2. The .ai format is imperative: if the file is in this format, you'll always be able to open and edit the file using Illustrator. However, you'll also want to save your work in a format optimized for sharing. For this purpose, vector graphics are most often saved in PDF, SVG, and PNG file formats. Save the file as a PDF now. Choose File > Save As (⌘-⇧-**S**) and then choose Adobe PDF from the format pull-down menu (**FIGURE 2.33**). The next dialog contains a

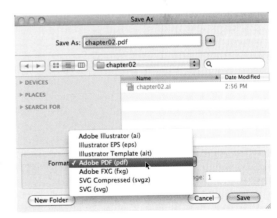

FIGURE 2.33 File formats, such as PDF, are available in the Format menu of the Save As dialog box.

lot of information about how the PDF will save, which is more thoroughly covered in Chapter 11, *The Grid* (Illustrator), and Chapter 12, *Continuity* (InDesign). For now, press the Save PDF button and view the two files in your folder. As described earlier in this chapter, you can use the same name on both files because the file extensions (which are, officially, part of the name) are different.

LAB CHALLENGE

Find or take a photograph of an athlete and develop a "tight" pencil illustration of her action or movement using the Pencil tool (or by exploring the Brush tool) in Illustrator.

CHAPTER 3
MODIFY BASIC SHAPES

THE EXERCISES IN this chapter will help you create complex graphic icons using three basic shapes: the circle, the square, and the triangle. You'll use the Pen, Add Anchor Point, Convert Anchor Point, Direct Selection, and Reflection tools and explore the Pathfinder panel.

Combining simple shapes to develop complex forms is a visual strategy employed by every illustrator or logo designer. As such, the three basic shapes should be well understood as psychological tools. Rudolf Arnheim, a master of perceptual psychology, declared that "visual experience is dynamic" [1]. He noted that shape and form are perceived in relation to every other lived experience and the simultaneous visual play within a composition. Compositions include "interplay(s) of directed tensions," which can be read as "psychological forces." Artist and Bauhaus instructor Johannes Itten said, "The character of the square is horizontal and vertical, that of the triangle, diagonal, and that of the circle circular" [2]. Each of these shapes can be harmonized or distressed by the horizontal, diagonal, or circular shape of the other.

REFERENCE [1] Rudolf Arnheim, *Art and Visual Perception: A Psychology of the Creative Eye* (Berkeley, CA: University of California Press, 1974). pg. 11.

REFERENCE [2] Johannes Itten, *Design and Form: The Basic Course at the Bauhaus and Later* (London: John Wiley & Sons, 1975). pg. 62.

REFERENCE [3] Itten, Ibid., pg. 62.

In Chapter 2, *Drawing Expressive Lines,* you learned to see how repeated lines are understood on a visual plane through shifting values and contrasting weights. In this chapter, you'll work with basic forms, while the lines will simply represent the perimeter of an object, or the difference between where a shape is present and where it is not. You'll notice how perception is influenced by the dynamic nature of shape relationships as you build your composite icons.

Since a shape is the culmination of a line that either curves or is angled back onto itself, it's no stretch of the imagination to follow a chapter study on lines with one on shapes. "To produce a work of art," wrote Itten, "creative imagination should have many possibilities to draw on. To find the simplest and clearest form, the thinking, in terms of variations and combinations, must be developed by means of exercises" [3]. Logo designers notoriously sketch hundreds of designs before arriving at their final compositions (**FIGURES 3.1 AND 3.2**).

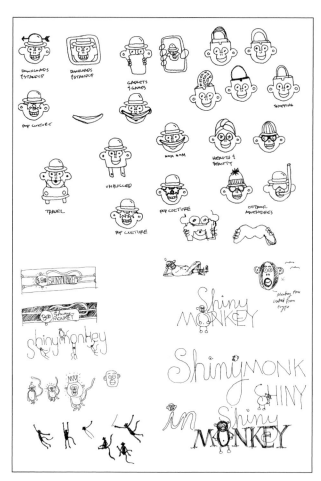

FIGURE 3.1 Logo/icon sketches by Ron Romain for MyShinyMonkey.com.

In this chapter, you'll work on two compositions. However, the lab challenge encourages you to continue this practice. The more relationships between these basic forms you can see and develop, the clearer you'll be able to see and think visually.

All complex shapes are created from the three basic forms. 2pxBorder, a web design firm in New Zealand, created a virtual kaleidoscope to mesmerize viewers who visit kaleidolism.com. In their "watermelon," "colored pencils," and "toolbox" kaleidoscopes, you can dynamically change the relationship between the circles, squares, and triangles in a web browser (**FIGURE 3.3**).

The exercises in this chapter will show you how to create two complex shapes based on circles and rectangles in Adobe Illustrator. You'll experiment with various modifications to the shapes to create recognizable graphic icons— a generic online profile image and a tree.

When you read about the contrast between something that is present and something that is not, you should connect this idea to binary digital relationships (off/on, yes/no, present/hidden), as well as to the formal design property of figure/ground or positive/negative space. Review the introduction to this section if this is unclear.

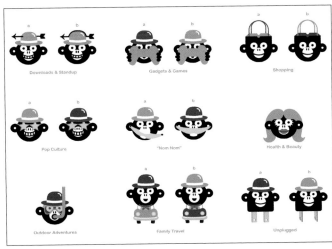

FIGURE 3.2 Final icons created by Ron Romain for MyShinyMonkey.com.

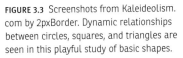

FIGURE 3.3 Screenshots from Kaleideolism.com by 2pxBorder. Dynamic relationships between circles, squares, and triangles are seen in this playful study of basic shapes.

SIGNS AND LOGOS

Read more in James Hoopes, ed., *Peirce on Signs: Writings on Semiotic* by Charles Sanders Peirce (North Carolina: University of North Carolina Press, 1991). Also see Roland Barthes, *Elements of Semiology*, trans. Annette Lavers and Colin Smith (New York: Hill and Wang, 1973) or *Mythologies*, trans. Annette Lavers (New York: Farrar, Straus and Giroux, 1972).

When basic shapes are combined into simple forms, they can become visual marks that are easy to remember. These forms act as visual signs to indicate a language-based idea. For instance, think about the signs you might see while traveling, eating out, or attending a public event. Charles Sanders Peirce, an American philosopher whose work in semiotics is applied to visual culture, posited that there are three types of signs: symbols, indexes, and icons. In the realm of graphic design, a successful logo might take any one of the formats described by Peirce. However, most logos are simple, abstract forms (more closely aligned with an iconic sign).

SIGNS

- Symbol: Stands in for an idea, such as a flag
- Index: Points to an idea as an indicator, such as an arrow
- Icon (or Likeness): Represents an idea in an abstract way, such as a stick figure or a smiley face

REFERENCE [4] David Airey, *Logo Design Love: A Guide to Creating Iconic Brand Identities* (Berkeley, CA: New Riders, 2010). pg. 22.

The first trademarked logo can still be seen on bottles of Bass beer: a red triangle in close proximity to the script-styled "Bass" (**FIGURE 3.4**). As David Airey wrote in his book, *Logo Design Love*, "a truly enviable iconic design will also be simple, relevant, enduring, distinctive, memorable, and adaptable" [4]. While this all may sound like a simple recipe, designing a logo to represent a company's brand that meets each of Airey's criteria is incredibly difficult. This chapter is a primer for those who seek further development on the study of logos, icons, mark making, and graphic design.

FIGURE 3.4 The logo for Bass Ale—registered as a trademark in the 1870s—was the first trademarked logo.

WHAT YOU'LL NEED

It's not necessary to download files to complete the exercises in this chapter. You'll benefit from the ability to perceive simple shapes within complex forms.

WHAT YOU'LL MAKE

In the exercises in this chapter, you'll create iconic graphics from simple shapes using the Pathfinder panel (FIGURE 3.5). Your digital composition will consist of a series of artboards showing the development of the altered shapes.

FIGURE 3.5 Iconic graphics created from simple shapes using the Pathfinder panel.

VECTOR CURVES

While you're modifying basic vector shapes in the following exercises, you'll notice that the straight paths are made up of anchor points, while curves are controlled by anchor points and Bézier handles. The handles allow you to control the Bézier curve, named for a French engineer who used them to design automobiles. You can move or reposition the anchor point at the midpoint of the curve with the Direct Selection tool and drag the end of the handle (there's one on each side of the midpoint) to lengthen or shorten it. The longer the handle, the softer (or smoother) the curve. Handles can also be repositioned with the Direct Selection tool to tweak the contour of a curve. If you're reading this without looking at a curve in Illustrator, it may seem abstract. You'll find Bézier handles a bit more intuitive after you modify some curves in Exercise 4.

EXERCISE 1

CREATE A DOCUMENT WITH ONE ARTBOARD

1. Create a new document in Illustrator as follows: press **Command(⌘)-N** or choose File > New Document. In the New Document dialog box, choose Profile > Print and then set the width and height to eight inches by typing "8 in" in each field (FIGURE 3.6). Change the units to Inches using the pull-down menu. Press OK.

2. Draw a circle, triangle, and square at the top of the document using a fill and no stroke. (I used a red fill—you can use any color.)

WORKSPACE > ESSENTIALS
Open Illustrator and set the workspace to Essentials by selecting it from the pull-down list in the Application bar or by choosing the Window menu > Workspace > Essentials.

FIGURE 3.6 Choose the Print profile and set the width and height to eight inches.

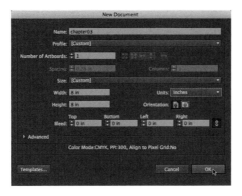

MAKING SHAPES

There are many ways to create a triangle. If you used the Pen tool, you made more clicks (and therefore more work for yourself) than was necessary! Draw a square; then use the Delete Anchor Point tool (**FIGURE 3.7**) to convert the four-point square into a three-point shape—a triangle (see **FIGURE 3.8** and **FIGURE 3.9**). You'll probably have to reform your triangle using the Direct Selection tool. Alternatively, use the Polygon tool (**FIGURE 3.10**) to create a triangle by clicking and dragging to create a multisided shape and then press the Down Arrow key to reduce the number of sides. For instance, if it begins as a six-sided shape, then you'll have to press the Down Arrow key three times (**FIGURES 3.11 AND 3.12**).

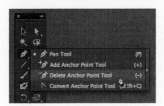

FIGURE 3.7 In the Tools panel, Delete Anchor Point is bundled with the Pen.

FIGURE 3.8 When an object is selected, its anchor points will be highlighted. Use the Delete Anchor Point tool to remove an anchor point, thereby changing the structure of the shape.

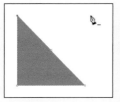

FIGURE 3.9 A triangle is created by deleting one of the anchor points on the original square.

FIGURE 3.10 The Polygon tool is bundled with the Shape tools in the Tools panel.

FIGURE 3.11 Click and drag to create a polygon and notice the number of sides.

FIGURE 3.12 While the mouse is depressed, pressing the Down Arrow key decreases the number of sides in a polygon.

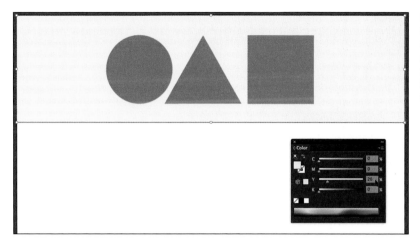

FIGURE 3.13 Fill the shape with 20% yellow using the Color panel in CMYK color mode. You can alter the color mode of this panel from the menu in its upper-right corner.

3. Set the three basic shapes aligned on a baseline at the top of the page— pay attention to a repetitive amount of negative space in the margins. Create a fill behind the three shapes with a light value. I set mine with the CMYK values seen in the Color panel in FIGURE 3.13. Those three shapes will be used to create more complicated forms while completing the exercises in this chapter.

ARRANGING THE STACKING ORDER OF PATHS IN ILLUSTRATOR

To arrange elements on the page, select the path and then choose the Object Menu > Arrange to position it with Bring Forward (by one level in the stacking order of the layers), Bring to Front (all the way to the top of the stacking order), Send Backward (back one level), or Send to Back (all the way behind other elements on the page). The key commands for arranging elements on the page are extremely handy:

- Bring Forward: ⌘-] (Close Bracket)
- To Front: ⌘-Shift(⇧)-]
- Backward: ⌘-[(Open Bracket)
- To Back: ⌘-⇧-[

If you simply remember that moving an element from front to back on the page involves selecting the element and pressing some combination of Command and Bracket (and possibly adding Shift to go all the way), you can move items efficiently.

1. Using the rest of the white space of the page, create two shape combinations. Combine the circles and squares as if you were making a silhouette of a person's head and shoulders (often used on the web to represent a generic "profile" icon) and use several copies of the circle to make a tree (**FIGURE 3.14**).

SMART GUIDES Choosing the View menu > Smart Guides will present alignment guides while you're working. In some situations, this can be extremely helpful, while in others it's an annoyance. The key command for Smart Guides is ⌘-U. It's one worth committing to memory!

ORGANIZING SHAPES Although it may be tempting, don't group your shapes at this point. You'll be organizing shapes in the next exercises.

2. Press ⌘-R to view rulers; then click and drag from the left ruler to four inches (dividing the page in half). A guide will be placed to help you to see how to distribute your work evenly within the positive and negative space in reference to this division (**FIGURE 3.15**). Guides are helpful visual aides; they will not appear in a printout.

3. Another way to find the halfway point between two endpoints is to draw a rectangle that starts at one point and ends at the other. Since every shape has an anchor point at the center, you can use a simple rectangle to determine the placement of a guide, and then delete it. Use this method to set a horizontal guide halfway between the row of basic shapes and the rest of the page (**FIGURE 3.16**). My rectangle is green—remember that it must be selected in order to see the anchor points. I deleted the green rectangle after my guide was in place.

4. Use the guides to help you organize the art on the page. I nudged my iconic graphics up a little so the center points in their bottom shapes (rectangles) intersected with the horizontal guide. I also nudged the graphics so they were equidistant from the vertical guide. Use your best judgment to use guides while aligning the art on the page.

FIGURE 3.14 Combine copies of the circle and square to create icons.

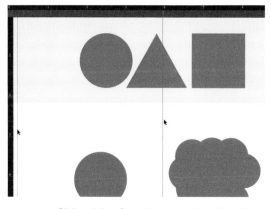

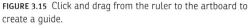

FIGURE 3.15 Click and drag from the ruler to the artboard to create a guide.

FIGURE 3.16 Draw a rectangle and use its anchor points to determine the placement of a guide.

EXERCISE 3 — DUPLICATE THE ARTBOARD AND UNITE THE PATHS

Since you'll use Option-drag key commands to duplicate the artboard, you'll want to see a lot of space in the application window before making a copy. Zoom out if you need to by pressing ⌘-- (hyphen or minus) or use the Zoom tool while pressing the Option key.

1. Use the Artboard tool to see the specifications of the current artboard in the Control area. Press **Option-⇧** as you click and drag a new artboard (or page) to the right of the current artboard (**FIGURE 3.17**).

COPYING You can Option-drag the new artboard to the top, right, bottom, or left of the original. Always use the Shift key to constrain the alignment of the artboards, paths, and objects.

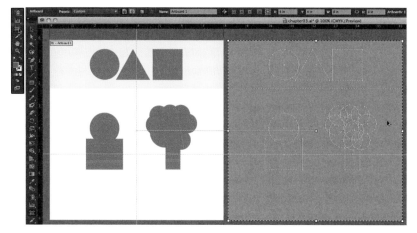

FIGURE 3.17 Duplicate the artboard with the Artboard tool using the Option and Shift keys as you click and drag the mouse.

FIGURE 3.18 Rename the artboard in the Control panel.

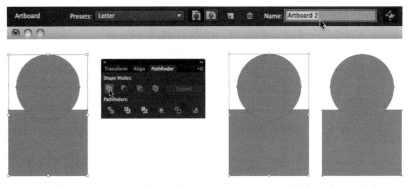

FIGURE 3.19 Select two paths and click the Unite button in the Pathfinder panel.

FIGURE 3.20 A side-by-side view of the two shapes when they are grouped (left) and when they are united into a single path (right). Notice that when the paths are selected, the perimeters of the full circle and square are visible in the grouped shape. The united path is transformed into a new shape that combines the original circle and square.

2. Rename the artboard **Artboard 2** in the Control panel (**FIGURE 3.18**). Complete Exercise 3 on this second page of your Illustrator document.

3. View the Pathfinder panel (Window > Pathfinder), where you'll join the shapes in the following steps. Select the first set of shapes (use the Shift key to select both paths or marquee around both paths with the Selection tool) that comprise the profile icon. Press the Unite button in the Pathfinder panel (**FIGURE 3.19**). Notice how the two separate shapes are now united into one continuous path (**FIGURE 3.20**).

4. Select the second set of shapes comprising the tree and unite the paths using the Pathfinder panel as you did in Step 4.

EXERCISE 4 DUPLICATE THE ARTBOARD AND MODIFY THE SHAPES

1. Duplicate the artboard again (see Exercise 3, Step 1). Rename it **Artboard 3**. Complete Exercise 4 on this third page of your Illustrator document.

2. Tear off the additional Pen tools by clicking on the Pen tool in the Tool panel and releasing your mouse over the sideways ("tear off") arrow (**FIGURE 3.21**).

FIGURE 3.21 Release the mouse over the sideways arrow in the Tools panel to tear off a group of tools.

3. Use the Convert Anchor Point tool to change the anchor point at the top-left shoulder of the profile icon from a sharp angle to a rounded edge—this action requires a click-and-drag action (**FIGURE 3.22**). You'll have to click directly on the anchor point to modify it with the Convert Anchor

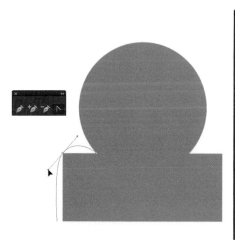

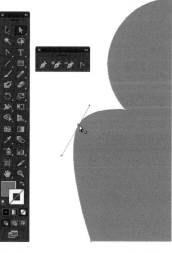

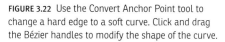

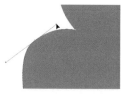

FIGURE 3.22 Use the Convert Anchor Point tool to change a hard edge to a soft curve. Click and drag the Bézier handles to modify the shape of the curve.

FIGURE 3.23 Move the anchor point with the Direct Selection tool to modify the path of a curve.

FIGURE 3.24 Modify the curve by altering the Bézier handles. The longer the handles, the softer the curve.

Point tool. The direction that you drag the mouse influences the curve of the path—if you find the path getting tangled into itself, drag the mouse in the opposite direction!

4. Modify the shoulder so it sits down, away from what would be the ear (if there were one), by moving the anchor point with the Direct Selection tool (**FIGURE 3.23**). Modify the softness of the curve by repositioning the Bézier handles (**FIGURE 3.24**).

5. To add a curve to the center of the tree trunk, you'll need to work in two steps. First, use the Add Anchor Point tool to add two anchor points at the center of the trunk (on the left and right sides) where you want to see the straight line bend (**FIGURE 3.25**). A straight line can become a curve only if there's an anchor point indicating its direction. Be sure to click on the path of the trunk to add anchor points.

MISSING THE PATH If you see the warning message "Please use the add anchor point tool on a segment of a path," then you missed the path when you clicked the mouse button. Press OK and try again.

FIGURE 3.25 Use the Add Anchor Point tool on both sides of the rectangle to establish where the tree trunk will bend.

You'll only modify one half of the profile body. Instead of repeating the action on the right side of the profile, you'll use the Reflect and Copy tool in the next exercise to ensure that the icon is symmetric.

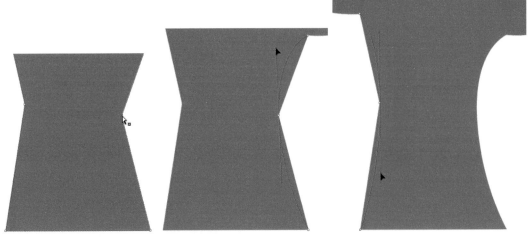

FIGURE 3.26 Use the Direct Selection tool to move the anchor points inward.

FIGURES 3.27 AND 3.28 Change the hard-edged anchor points to a curve by clicking and dragging on the anchor point with the Convert Anchor Point tool.

SCREENCAST 3-1 MODIFY PATHS WITH THE PEN AND DIRECT SELECTION TOOLS

The Pen and its related tools can be difficult to master. Working with anchor points is not as intuitive as drawing with a pen (perhaps the tool is misnamed). In this online extra, the author demonstrates adding and modifying anchor points and Bézier handles.

All screencasts are available on the companion website, www.digitalart-design.com, or on the YouTube playlist, www.youtube.com/playlist?list=PLAy6P5IoEjy2v3kZKCt8spqJ50nLb2XQI.

You can alter the order of the last two steps. Instead of pushing the anchor points inward before adding the curve, you could have converted the anchor points and then moved them. However, if the anchor points are still along the path of the tree trunk, the direction of your mouse movements won't be too obvious.

6. Use the Direct Selection tool to move the new anchor points in toward the center of the trunk (**FIGURE 3.26**). This creates the new dent in the shape, but the edges are still angular rather than curved.

7. Click and drag, one at a time, on each of the new anchor points with the Convert Anchor Point tool to convert the sharp angle to a curve. I dragged the right anchor point toward the top of the page (**FIGURE 3.27**) and the left anchor point toward the bottom (**FIGURE 3.28**).

8. Make any further adjustments to the trunk with the Direct Selection tool on the anchor points or Bézier handles.

EXERCISE 5 · REFLECT AND COPY A SECOND HALF ONTO THE PROFILE ICON

1. Create a duplicate, fourth artboard. Name it **Artboard 4**. Complete Exercises 5 and 6 on this page of your Illustrator document.

2. Create a vertical guide at the center of the profile icon. Draw a rectangle (use a new color so you can differentiate between the two paths) that starts at the intersection of the guide and ends well outside (covering) the right half of the profile icon (**FIGURE 3.29**).

3. Use the Selection tool to select both the visible half of the profile (with the rounded shoulder) and the box on top of the second half of the profile. Press the Minus Front button in the Pathfinder panel (**FIGURE 3.30**). The right half of the profile will be deleted because it was included in the "front" shape area.

4. With the left half of the profile still selected, choose the Reflect tool in the Tools panel. It's hidden beneath the Rotate tool, so you may need to click and hold the mouse on the Rotate tool before dragging to select the Reflect tool (**FIGURE 3.31**).

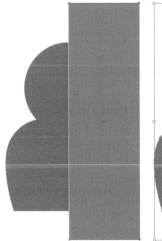
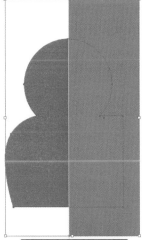

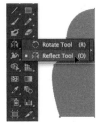

FIGURE 3.29 A rectangle covers the right half of the profile icon.

FIGURE 3.30 The Minus Front button in the Pathfinder panel can be used to delete parts of an object according to a path placed in front of it.

FIGURE 3.31 The Reflect tool is bundled under the Rotate tool.

Guides are helpful when you're aligning elements in a composition. However, sometimes they obscure your view of design elements. It's just as important to know how and why to draw guides as it is to know how to hide or delete them. Both operations can be carried out by choosing the View Menu > Guides. However, there are two things you should know:

- The easiest way to hide and show guides is by pressing ⌘-; (semicolon). Use this key command to hide guides; then use it again to show them. Or you can choose the View menu > Guides > Hide/Show Guides.

- Deleting guides can be annoying because, by default, Illustrator locks guides. So you'll need to unlock your guides (View Menu > Guides > Unlock Guides) and then select a guide with the Selection tool and press the Delete key on your keypad.

5. Double-click the Reflect tool. In the Reflect dialog box, check the Vertical radio button, make sure the angle is set to 90 degrees (the default), and press the Copy button (**FIGURE 3.32**). Since you're making a copy, the second half of the profile icon will appear; however, it may be misplaced.

6. Use the Selection tool to align the second half of the profile icon (use the guide you created). Once selected, I nudged the right half by holding Shift while pressing the Right Arrow key. Zoom in so you can make sure there's no negative space between the halves. Select both halves and then press the Unite button in the Pathfinder panel to join the two paths into one shape (**FIGURE 3.33**).

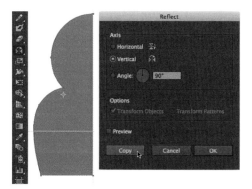

FIGURE 3.32 The Reflect tool dialog box. Notice that you can exit the box by clicking the Copy, Cancel, or OK buttons.

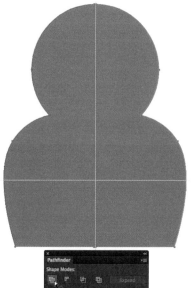

FIGURE 3.33 The Unite button, found in the Pathfinder panel, is used to combine multiple paths.

EXERCISE 6: BRUSH DETAILS INTO THE TREETOP

1. Use the Paintbrush tool with white or any color that will be visible on your tree icon assigned to the Stroke (no color assigned to the Fill) to add curvy lines in the treetop (**FIGURE 3.34**).

2. Add a few more lines and set them at half of the stroke weight you used in the previous step (**FIGURE 3.35**).

3. Select the tree and brush strokes and then try using the Minus Front button in the Pathfinder to see how these shapes relate. You'll notice that since the brush strokes are not closed paths, the Pathfinder panel will close the path for you before making adjustments (**FIGURE 3.36**). This results in unwanted visual effects.

FIGURE 3.34 Add loose white lines with the Paintbrush tool.

TIP Adjust the Stroke value in the Control area to apply more or less weight to the line settings.

FIGURE 3.35 Adjust the stroke weight to create contrast between thin and thick lines.

FIGURE 3.36 Adjustments made using the Pathfinder panel will often close paths. This may result in unwanted or unpredicted effects.

4. Choose Edit > Undo or press ⌘-Z to undo the last step. Before you can use the Pathfinder panel successfully, you'll need to expand each of the brush strokes into its own closed path. Marquee over the entire tree using the Selection tool; then hold the Shift key while clicking on the tree trunk (where there are no curvy lines). You'll have selected all the brush strokes and deselected the tree. Choose Object > Expand Appearance (**FIGURE 3.37**).

5. Now that the brush strokes are separate, closed paths, you can use the Minus Front button in the Pathfinder panel to render the strokes as transparent "holes" in the treetop (**FIGURE 3.38**). Be sure to select the whole tree, including the brush stroke paths, before pressing the Minus Front button.

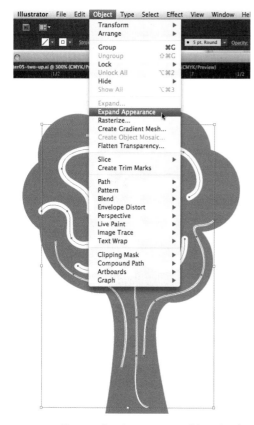

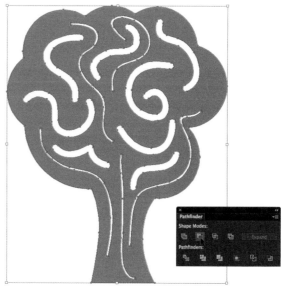

FIGURE 3.37 By expanding the appearance of the painted lines, the "lines" are converted to Illustrator "shapes."

FIGURE 3.38 Use the Minus Front button to render the strokes as "holes" or areas of negative space rather than white paint.

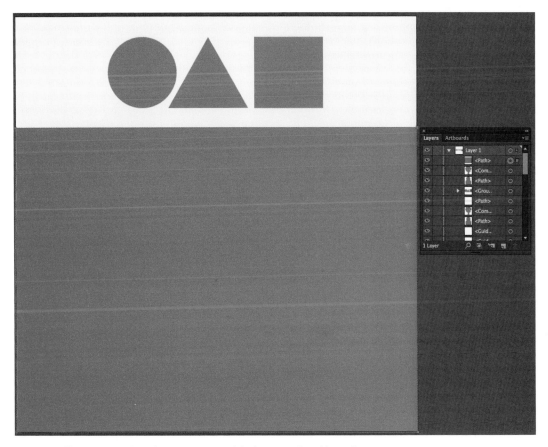

EXERCISE 7 · ADD A BACKGROUND COLOR AND SAVE A MULTIPAGE PDF

1. Create another duplicate artboard. Name it **Artboard 5**. Complete this exercise on the fifth page of your Illustrator document.

2. Draw a red (or whatever color you've been using for your graphics) rectangle from the bottom-left corner of the page to the lower-right corner of the yellow rectangle at the top of the page. For a moment, you'll lose your graphics in a sea of one color (**FIGURE 3.39**). This would be a good time to notice that the new path is on the top of the Layer panel stacking order.

FIGURE 3.39 The new rectangle path appears on top of the Layer panel stacking order.

3. While the path is selected, use the top-right pull-down menu in the Color panel to select Invert (**FIGURE 3.40**).

4. Press ⌘-⇧-[to send the background path to the back of the document (**FIGURE 3.41**).

5. The graphic icons have shifted in shape and size as you've made many modifications to their design. Set a guide to divide the page in half (vertically) and align your graphics toward the center of the bottom area of the page (**FIGURE 3.42**). Leave a little extra space on the bottom as the eye naturally pulls a composition down in space. (This is sometimes referred to as designing the composition in a space that is *bottom heavy.*)

FIGURE 3.40 Colors can be inverted from the Color panel.

FIGURE 3.41 The background path should appear in the back of the document.

FIGURE 3.42 Align the graphics evenly, with bottom weight.

6. Save the master (.ai) file. Then choose File >
   Save As and select Adobe PDF from the Format
   pull-down menu. Notice that you can save a
   range of pages since the document contains
   multiple artboards (FIGURE 3.43). Leave the
   default radio button for "All" selected, as you'll
   want to see all five pages in your PDF. Press the
   Save PDF button in the following Save Adobe
   PDF dialog box.

7. Open the PDF to see your icons develop in
   stages, demonstrating the exercises in this
   chapter. In the future, you might use this
   technique to create a multipage document
   demonstrating several compositions for one
   project, different stages of an interactive work,
   or frames of an animation.

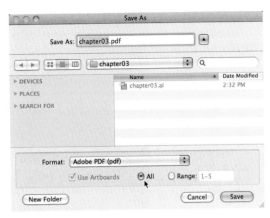

FIGURE 3.43 Save all five pages as a single PDF.

 ## LAB CHALLENGE

Add another artboard or two to your document and develop two more complicated, unified shapes. Start with a combination of the circle, square, or
triangle. Use the Direct Selection and Pen tools as well as the Pathfinder panel
to unify and modify your shapes.

FIGURE S2.1 In Santa Monica, California, you can walk into a room-sized camera obscura to see a view of the Santa Monica pier projected onto a disk. The top image portrays the room's ceiling, where the lens in the roof collects light that's projected onto the disk beneath it via carefully positioned mirrors.

SECTION 2
DIGITAL PHOTOGRAPHY

THE GREEK ROOTS of the word photography loosely translate to "drawing with light." In this sense, digital photography is no different than photography using analog methods, but of course the digital camera lets you save files rather than negatives and create prints without a wet lab. Photography developed as an art form at the intersection of the sciences and technology. The camera obscura (FIGURE S2.1), a forerunner of the camera we know today, was a dark room that projected a scene onto its wall as a result of distributing light through a hole in the building (or later, a box). It was used as a drawing aide by Renaissance artists such as Leonardo da Vinci.

Kodak developed the Brownie camera, one of the first snapshot technologies in the early 1900s. As the company's advertisement demonstrates (FIGURE S2.2), it was so easy to use that even a woman could operate the device (sarcasm intended in my interpretation). Digital art and design students have access to a broad range of tools. Some use a digital single lens reflex camera (DSLR), while others primarily rely on a camera phone to create their imagery.

FIGURE S2.2 An original advertisement for Kodak's Brownie camera. Adjusted for expected inflation in 2013, the cost for each camera was approximately $27. Image courtesy of Ellis Collection of Kodakiana—Database #K0430, Emergence of Advertising On-Line Project, John W. Hartman Center for Sales, Advertising & Marketing History, Duke University, David M. Rubenstein Rare Book & Manuscript Library, http://library.duke.edu/digitalcollections/eaa/.

This section will heighten a digital artist's or designer's awareness of the digital photographic image, regardless of her capturing device. The process of creating a photograph is nearly the opposite of the process of creating vector illustrations (reviewed in the first section of this book). For instance, when you begin to create a vector illustration, you start with a blank page (or a white Adobe Illustrator artboard). Vector illustration is an additive process—you add dots, lines, or shapes to the composition. Photography necessitates a process of selective reduction. Instead of adding to the empty canvas, photographers frame their surroundings to capture just the right moment in time. Compositional design elements are still active within the frame, but technological components relating to the camera—we might call this the "hardware"—play a large role in the resulting image. The chapters in this section will help you understand the interplay between composition and lighting by first teaching you the mechanics of your digital camera and then explaining how to identify the compositional attributes that apply specifically to the photographic frame and how to adjust the digital histogram that renders the tonal scale within the image.

Of course, photographs (digitized by the camera or the scanner) are made of pixels, and you'll edit or manipulate pixels in Adobe Photoshop. If you're new to this material, this section of the book may be your first experience with bitmap images. It would be convenient if I could assert that the pixel is to the digital photograph what the anchor point is to the vector illustration, but that just isn't accurate. The two systems of image construction are so different that an analogy is not possible. A pixel is a single unit of color, sampled from the original image. If the bitmap image is created with a digital camera, then each pixel is sampled from the scene at the time of the photograph, according to the specific lighting conditions and camera settings. If a bitmap image is created by scanning a print, then the pixel is a sample taken at the time of scanning according to the input specifications in the scanner software. Pixels are finite. You can resample pixels, and there are ways you can add pixels to a document, but for most people who operate some version of Photoshop and want to print on their home inkjet printer, you'll have only as many pixels as were sampled at the time the bitmap image was created. This means that unlike vector art, bitmap images are not infinitely scalable.

The exercises in Chapter 4, *Creating and Organizing Digital Photographs,* will teach you to use settings that might be available on your digital camera. You'll also learn to organize your files using Adobe Bridge, which can be especially helpful as you're editing the many photographs you'll take while exploring your camera.

In the mid-twentieth century, Ansel Adams developed the infamous zone system with Fred Archer: an 11-step scale (counting step zero) to delineate, pre-visualize, and understand the relationship between the luminance of the scene, the density values of the negative, and the final printed image. Using Roman numerals to avoid confusion with so many other numbers on the camera, the scale starts at Zone 0, a black part of a photograph with no texture or image details. It ends at Zone X (ten) where white appears in the print with no texture. The middle point, Zone V (five), is considered middle gray, though it's about an 18% gray value. (When we review the zone system for digital photographers, you'll learn that this percentage decreases a bit.) While the zone system directly helps photographers with the craft of printing, and although "negative densities" may not seem relevant to digital images, understanding the zone will help you see what Adams describes as a "practical interpretation of sensitometry" [1]. Since the zone system is so specifically related to value, I've included a study of an adapted zone system for digital photographers in Chapter 5, *Resolution and Value.*

REFERENCE [1] Ansel Adams, *Camera and Lens* (New York: Morgan & Morgan, 1970). pg. 22. If you really love it, you can check out Adams's series, *The Camera, The Negative, and The Print.* The zone system is most thoroughly explicated in Book 2, *The Negative.*

Contemporary artists continue to use the zone system as a method for understanding the values and tonal range in a photographic image. Terry Flaxton's *In Re Ansel Adams* was created in homage to one of Adams's seminal photographic images—the resolution of the digital image is more robust than the tonal range in the original print (FIGURE S2.3). Add the movement of the video and the soundtrack of the waterfall, and the scene comes to life (FIGURE S2.4).

The exercises in Chapter 5 will help you learn to see the zone system in a digital photograph. You'll understand the image's histogram and learn to modify the tonal range to increase the contrast of the composition.

FIGURE S2.3 Terry Flaxton operates a high-resolution camera during the making of his *In Re Ansel Adams.*

FIGURE S2.4 View Terry Flaxton's video at www.visualfields.co.uk/ANSELembed.html.

The exercises in Chapter 6, *Color Models,* will help you understand essential properties of color including harmony, contrast, and digital color modes.

In the days of analog photography, working in color was vastly different from shooting, processing, and printing with black-and-white film. For most photographers, working in color implied that they were unable to process their own film (where much experimentation took place with negatives) and necessitated the use of a color lab for printing. This was not nearly as affordable as a black-and-white darkroom you could rig in your home. Shifting to color typically changed the experience for the photographer from working in solitude with complete control over film processing to working in a shared lab with far less control over film processing. The digital camera, especially the DSLR, has mostly returned the photographer to solitude (if she wishes to work in this manner), where post-production takes place on a home computer. Shooting in color, from the perspective of processing, is the same as shooting in black and white—in both situations, you will "process" the images on your computer. Color is a basic design element that should be learned alongside value. We'll study color with bitmap images, although the same principles of color apply to vector graphics.

REFERENCE [2] Ibid., Foreword to *Camera and Lens.*

LINK The Masters of Photography website, www.masters-of-photography.com, provides a substantial introduction to historically relevant photographers of the twentieth century.

In these three chapters, you'll work with the foundation elements of digital photography: the photographic image, value, and color, and you'll be encouraged to think about the relationship between these design elements and digital technologies. As Ansel Adams wrote, "With photography we touch the domains of science, illustration, documentation, and expressible art" [2]. Keep the lessons of the first three chapters in mind, too. You'll continue to see dots (maybe in the form of pixels), lines, and relationships between shapes while you're interpreting value and composing with the rule of thirds.

CHAPTER 4

CREATING AND ORGANIZING DIGITAL PHOTOGRAPHS

THE EXERCISES IN this chapter will explain the camera mechanics involved in creating a photograph and demonstrate how to organize, rename, and set up a digital "contact sheet" via a PDF of your images. You'll explore your camera and use your files or those from the companion website to learn some of the best file management tools available in Adobe Bridge.

Light is essential for creating a photographic image. How the light is measured and captured in the camera will affect the resulting image. In this chapter, you'll learn to control how much light is rendered in your "light drawing" or photograph. In the following chapters, you'll learn to compose within the frame of the viewfinder and to adjust the tonal range during the post-production process. Since outdoor light is a direct product of the sun and moon, the amount of natural light in a photograph also relates to the time of day. Conceptually, time, considered as both duration and as the shift in lighting as day passes to night is a rich theme for photographers and artists to explore and interpret. The new media artist duo Jon Thomson and Alison Craighead

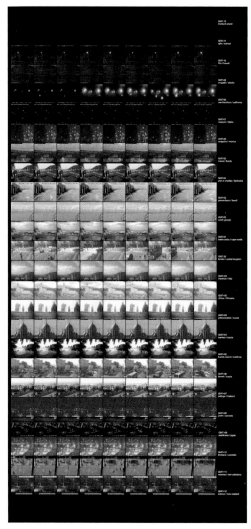

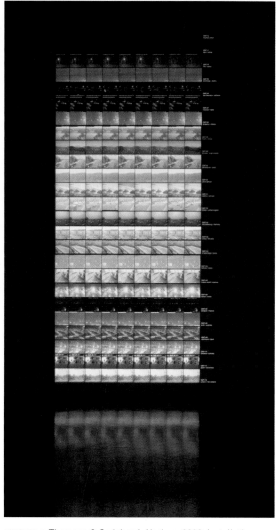

FIGURE 4.1 Thomson & Craighead, *Horizon*, 2009. Screen view, Dundee Contemporary Arts. Image provided courtesy of the artists.

FIGURE 4.2 Thomson & Craighead, *Horizon*, 2009. Installation view, Dundee Contemporary Arts. Image provided courtesy of the artists.

(known simply as Thomson and Craighead) created an installation titled *Horizon* that displays a representation of the time at one specific location—the horizon (**FIGURES 4.1 AND 4.2**). On their website, they write:

REFERENCE [1]

See www.thomson-craighead.net/docs/horizon.html

Horizon is a narrative clock made out of images accessed in real time from webcams found in every time zone around the world. The result is a constantly updating array of images that read like a series of movie storyboards, but also as an idiosyncratic global electronic sundial [1].

Your camera may offer you anything from no control over the way light is registered on the digital sensor (which is ultimately responsible for the resulting image file) to complete control in manual mode. Some of the information in the Camera Mechanics exercise won't apply to your situation if you're using a point-and-shoot camera or a mobile device. However, most of my students have access to consumer- or prosumer-level (not quite professional but a step above the consumer level) digital cameras and many have digital single lens reflex (DSLR) cameras. This range offers the photographer some degree of or even full control.

Photography began as a technical and scientific pursuit of creative and documentary expression. The pervasive nature of digital cameras makes it difficult for some people to conceive of the craft as specialized. For many, the camera is just another gadget. Harrod Blank's *Camera Van* (FIGURE 4.3) includes one of every Polaroid camera ever made along its front grill, and that's just the beginning. The word "SMILE" is printed across the top of the van, each letter formed of Kodak Instamatic cameras (FIGURE 4.4). On the driver's side, a camera-mural of the Kodak Instamatic is made of mounted Instamatics. Do they work? Yes, they do! Screens display photos taken with the van (FIGURE 4.5).

FIGURE 4.3 Harrod Blank, *Camera Van*, 1995 and ongoing. www.cameravan.com. Photo by Hunter Mann.

Blank showcases image galleries for each set of audiences he's driven past in *Camera Van* (FIGURE 4.6). After learning of the many ways to control the production of a single photographic image, even skeptics should agree that the craft is as rich and complicated today as it was in the days of glass negatives.

FIGURE 4.4 Harrod Blank, *Camera Van*. www.cameravan.com.

FIGURE 4.5 Harrod Blank, *Camera Van*. www.cameravan.com.

FIGURE 4.6 Harrod Blank, *Soy Bean Farmer, MN*. Photograph created by the Camera Van.

MEASURING LIGHT

PHOTOGRAPHIC VALUES
The zone system for understanding value shifts across
the image is more thor-
oughly covered in Chapter 5,
Resolution and Value.

The amount of light required to make a photograph is measured with a meter. In the predigital era, some SLR cameras had built-in light meters, while large-format cameras did not. External light meters are still used today in photography studios. Digital cameras include a built-in light meter. The light meter registers the amount of light that's either in the center of the frame, averaged throughout the frame, or—for some cameras with the "spot" option—at a specific location within the frame. Understanding how to adjust your camera settings to comply with the light meter specifications requires you to understand the role of the f-stop and shutter speed camera controls. The light meter reading will show you how much light will be required to make a legible exposure for a balanced combination of f-stop and shutter speed settings discussed in Exercise 1. Generally, the purpose of your exposure will be to present photographic details at the extreme areas of contrast in the image. That means you'll want to capture details in the highlights and details in the shadows.

If you're shooting in automatic mode or can't control these settings, you'll simply point and shoot, and then hope for the best. Be careful when composing images in high-contrast lighting situations. Avoid shooting at or near noon, when the sun and shadows are strongest. And avoid low-light situations.

If you're working in manual mode, once you know how much light you need, balance the f-stop (which governs the diameter of the aperture) and shutter speed (which controls the duration of the shutter release) settings. Your choices about these two settings will depend on the depth of field (in the case of aperture) and movement (shutter speed) you want to include.

Some cameras let you create photographs in "aperture priority" or "shutter speed priority" modes. This means you can choose which of those two features you want to control. The camera will set the opposing lighting variable according to the choice you make.

RULE OF THIRDS

In addition to your camera setting choices, you'll be making decisions while creating a composition. As you can imagine, there are a lot of technical and aesthetic choices to make while creating powerful photographic imagery. In Exercise 5, you'll learn to see the compositional space using crop guides that make visible the "rule of thirds." This is a common way to understand the photographic frame, which is most often a two-dimensional environment with a 3:2 ratio. (4:3 and 16:9 are also common ratios among a variety of digital

Two additional pieces of advice that I give to new students are not specified by the rule of thirds:

- Get closer. By that I mean physically move your body and your camera closer to your subject.

- Watch the edges of the frame. The viewer shouldn't be left in no-man's-land at the edges of the frame. Be conscious about using the full frame to tell your visual story.

FIGURE 4.7 An image composed adhering to the rule of thirds.

media.) The premise of the rule of thirds is to evenly divide the frame by two horizontal and two vertical lines before composing the subject matter along the intersections of those guides (FIGURE 4.7).

One desired result of the rule of thirds is the elimination of the number one newbie mistake: centering the subject in the middle of the frame. You'll also start to see and weigh the visual balance of your subject matter by thirds, bringing more tension and energy to the overall composition. The more you're aware of the compositional space, the more likely you'll be to create a composition that leads the eye to your desired focal point.

RATIOS A ratio is a relationship between pairs of numbers. For instance, if you're cooking rice at a 1:2 ratio with water, you'll add one part of rice to the pot for every two parts of water. Instead of instructing someone to cook one cup of rice with two cups of water, it's more scalable to advise the ratio.

ADOBE BRIDGE

Admittedly, when Bridge was first released for Adobe Creative Suite 2, it was, how shall I put this, not terribly user-friendly. I didn't use it. My students didn't use it. No one I knew used it. We might have tried it a few times, but it just didn't seem worth the effort. After several revisions, Bridge has become an organizational tool that is absolutely worth learning. Bridge was primarily developed to allow you to organize and view file information relating to all the various types of files you generate using Creative Cloud.

WHAT YOU'LL NEED

Download the following source materials to complete the exercises in this chapter:

✔ The **chapter4-start** folder from the Chapter 4 downloads area on the book's companion website includes a **rule-of-thirds** folder and a **batch-rename** folder for those exercises.

You'll begin the exercises in this chapter by exploring your digital camera.

WHAT YOU'LL MAKE

In the exercises for this chapter, you'll organize your digital photographs in Bridge and create a PDF that showcases a series of images (**FIGURE 4.8**). This serves the same purpose as and looks similar to the contact sheets that photographers have used for decades. Your PDF will contain images, and it will display your file naming system.

FIGURE 4.8 Completed PDF contact sheet created in Chapter 4 exercises.

In the following exercises, you'll learn how to rename a folder of files, label (or rate) your files, and generate a contact sheet in a PDF, all at the click of a button. In Chapter 16, Automation, you'll use Bridge to apply Photoshop actions.

CAMERA MECHANICS

Basic operations take place when you create a photograph with your digital camera. There may be many adjustments to the camera that you can make, if your camera gives you control over them. These will have a direct result on the aesthetics of the resulting photograph. Most cameras also have an automatic setting, which lets you simply point and shoot. Even if you're just pressing the button, each of the following steps will take place. Details about each step are included in Exercise 2.

- Before shooting, consider adjusting the white balance, ISO, and file size settings. Or, just let the camera do that work for you. (Your camera might not allow you to control some of these settings.)

- Frame a scene by placing your eye to the viewfinder or by peering at the LCD screen on the back of the camera. Many DSLRs don't allow use of the LCD during shooting. If you have both options, consider the pros and cons of each (TABLE 4.1).

- After the image is framed, decide whether to shoot in automatic or manual mode. Do you want the camera to control the amount of light on the sensor, or do you want to control it by balancing the relationship between the f-stop (the diameter of the aperture) and the shutter speed (the quickness of the shutter release)? You'll learn more about f-stop and shutter speed settings in the next step.

- Press the shutter release button. Hold the camera tightly and try to eliminate body movement.

- The shutter will open, and the aperture will enlarge or decrease according to the f-stop settings.

- Light will be recorded on the digital sensor.

- The shutter will close based on the duration of time indicated by the shutter speed settings.

- You can preview your image immediately as it is saved on a memory card.

This choice is dictated by personal preference and limitations presented by the type of camera you're using. When using my DSLR, I always use the viewfinder. However, on my iPhone, I'm forced to use the LCD.

LCD	VIEWFINDER
Accurately represents the framed image space	Can be slightly inaccurate in consumer cameras due to what is called "parallax" as the viewfinder location is slightly above and to the left of the lens
Can lead to instability: since you'll hold the camera away from your face to see through the viewfinder, the camera is less stable than it would be if you were holding it closer to your balanced body.	Often leads to greater stability: you'll hold the camera to your face while making the photograph. Remember to square your hips and be still while you shoot.
Drains battery power	No extra battery power is required for composing through the viewfinder.

TABLE 4.1

CAMERA SETTINGS

The following items are elements you might be able to control when making a photograph. All digital cameras have different user interfaces. I've indicated where these items typically appear on the cameras I've seen in my classroom. Yours might be different. The best thing to do is read your camera's manual, or at least view the page containing the illustration of the camera and its settings! Did you lose it (or throw it away with the box)? Most manuals can be downloaded from the manufacturer's website.

- **File Size, Compression, and/or File Format.** These typically appear in the camera menu or function area.

  Even if your camera isn't terribly fancy, you may have a choice of creating small, medium, or large images, or you might even have a specific set of resolutions, via pixel dimensions or megabytes, to choose from in the File or Camera menu.

  You also might be able to choose to shoot in JPG, TIFF, or even RAW mode. Shooting in RAW mode yields the most information and adaptability, but processing a RAW image is outside the scope of this book. (There are plenty of books that deal specifically with Camera RAW, and I encourage photography students to become familiar with these details.) If you can choose between shooting in JPG or TIFF modes, you should know that the JPG will be more compressed (and usually a smaller file size) than the TIFF.

- **ISO.** ISO typically appears in the Camera or Function menu.

The ISO rating is analogous to what was once referred to as the *film speed*. Silver nitrate is the light-sensitive chemical found in film. The amount of silver in the film stock directly correlates to its ISO rating.

- **Low ISO.** A low ISO rating (25 or 50 in special films, 100 or 200 in the kind of film you can purchase at the drug store) indicates that there's little silver nitrate in the film. This in turn means that you'll need a lot of light in order to register the image on the film. If you're shooting outside on a bright day, set the ISO to a low setting. What's the advantage of using a super low ISO setting? In the film world, you'll see less film grain in the resulting print. In the digital world, the same rule applies— though we'll just call the film grain "digital noise." If you're shooting in a studio and you want to create a high-quality print devoid of noise, use the lowest ISO your camera offers and set up plenty of lights.

- **High ISO.** A high ISO rating (800, 1600, 3200 in special films, 400 in common film stocks) indicates that there's a large quantity of silver nitrate in the film. This in turn means that you'll need little light in order to register the image on the film. If you're shooting indoors, in the late evening, or at night, you'll probably need to set the ISO to a high setting. The advantages of using a high ISO setting are that you have greater flexibility in low-light situations. However, you'll see the grain of the film or some digital noise in your files (**FIGURE 4.9**).

FIGURE 4.9 Although high ISO settings make it possible to create images in low light, they often result in digital noise. Photograph by Thomas Van Deusen.

- **White Balance.** Along with ISO, this typically appears in the camera or function menu.

  Setting the white balance on your camera, if you're able, will ensure that the whites appear as a true white, and that the rest of the colors in the spectrum of the photographs are not the victims of a nasty "color cast" (FIGURE 4.10).

  The following are typical (self-evident) setting labels or icons you might find in a menu or function area. Match the white balance lighting to your situation: Auto (A-WB), Daylight (sunshine icon), Cloudy (cloud icon), Tungsten (lightbulb icon), and Night (moon or flash icon).

- **Aperture.** If you can control the aperture, you'll typically do so with a dial or button near the top of the camera body.

  The aperture is the size of the opening that light travels through the lens to the digital sensor. The wider the aperture opens, the more light you'll send to the digital sensor; of course, the inverse is true, too (FIGURE 4.11). The aperture's diameter size is controlled by the f-stop. Here's the tricky part: the smaller the f-stop number, the wider the aperture is open.

DAYLIGHT SETTING

TUNGSTEN (OR INCANDESCENT) SETTING

"SHADY" SETTING

FIGURE 4.10 Three photographs of the same scene made in natural daylight demonstrate the results of different white balance settings. If the white balance setting on the camera does not match the situation, the result may be an unpleasant color cast.

UNDERSTANDING F-STOP VALUES

The trick is to remember that the f-stop is a ratio, which means that the f-stop number you select on your camera refers to the denominator of a fraction where the numerator is 1. There is an inverse relationship between the size of the number and the size of the aperture opening. A small denominator corresponds to a big ratio (or a wide aperture).

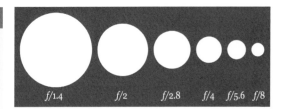

FIGURE 4.11 This illustration demonstrates decreasing aperture sizes. Created by Cbuckley and updated by Dicklyon on Wikipedia.

- **Depth of Field.** When the aperture is wide open (for example, f/2) the resulting image has a small area of focus; a large f-number (for example, f/22) generates a large area of focus in the image. Photographers refer to this optical phenomena as "depth of field." Shallow depth of field is created with lower f-stop numbers (**FIGURE 4.12**), while greater depth of field is seen in photographs made with larger f-stop numbers (**FIGURE 4.13**). Figures 4.12 and 4.13 showcase the results of using lower and higher f-stop values and the types of visual situations where one is preferred to the other.

FIGURE 4.12 Lauren Thompson, Snow White series, 2012. In this image, a low f-stop was used to create shallow depth of field. The focus on the figure's face contrasts with the blurriness of the tree branches she stands behind.

FIGURE 4.13 Tracey Cole, 2012. In this photograph, a high f-stop is used to capture the details in the glass object.

FIGURE 4.14 Ashley Tingley, *Untitled*, 2012. Photographs captured at a fast shutter speed appear to freeze time.

FIGURE 4.15 David Le, *Untitled*, 2012. Slower shutter speeds record movement.

- **Shutter Speed.** If you can control the shutter speed, you'll typically do so with a dial or a button near the top of the camera body.

  - The shutter speed indicates how quickly (or slowly) the shutter will open and close. In automatic mode with a reasonable amount of light, the shutter will probably release at about 1/60th of a second.

  - Anything above 1/60th of a second (which might just be indicated by the number "60" on your digital camera) is considered somewhat fast. A fast shutter speed will appear to "freeze" time, allowing viewers to see a moment that often escapes us. A cup filled with liquid in midair, for instance, can be recorded before it spills (FIGURE 4.14).

  - A slower shutter speed (1/15th of a second, 1/8th of a second, or more) will result in images that record subject matter movement. In FIGURE 4.15, the musicians and lights are blurred as they move rapidly on the stage.

SHUTTER SPEED AND SHAKY PHOTOGRAPHS

Your photographs will not display movements due to your physical inability to remain completely still at a shutter speed of 1/60th of a second or less (1/125th of a second, 1/250th of a second, and so on). With practice, you can probably even seem to hold the camera still at 1/30th of a second. Some people claim to be able to get a still image while hand holding the camera at 1/15th of a second (but that has never been the situation for me). If you plan to shoot at a slower shutter speed, use a tripod or steady the camera without human interference.

- **Exposure Value (EV or E/V).** If you can't control the f-stop or shutter speed, you may be able to alter the exposure value, typically accessed by a button on the back of the camera near the LCD. This button will normally allow you to take a photograph with slightly lighter and darker exposure values. On some cameras, you can press a Plus (+) or Minus (-) button; on others, you just spin a dial to move across a sliding scale. Altering the exposure value is an essential skill to learn so you can bracket your exposures while you're still learning to create photographs.

BRACKETING

Like the rule of thirds (see Exercise 5), bracketing is one of the first lessons new photographers learn. Since you're drawing with light when you create a photograph, the exposure of light that you set in your camera has one of the biggest visual impacts on the photograph. Bracketing is a method of increasing and decreasing the exposure value on the same scene in order to understand the visual results of an array of exposure values in a particular lighting situation. If you're new to photography, bracketing in as many lighting situations as you can will help you understand how light will register in the visual image made by your camera.

On any camera where you can control the exposure value, use the bracketing technique by shooting the same scene at least three times (TABLE 4.2). First, take a photograph using the most accurate exposure value according to your light meter (built in to DSLRs or likely whatever the automatic mode will indicate on consumer cameras). Then create another photograph of the same scene with one stop of additional light (a single shutter speed setting or f-stop setting). Follow this by creating one more photograph of the same scene by decreasing the amount of light to the sensor by one stop (a single shutter speed setting or f-stop setting in the opposite direction), starting from the "center" or original metered reading (FIGURE 4.16).

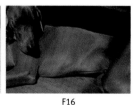

| F 5.6 | F 8 | F 11 | F16 |

FIGURE 4.16 Bracketed photographs. If you're only bracketing with three images, watch out for digital cameras that include half-stops. It's best to bracket at least five or eight times if you're brand new to the concept. You'll learn how your camera operates by experimenting.

	DSLR If you can control the f-stop and shutter speed settings, use the following list.	CONSUMER CAMERA If you simply have the Exposure Value (EV or E/V) button on your camera, use the following list.
Photo 1	Use the most accurate exposure value according to your light meter. You may need to manually adjust your shutter speed or f-stop value, or both, to achieve a balanced meter reading.	Use the most accurate exposure value according to your light meter. You'll probably see in the Exposure Value (EV or E/V) area of your camera settings that there's a dotted or dashed line, or perhaps a series of vertical straight lines with an indicator (a dot, usually) of the current exposure value. In automatic mode, the exposure value will likely fall in the center of the line. Pressing the EV button (or spinning a dial) will let you register that dot to the right or left of the center mark, which increases or decreases the exposure value.
Photo 2	Lighten the exposure value by one f-stop or by one notch on the shutter speed scale. For instance, if Photo 1 was taken at 1/60th of a second, take Photo 2 at 1/30th of a second to lighten the exposure value by one notch down on the shutter speed scale. (The shutter will remain open longer, allowing more light to register on the digital sensor.) Or, if Photo 1 was taken at f/5.6, take Photo 2 at f/4 to increase the amount of light through a wider aperture.	Lighten the exposure value by one notch to the right of the center on the exposure value line. You'll have to figure out how to add and subtract a notch on the EV scale.
Photo 3	Now decrease the exposure value. Create a photograph that's darker by one f-stop or one notch on the shutter speed scale. For instance, if Photo 1 was taken at 1/60th of a second, take Photo 3 at 1/125th of a second to darken the exposure value by one notch up on the shutter speed scale. Or, if Photo 1 was taken at f/5.6, take Photo 3 at f/8 to decrease the amount of light through a narrower aperture.	Darken the exposure value by one notch to the left of center on the exposure value line.

TABLE 4.2

 EXERCISE 4

BEFORE YOU SHOOT

Before you take off with your camera for a photography session, set aside an intentional moment where you consider some of the camera settings that may not change throughout your shoot:

- Prepare for the lighting situation: Is it daylight? Is it near evening?

  - Set the ISO for the amount of light you expect to capture.

  - Set the white balance for the type of lighting condition.

- Where will the photographs be published or printed? Do you need high-resolution images or are these just "practice shots?" Will the photographs be published strictly on a website?

  - Set the image size or resolution. (Use the largest size if you plan to print your images, and a medium or smaller size for experiments or web content.)

  - Set the format of the file. Use RAW only if you know how to process the RAW formatted images. If this is currently beyond your expertise, it may not be worth saving such large image sizes at this point in time.

- If you have the option, do you want to shoot in full manual mode, shutter speed priority, or aperture priority? Set the mode now.

 RULE OF THIRDS

As you've seen, the rule of thirds is a compositional concept that photographers use while framing the image during its production. Some cameras have a rule-of-thirds grid that you can superimpose in the viewfinder to see the guides while you're creating the photograph. In this exercise, you'll see how to use this compositional structure in Photoshop to assist you during post-production editing.

WORKSPACE › ESSENTIALS
Open Photoshop and set the workspace to Essentials by selecting it from the pull-down list in the Application Frame or by choosing the Window menu > Workspace > Essentials.

1. Open the file **dog-beach.psd** from the **rule-of-thirds** folder.

2. I've purposefully selected a lousy composition for you to work with in this exercise. Where are the first and second focal points? What's happening at the edges of the frame? Notice that the middle dog and the large branch are two main areas of focus. Where are they positioned in the frame? The top of the frame is full of distracting information: the cone, the volleyball net, and the houses in the background are all unnecessary to the activity in the primary focal area. In the next step, you'll reframe this image.

3. Choose the Crop tool from the Tools panel and set the tool options to Unconstrained and View: Rule of Thirds (**FIGURE 4.17**) in the Options panel.

4. Pull the Crop anchor at the middle of the top frame down so the top of the frame touches the tip of the red dog's tail (**FIGURE 4.18**).

5. Notice where the rule-of-thirds guides are located on the image. The branch is located precisely in the central square. You'd rather see main elements on one of the vertical or horizontal lines than inside what would be a cell if you think of the grid as a table. Move the crop guide on the left edge of the frame toward the middle of the image until the branch is more or less aligned on the left vertical rule-of-thirds guide (**FIGURE 4.19**).

6. Let's eliminate some of the bottom area of the image, just as you did with the top—the information at the bottom is simply distracting the viewer from the activity. Move the bottom crop guide toward the top of the image, keeping the idea of a two-thirds to one-third compositional ratio in mind. I adjusted the bottom crop guide so that the Weimaraner's front left paw is planted on the top horizontal guide (**FIGURE 4.20**).

7. You can continue to adjust the crop guides until you're satisfied with the crop. Notice that while you're cropping the image, the Layers panel indicates that you're in a Crop Preview (**FIGURE 4.21**). Press the Commit Current Crop Operation button in the Options panel when you're finished (**FIGURE 4.22**).

Save the file as **dog-beach-cropped.psd** to complete the exercise.

FIGURE 4.17 The rule-of-thirds grid can be viewed by using the Crop tool.

FIGURE 4.18 Adjust the Crop anchor to eliminate distracting information.

FIGURE 4.19 Align the subject on the rule-of-thirds grid.

FIGURE 4.20 Pay attention to the edges of the photographic frame when cropping the image.

FIGURE 4.21 The Layers panel will display the layer as Crop Preview while you're working with the Crop tool.

FIGURE 4.22 Starting with Photoshop CS6, you have the option to retain or delete cropped pixels. I prefer to retain pixel information, so I leave the Delete Cropped Pixels button unchecked, as seen here. Click the checkmark icon to exit the Crop tool or press the Return key.

EXERCISE 6 BRIDGE WORKSPACES

For the following exercises, you may use the images from your photo shoot or the series of photographs in the **batch-rename** folder. To demonstrate the following exercises, I used 12 daguerreotype photographs taken by Mathew Brady with the words "unidentified woman" in the title, which I downloaded from the Library of Congress website. Place the files in one easily accessible folder. I copied mine to a **chapter04** folder on my desktop.

1. Launch Bridge from the Mac dock or the PC Start menu, as you would open any other application. However, if you're opening Bridge, you probably have a particular set of files in mind that you want to review. An easy way to get into Bridge is to drag and drop the file of folders you want to view directly on the Bridge application icon. This method of opening the application forces a specific set of images to be on view immediately, once Bridge is open. Drag your folder of photographs on the Bridge icon (**FIGURE 4.23**).

2. To ensure that your screen looks similar to mine, choose the Window menu > Workspace > Essentials.

3. Notice that the content of the folder you dragged on the Bridge icon appears in the main window (the second of three columns) beneath a tab labeled Content. The file path to this content appears on the top left of the application window (**FIGURE 4.24**).

4. The top of the first column holds a set of tabs for Favorites and Folders. If your folder isn't displaying in the Content area, you can use one of these two tabs to navigate to the folder you want to view. (For instance, if your folder is located on the desktop, you can click the Desktop button from the Favorites list and then double-click the appropriate folder in the Content area.) Locating your files within Bridge is essential because you won't be able to do anything to your files unless you can see them in the Content area.

5. Drag the slider in the lower right of the Content area to enlarge or decrease the thumbnail view of your files (**FIGURE 4.25**). Since I only have 12 files in my folder, I zoomed out enough to see all of them on the screen at once.

FIGURE 4.23 Open a folder by dragging it onto the Bridge icon.

FIGURE 4.24 In Bridge, the file path to items in the Content area is a reminder of the location of files on the hard drive.

FIGURE 4.26 Information about the file appears in the Metadata Placard. If I'd used my DSLR to take these images, I would also see f-stop, shutter speed, and ISO information.

FIGURE 4.25 You can use the slider near the lower-right corner of the Content area to increase or decrease the size of the thumbnails.

FIGURE 4.27 When a file is selected, its properties appear in the Metadata Placard.

6. The column on the far right contains the Metadata tab. This provides you with the most information about your files. Click once on any of the images in the Content area—be careful not to double-click, as this may open your file in another application! Meta information (or information about the selected file) appears in both the Metadata Placard (FIGURE 4.26) and the File Properties menu. The Metadata Placard is especially helpful if the images were created on a digital camera that stores metadata within the image file. (For instance, digital single lens reflex cameras will store this information.) If the files were downloaded from a website (as mine are), the Metadata Placard won't show as much information. However, the File Properties menu will enable you to learn about the file's format (or document type), size, pixel dimensions, color mode, and more (FIGURE 4.27). Quick access to this type of information can be extremely helpful when you have a folder with many similar files.

BE CAREFUL! Double-clicking on a file in Bridge may open that file in a different application, such as Photoshop or Illustrator. You can alter these settings in the Preferences dialog, **Command(⌘)-K**, by selecting File Type Associations from the list in the left column and choosing an application to open for files in the JPG (or other) format.

EXERCISE 7 BATCH RENAME

KEY COMMANDS

Press ⌘-A to select all the files in the folder (that is, all files present in the Content area). Use the Shift key to select files that are next to one another. If you accidentally include a file in your selection, hold the Command key while clicking on it once to deselect it from the group.

The tool I use most in Bridge is Batch Rename. This command lets you assign a new file name to a group of files. You can rename an entire folder of files or just a few files selected within a folder.

1. The file names that I've assigned to the 12 photographs are long. I included a number, the source ("loc" for "Library of Congress"), the photographer's last name, and the name of the series. Let's assume that you're going to select half of these original files to modify in your own work. You want a new folder for your work, and you want to rename the files with your first initial, last name, and a sequence number (for example, **x-burrough01.jpg**). Before running a batch rename, decide on a system for renaming the files. Start by selecting the files you want to use. In this hypothetical situation, I'll select every other file by holding the Command key as I click on each of them in the Content area (**FIGURE 4.28**).

2. With the files actively selected (you'll see an outline around the selected file thumbnails), choose the Tools menu > Batch Rename. In the Batch Rename dialog box, you'll make several choices as follows.

FIGURE 4.28 To select multiple files in a row, press the Shift key and click from the first to the last file. To select multiple files that are not positioned next to each other, press the Command key while clicking one time on each image.

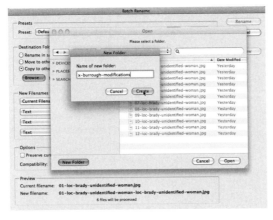

FIGURE 4.29 Create a new destination folder during the Batch Rename process.

FIGURE 4.31 Change the first filename field to Text.

FIGURE 4.30 Rename files using the new filename fields. Add and delete fields by pressing the plus and minus icons to the right of each field.

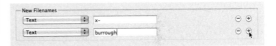

FIGURE 4.32 Add an additional filename field after the second one by clicking on the plus icon.

3. In the Destination Folder area, press the radio button next to "Copy to other folder" because you are going to create a copy of the original files with a new name. Press the Browse button, locate your **chapter04** folder (or the folder where you're saving the images in the Content area), press the New Folder button, name the new folder (**FIGURE 4.29**), and then press the Open button.

4. In the New Filenames area, I pressed the small Minus (-) radio button to the right of several of the Filenames fields (**FIGURE 4.30**). The original file name was lengthy, and I find it easier to start anew.

5. Change the first Filenames field to Text and then enter the first initial of your name followed by a dash (-) in its field (**FIGURE 4.31**).

6. Press the Plus (+) radio button to the right of the first Filename field you just set to add more information to the filename.

7. Select the Text option again and enter your last name in the field. Press the Plus button (**FIGURE 4.32**).

8. Choose the Sequence Number option from the pull-down list. Be sure the numbering starts with "1" and choose Two Digits from the pull-down list to the right of the field (**FIGURE 4.33**).

BE CAREFUL! I usually rename my files in the same folder rather than copy my files to a new folder. However, consider yourself warned. When you rename files in the same folder, you'll have lost the original names. You can't undo a batch rename.

You may not need to "clean" your Filenames fields area. You'll add new fields in the Step 6.

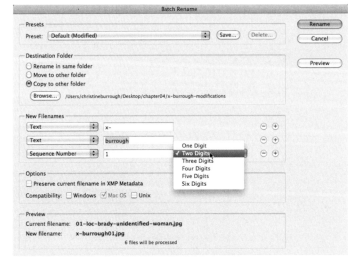

FIGURE 4.33 If it's possible, you'll end up with more than 99 images, so choose a name with three digits. A folder with fewer than 99 files should be saved with two digits if you're using sequence numbers in the name in order to keep the 10th through 99th files organized. You can see the file path to the location of the saved new folder next to the Browse button in the Destination Folder area. Also, you can see a preview of the new file names in the Preview area.

FIGURE 4.34 Double-click the folder (left part of the screenshot) in the Content area to open its contents (right part of the screenshot). Notice the file path at the top of this window area.

9. Review your selections. You should see the proper file path to the new folder. An example of the new file names appears at the bottom of the dialog box, as well as a message about how many files will be renamed. If all of this seems accurate, press the Rename button.

10. Scroll down in the Content area if you need to and find the new folder you created. Double-click the folder to open its contents. You should see your six renamed files in the Content area (**FIGURE 4.34**).

SCREENCAST 4-1 RENAMING AND RANKING FILES IN BRIDGE

Renaming files in Bridge using the Batch Rename tool is simple, but it comes with a heavy price: there's no going back! Watch a short video demonstrating this process.

All screencasts are available on the companion website, www.digitalart-design.com or on the YouTube playlist, www.youtube.com/playlist?list=PLAy6P5IoEjy2v3kZKCt8spqJ50nLb2XQI.

EXERCISE 8 · GENERATE A PDF TO SHOWCASE YOUR FILES

If you had one or several sheets of negatives to preview, you'd go to the dark-room, press the negatives directly onto a sheet of sensitized photographic paper with heavy glass, and expose the glass-negatives-paper sandwich with the light of an enlarger. The resulting proof is called a *contact sheet* because of the direct (negative in contact with the paper) printing process. Digital images can be previewed on the camera, so in a sense the need for contact sheets is not terribly urgent. Yet it's extremely common to share a set of images, mock-ups, or compositions with others in a single file. Earlier versions of Photoshop (before CS4) included an automated process for creating these types of documents, aptly titled *Contact Sheet*. Starting with CS4, the Contact Sheet automated task was transferred to Bridge. In the following exercise, you'll create a PDF of thumbnail (or larger)-sized images using Bridge's Output Workspace.

1. View the contents of your **chapter04** folder (my set of 12 images or your own photos) in Bridge. I had to choose the View menu > Show Reject Files to see all 12 images. You may also see the folder you created in Exercise 3.

2. Press ⌘-**A** to select all the files. Press the Command key while deselecting the folder or any other files you don't want to include in the PDF (**FIGURE 4.35**).

FIGURE 4.35 To select all the files without selecting the folder press ⌘-**A** (to select all) and then hold the Command key while clicking once on the folder to deselect it. Click and drag to move the files into the deselected folder.

FIGURE 4.36 Select files in the Output workspace to save them as a PDF.

3. Notice that the selected items appear in the Preview tab in the top-right column.

4. Press the Output button in the top-right area of the application window or choose Window > Workspace > Output (**FIGURE 4.36**). Notice that the layout of the tabs in Bridge changes. The selected content items are organized in a single row along the bottom of the application. The main area is reserved for the Preview tab. The right column is dedicated to the Output tab and menus beneath it.

5. Starting at the top of the Output tab, make the following selections:

    A. Press the PDF button. (It's selected by default.)

    B. In the Document menu, choose a page preset (I selected US Paper), a size (Letter), and set the Quality slider to the resolution of your choice. If you're just sharing files for a screen presentation, you can set the resolution as low as 72 or 96 DPI. I typically ask students to set the quality to 150 DPI so you can zoom in on images without seeing them pixelate during a critique session.

    C. In the Layout area, set the number of columns and rows you want to see. The more columns and rows you choose, the smaller the images will be on the page. I set mine to 2 by 2 and checked the Use Auto-Spacing box.

FIGURE 4.37 Modify the Output panel to customize your PDF. I tend to keep Overlays active in order to see the file name beneath each thumbnail in the PDF.

FIGURE 4.38 Collapse areas of the Output panel that you're not using by clicking on the sideways arrow to the left of the menu name.

D. The Overlays area lets you include a file name with your image. I keep the box next to Filename checked, because I like to see the filename so I can check how my students are naming their files (FIGURE 4.37). Also, it easily allows you to reference an image by name, rather than by description.

6. Scroll down in the Output area. I don't often use the Header, Footers, Playback, or Watermark menus, but they're clearly labeled should you want to add those features to your document. You can collapse the menus you don't want to use by pressing the sideways arrow to their left (FIGURE 4.38). Finally, check the View PDF After Save box and then press the Save button.

7. Save the PDF in your **chapter04** folder. Open it if it doesn't open automatically (if you forgot to check the View PDF After Save button, for instance) and preview your files.

8. Check the PDF file size on your operating system. On a Mac, you can see the file size by viewing the files in list format or by clicking on the file once and then choosing File menu > Get Info in the Finder or Desktop area. On a PC, you can right-click the file and view the file size in the Properties area. Since I set the resolution to 150 DPI (which is relatively low), my document showcasing 12 images is less than 4 megabytes—a reasonable size for emailing or uploading the file.

 ## LAB CHALLENGE

Find or take a series of photographs to demonstrate the theme "time passing." This is a classic photography assignment for which many people have photographed a flower throughout its growth and death stages. Don't choose to document a flower! What other visual references to the passing of time can you develop? (Stretch your imagination and avoid imagery of clocks, too). Take several shots based on one idea and place them in a single PDF using Bridge.

CHAPTER 5

RESOLUTION AND VALUE

THE EXERCISES IN this chapter will provide a technical lesson and a set of aesthetic exercises focusing on values that make up the tonal range of the composition. You'll explore the file size and resolution of a bitmap image to understand the nature of an image created by pixels. Then you'll study the values in a grayscale digital photograph. You'll learn to apply a zone system to gray values and to use a digital camera with this system in mind, for readers who opt to shoot in manual mode. Finally, you'll create a PDF to showcase your organized files in Adobe Bridge.

REDISTRIBUTING AND RESAMPLING PIXELS VIA RESOLUTION

The Image Size dialog box will be the main area of study in the first exercise. This dialog allows you to control the file resolution in relationship to your output preferences. Remember: the number of pixels captured is determined at the moment the digital photograph or scan is made. If you need to change the file's resolution, you will have to decide whether you want to redistribute or resample those pixels.

In the first exercise, you'll choose the Image menu > Image Size to review or modify the way that the pixels are distributed within the file. Most people think of this dialog box as the place where you adjust the file resolution. To avoid confusion, think of this as the place where you either redistribute or resample pixels.

To *redistribute* pixels is to compress or spread out the existing pixels, those native to the document. You can tell the document to pack as few or as many pixels into each inch of screen or printed space, but redistributing will not add or subtract pixels. Therefore, when you redistribute pixels, the file size will remain the same. If you *freeze* the number of pixels in the document by unchecking the Resample Image check box, then decreasing the resolution will result in spreading the existing pixels over more inches. This in turn increases its printed size. This process puts a finite limitation on how much you'll be able to increase the image size and get acceptable results. Depending on the values you see in the Image Size dialog box, you might not want to increase the size at all.

To *resample* pixels is to either throw them away (therefore reducing the document file size) or add new pixels, which generally is not a good idea. You should only resample the image if you need to throw away pixels to decrease the size of the document.

WHY SHOULDN'T I ADD PIXELS VIA RESAMPLING THE IMAGE?

Photoshop will use a sample of pixels from within your image to determine the best pixel values for the new ones it creates. This isn't a good idea because Photoshop was not on location when you shot the picture. (This is even truer for screen captures or images where you have introduced text or graphics; they will become fuzzy.) So the rule is that it's safe to delete pixels, but you should not add them to the document.

VALUE AND THE TONAL RANGE

Following the exercise on resolution, you'll learn to see values in a bitmap image by reading its histogram. You'll apply an adjustment layer to an image to alter its set of values, or the *tonal range*. The ability to control the tonal range in a photographic image lets you express its mood precisely. The tonal range might be a result of purposeful play between light and shadow, or it may be limited by the printing technique selected by the artist.

During the 1920s (the same decade that Walter Gropius led the Bauhaus school in Weimar and delivered a paper on unity among art, science, and technology), the artist Man Ray created a series of "rayographs" in reference to his version of the popular camera-less image-making process, the *photogram*. Man Ray's work influenced László Moholy-Nagy, who taught at the Bauhaus and also made photograms, but these were not the first set of light and object studies created with the photogram process. More than 70 years earlier, Anna Atkins created a book of cyanotype prints titled *Photographs of British Algae: Cyanotype Impressions*. These images are a result of placing an object (or objects) directly on sensitized paper before exposing the paper-object combination to light (FIGURE 5.1). The white imprint of the image (its *there-ness*) is mildly set apart from the cyan negative space where unobstructed paper receives a full exposure. A short shadow may be visible due to the close proximity between the object and the paper. The presence and absence of the representation of the object(s) might remind you of the binary nature of computing, where a bit is either "on" or "off." Of course, objects with some level of transparency (fruit slices, mesh fabrics, tracing paper, and so on) will also have an effect on the tonal range of the image. The digital version of a photogram is a scanogram, whereupon objects, rather than prints, are placed on the scanner bed.

FIGURE 5.1 Anna Atkins, *Cystoseira foeniculacea*, in *Photographs of British Algae: Cyanotype Impressions, Part I*. 1843–53. Courtesy of the Spencer Collection, The New York Public Library, Astor, Lenox, and Tilden Foundations.

Stark images with high contrast have a shallow tonal range. They can express an intensity as seen in Kevin McCarty's 2006 *Monster*, a portrait of a young

FIGURE 5.2 Kevin McCarty, *Monster,* from the series *I'm Not Like You,* 2006. Photograph courtesy of the artist.

FIGURE 5.3 Christopher James, *Nelske,* 2010. Photograph courtesy of the artist.

punk with spiky, dark hair (**FIGURE 5.2**). The separation between the subject's hair and background shadow area is defined with precise lines. The viewer is drawn to the contrasting tones in her face and the bright hue of her neck scarf.

If high-contrast images with sharp contours and few tones imply an ideological position, those with a soft, full tonal range may suggest uncertainty. For instance, Christopher James's 2010 portrait *Nelske* has a dreamlike aesthetic quality (**FIGURE 5.3**). In this wet plate collodion print, the artist painted a sodium thiosulfate concentration in specific sections of the plate before baking it in the summer sun. The result is a range of gray values that spread across the subject's face and hair before blending into the background. Where the face of the subject in *Monster* is harshly defined, in *Nelske* it is soft. Her eyes remain unknowable.

You might notice similarities between controlling the set of values in an image and using a square, circle, or triangle as a primary shape in a design. The tonal range informs the viewer (consciously or subconsciously), just as basic shapes signify visual meaning. In the following compositions, you'll learn to control the tonal range in the camera and see how it affects human perception.

ZONE SYSTEM REDUX

As mentioned in the introduction to this section, Ansel Adams first published a method for determining photographic values in his series of books, *The Camera, The Negative,* and *The Print.* The zone system is referenced in all three books, but it's most thoroughly described in *The Negative.* Since different readers of this text will have varying amounts of control over camera settings, you'll learn about the zone system for digital cameras here briefly. If you have little or no control over your camera exposure settings, the following may not apply to your current situation.

For a more lengthy explanation of the zone system for digital photographers see Chris Johnson, *The Practical Zone System for Film and Digital Photography* (Waltham, MA: Focal Press, 2012).

The zone system enables a photographer to divide her subject into 11 areas of value (10 steps) from black to white, as seen in FIGURE 5.4. The first, zone zero, is pure black. The last, zone 10, is pure white.

If you can shoot in priority or full manual mode, you'll use your light meter to determine how much light is required to obtain an exposure resulting in visible details in the highlights and shadows. Typically, this metering is averaged throughout the scene, and the exposure values you choose will likely place middle gray in the Zone V area. In other words, the traditional (analog film) method for utilizing the zone system was to expose the film for middle gray. The digital "rule" is to use the zone system to expose for the most important highlight values (usually occurring in Zone VII). The reasons for this rule are expressed eloquently by Chris Johnson in *The Practical Zone System for Film and Digital Photography* (referenced in the margin), but I will not get into them here. This is a major paradigm shift for those who learned to use the zone system with film and have converted to digital media. If the zone is new to you, then you can simply learn the digital zone and work with a system whereby exposing for Zone VII will give you the most flexibility with your digital file. To do this, you'll need to either fill the frame with a Zone VII element in the shot, or set your camera metering to *spot*. In Exercise 3, you'll learn to "see" the zones throughout a photograph, and in Exercise 4, you'll see why a slightly overexposed digital file will produce better results with digital processing.

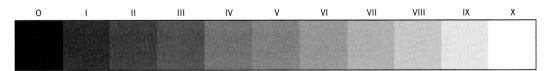

FIGURE 5.4 Zones 0 through X (11 values in 10 steps) between black and white are seen in this traditional scale representing the zone system.

WHAT YOU'LL NEED

Download the following source materials to complete the exercises in this chapter:

✔ The **chapter5-start** folder from the Chapter 5 downloads area on the book's companion website includes four photographs.

You could also use your own digital photographs, although your settings will undoubtedly differ from mine. You'll benefit from the ability to see changes in value across all areas of the image.

WHAT YOU'LL MAKE

In the exercises in this chapter, you'll create a study of value by noticing and placing the zone system on a photograph (**FIGURE 5.5**). You'll also learn to modify the tonal range in a photograph using a Levels adjustment layer (**FIGURE 5.6**).

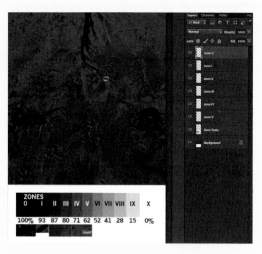

FIGURE 5.5 The exercises in this chapter will help you see the values in a photograph using the zone system.

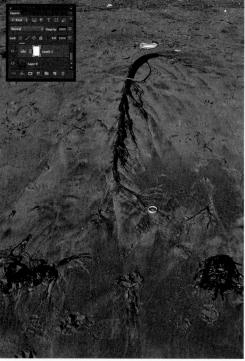

FIGURE 5.6 The adjustment layer for Levels is added to the photograph on the right. Notice the difference in the tonal scale between the original (left) and adjusted (right) images.

EXERCISE 1

REDISTRIBUTE PIXELS FOR PRINT RESOLUTION

1. Download the **chapter05-start** folder from the companion website.

2. The **chapter05** folder includes one photograph named according to its f-stop and shutter speed settings (as a point of information) and a digital representation of the Zone System named **zone-scale.jpg**. Open **f11-shutter640.psd** in Photoshop. Reset your workspace to Essentials mode, Window > Workspace > Essentials.

3. The photos were captured in color, but for these exercises we'll focus on the tonal range. This is much easier to see in grayscale color mode. Choose the Image menu > Mode > Grayscale. Press the Discard button to lose color information.

4. Choose the Image menu > Image Size to evaluate the pixel dimensions, document print settings, and resolution of the file (**FIGURE 5.7**).

5. There are two distinct areas within the Image Size dialog box: Pixel Dimensions and Document Size. (There are also check boxes at the bottom, which I'll discuss later.) The two reasons you'll most likely find yourself entering this dialog box are to alter the resolution to fit the type of output you intend or to modify the document dimensions (probably in pixels or inches). Let's assume that you want to print this image on a home inkjet printer as large as it can be printed without compromising the quality of the print. If your viewers will experience your file on paper or through some type of printing process, then the file resolution should be approximately 300 dots per inch (or DPI). Most consumer inkjet printers will produce a fine print at 240 DPI, so there's a little wiggle room for files that aren't quite large enough at the time of printing. This image is 5.357 by 8 inches at 300 DPI. If you want to see just how large you might print the image, you can reduce the resolution to 240 DPI, but you have to keep an eye on one important setting: the *Resample Image* check box. Uncheck Resample Image because you don't want to add pixels to the document. Instead, you'll redistribute the pixels within the document. Notice that when this box is unchecked, the Document Size settings are locked together, and the Pixel Dimensions area is grayed out (indicating that it's frozen). Now change the file resolution to 240 DPI, and you'll notice that the largest print you can make is 10 inches tall (**FIGURE 5.8**). Press OK to exit the dialog box and notice that nothing appears to change because your file still contains the same number of pixels—you simply told the file how to distribute the pixels at the time of printing.

6. Choose File > Save As and save the native file as **chapter05-print.psd**.

REMINDER You'll learn to add an adjustment layer for Levels in Exercise 4. When you're comfortable with adjustment layers, you can choose whether you want to discard color information as you did in Step 3 of Exercise 1 or "hide" the color information by using an adjustment layer. When the color is "discarded," it is literally removed from the file.

MODE SUBMENU
Notice that all of the modes of color, or digital color spaces, are listed in this submenu of the Image menu.

Seeing is believing. Save two versions of the same document. Redistribute the pixel resolution in one document to 72 DPI. In the other, redistribute the resolution to 300 DPI. Print each file and notice the difference in both the size and quality of the printed image.

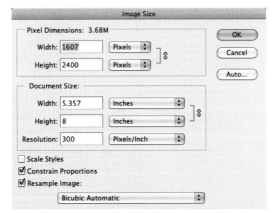

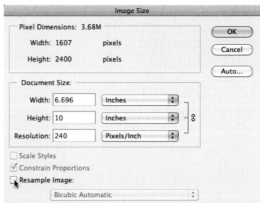

FIGURE 5.7 Notice the two distinct areas in the Image Size dialog box: Pixel Dimensions and Document Size.

FIGURE 5.8 Uncheck the Resample Image check box in the Image Size dialog box to redistribute the existing pixels in your image. *Resampling* means removing or adding pixels.

PRINTING RESOLUTIONS

If you're printing with a commercial lab, always ask the printer for the correct file resolution before setting up and sharing your documents. The paper and printing process may both have an effect on determining the best resolution (or dots printed in an inch). For instance, most newspapers specify that the file should be saved between 150 and 200 DPI, which is lower than the resolution you'll use on your home inkjet printer because the printing process and paper qualities are both different. I can print decent quality inkjet prints at home at a resolution of 240 DPI, while the laser printer in the lab where I teach has generated decent prints at 180 DPI (though those are noticeably less fine than prints sent to the laser printer with a file resolution of 300 DPI).

EXERCISE 2 — RESAMPLE PIXELS FOR SCREEN RESOLUTION

Now we'll assume that instead of formatting the image for printing, you want to format it for sharing on the web. If your viewers will experience your file on a screen (for instance, on a webpage, tablet, mobile device, digital video, and so on), then the file resolution should be approximately 72 pixels per inch (or PPI). There are specific resolutions for each type of electronic media, but most of the time you're likely to be saving for the web at 72 PPI. The smaller the file resolution, the fewer pixels occupy one inch of space, therefore the file size is smaller—with resampling. When the file size is small, it's more easily shared over a network. So for the end user, the download time decreases as the file size of the image or document to be downloaded decreases.

SCREEN RESOLUTIONS

A basic website will contain images that are likely saved at 72 PPI. Sometimes people share large files (in which case, the sharing of the bigger file is more essential than a smaller download time), so 72 is not exactly a magic number. To add to this confusion, iPads display graphics best at 132 PPI. Content developers creating media for tablets keep this resolution in mind. Ultimately, digital devices control the display of the file. In Photoshop, choose the View menu > Actual Pixels (⌘-1) or double-click the Zoom tool to see the size of the file at 100% (or its *actual* size on your digital display).

1. Choose Image menu > Image Size or press **Command(⌘)-Option-I**.

2. In the Image Size dialog box, you'll likely see the same settings you just left at the end of Exercise 1. (If not, uncheck the Resample Image check box.) With resampling turned off, redistribute the pixels to place only 72 pixels in an inch (**FIGURE 5.9**). Notice that at this resolution the document size is gigantic—just over 22 by 33 inches. This digital image would expand larger than most web browsers as it takes up a lot of screen space. Of course, a print made at 72 DPI would lack quality due to blurriness or pixelization. Keep the Image Size dialog box open for the next step.

3. In addition to redistributing pixels in order to modify the file resolution, you'll also throw away some pixels because this file has a larger width than webpages are designed to fit. Check the Resample Image box. From the pull-down menu, choose "Bicubic Sharper (best for reduction)" and then change the width to 800 pixels in the Pixel Dimensions area (**FIGURE 5.10**). Notice that your file size will be approximately 933KB, nearly one-fourth the file size of the original (3.68MB)

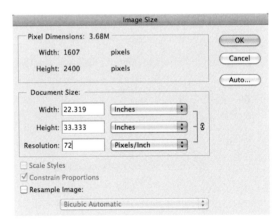

FIGURE 5.9 Screen resolution is 72 dots or pixels per inch (DPI or PPI). Notice how the document size increases when pixels are redistributed for screen resolution.

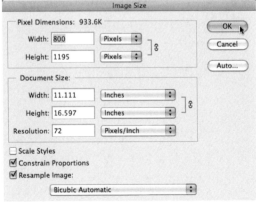

FIGURE 5.10 With the Resample Image check box checked, it is possible to remove pixels from the document in the pixel dimension area of the Image Size dialog box.

4. Press OK to exit the dialog box. Your file should have been visibly reduced in size because you threw away pixels by using the "Resample Image" check box inside the Image Size dialog box. Press ⌘-1 or View > Actual Pixels to see your file at 100% and confirm its digital size.

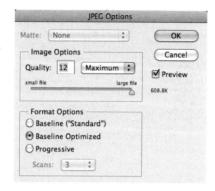

FIGURE 5.11 The JPG quality slider that appears when you choose the JPG format from the Save As option in the File menu.

You'll learn to save files for the web with the Save for Web dialog box in Chapter 13, *Graphics on the Web*.

5. Choose File > Save as and save this file as **chapter05-web.jpg** by choosing JPG from the Format menu. Press the Save button and then drag the quality slider to 12, saving this image with the highest amount of quality (FIGURE 5.11).

6. Look at the difference in file sizes within your **chapter05** folder. My print file is 3.9MB (almost 4 megabytes) while my web file is 635KB (a little more than half a megabyte). The web file has far fewer pixels saved within the document, and it was saved in a format that further compresses the file size. Print files are typically larger than files saved for viewing on a screen because they require larger file resolutions to maintain their quality.

ANALYZE A PHOTOGRAPH USING THE ZONE SYSTEM

EXERCISE 3

You'll know you've resampled rather than redistributed pixels when the file becomes visibly larger or smaller on your screen. If you didn't intend to add or delete pixels, choose File > Undo or use ⌘-Z to step backward and try the process again.

1. Practice redistributing pixels by changing the resolution of **chapter05-web. jpg** to 240 DPI without resampling the image (FIGURE 5.12). Press OK to exit the dialog box and nothing should appear to change on your screen.

2. Let's use an image of the zone system created for use in a digital file within this document. To expand the space in your image document for the next steps, choose the Image menu > Canvas Size. Here you can add dimensions to either or both sides and specify where the extra space will be added in relation to the image by placing an *anchor*. Change the height to 6.25 inches. Next to the Anchor field, click in the top, middle box. This tells Photoshop that you want the image to remain in the center (horizontally) and top of the new space (FIGURE 5.13). Since you're not adding to the width value, you'll simply see new document space at the bottom of the image.

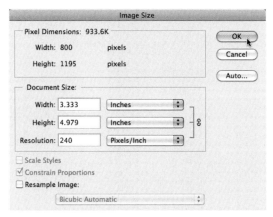

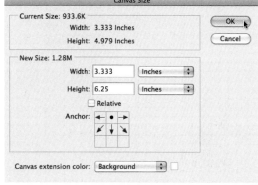

FIGURE 5.12 Redistributing pixels in the Image Size dialog box. (Notice the Resample Image check box is not checked.)

FIGURE 5.13 The anchor in the Canvas Size dialog box is used to position the page opposite the location of the additional "canvas" (or document) size.

THE ZONE SYSTEM SCALE

I created the zone system scale by following Lee Varis's steps from a tutorial on his website, www.varis.com. The tutorial, called "Digital Zone System–Part I," can be viewed at www.varis.com/DigitalZoneSystem/Digital_Zone_System-Part_1.html.

3. Open the file **zone-scale.jpg** in Photoshop and notice that the new file opens in a new tab.

4. In this step, you'll select, copy, and paste. Since Photoshop reads the entire image as a collection of pixels, "copy" is understood only when a selection of pixels has been indicated. Therefore, the copy action will be available only if something is selected. Since these are common actions, I'll direct you to do this with key commands and mouse strokes. I prefer using the keys for such repeatable actions. Press ⌘-A or choose the Select menu > All to create a selection around the entire image. Press ⌘-C or choose the Edit menu > Copy to copy the selection. Click on the **chapter05-web** file tab. In this file, press ⌘-V or choose the Edit menu > Paste to paste the image (**FIGURE 5.14**).

5. The image of the zone scale will paste in your document window on a new layer. It will be visibly on top of the photograph. Move the zone scale to the bottom area of the composition by clicking and dragging it with the Move tool (the first tool in the Tools panel).

CANVAS COLORS
The new "canvas" space will be transparent if the document was originally set up with a transparent background, or it will use the background color set in the Tools panel.

LAYERS When you paste new content in a Photoshop document, it "lands" on a new layer. You'll learn more about using, moving, and modifying layers in Chapters 6, 7, and 8.

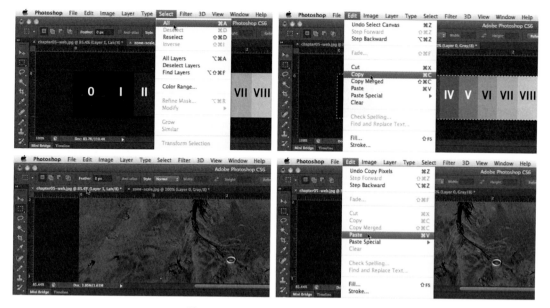

FIGURE 5.14 It's common to select all pixels on a layer in one Photoshop document, copy them, click on the tab to a different document, and paste the copied material. Memorize this process using the following key commands: ⌘-A (select all), ⌘-C (copy), ⌘-V (paste).

MOVE TOOL The Move tool acts only on the active layer. If you've made a selection, it will move only the selected pixels or object. If you haven't made a selection, the entire layer will be displaced.

Different digital color modes will register this middle gray at slightly different values. Middle gray is consistently a little higher than 50% in RGB, CMYK, and Gray-scale color modes.

6. Notice that the zone system demonstrates each zone, o through X. The darkest shadows are on the low end of the zone. Zone o is as close to pure black with no image details as you can get—most of the time you won't want to see Zone o in your photographs. Zone X, likewise, is as close to pure white with no image details—another Zone you probably don't want to see in your images. Zone V is approximately middle gray. In some images, you'll want a compacted tonal range, with values that fall into only a few zones. In other images, you may want to see a tonal range that spans zones II through IX. The photograph is dark in value overall because its exposure was based on a light-meter reading of the highlight values in approximately zone VIII (the plate). You'll correct the tonal range for the image in the next exercise, where you'll learn why the image was exposed for the highlights rather than middle gray.

WHY IS THE ZONE SYSTEM LABELED IN ROMAN NUMERALS?

Ansel Adams labeled the zones in Roman numerals to set them apart from so many of the other numbers that photographers dealt with during the camera, negative, and development phases of the photographic process.

FIGURE 5.15 A rectangular selection of a dark tone in the image.

7. Also, notice that the zone system includes a range of percentages below the shades of gray from black to white. The percentages indicate the amount of black value present in each zone. Zone 0 is 100% black, while Zone V is 62% black in Grayscale color mode. Zone X is 0% black. The zones are not evenly distributed in Grayscale color mode. (As noted, different digital color modes will register the zones with slightly different percentages.)

8. Now evaluate parts of the image that fall into particular areas of the zone system. Click once on the **Background** layer in the Layers panel to activate it. Use the Rectangular Marquee tool (second in the Tools panel) to select a small area of the image containing a consistent value in what you believe will be Zone 0 by clicking and dragging a box around it (**FIGURE 5.15**).

FIGURE 5.16 The pasted image selection is moved beneath the zone scale.

9. Press ⌘-C to copy the portion of the image you selected on the **Background** layer. Then press ⌘-V to paste it. You might think nothing happened, but check your Layers panel. Pasting should have created a new layer. The pasted image is directly on top of the copied image. Trust that it's there and use the Move tool to move the image part near the zone system scale (**FIGURE 5.16**).

10. Let's try this again on Zone I in a slightly different way. This time, create a rectangular selection that matches the width of Zone I. It doesn't matter what layer is active while you're clicking and dragging to create the selection. Once the selection is in place, be sure to click on the **Background** layer to activate it (**FIGURE 5.17**).

11. When a selection has been made and while you're still using a selection tool (such as the Rectangular Marquee tool), you can place the tool inside the selection and then click and drag to move the selection around the image. *This is different from moving an image—instead, you're moving a selection on an image.* Put the Rectangular Marquee selection tool inside the box and click and drag to move it to an area of the photograph that you think registers Zone I values (**FIGURE 5.18**).

FIGURE 5.18 After a selection is created, it can be moved by clicking and dragging with any of the selection tools. In this screenshot, a selection was made to fit the width of the Zone I box, and then it was moved to a location in the photograph that includes an extremely dark area.

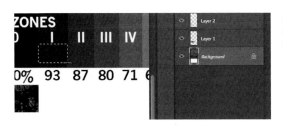

FIGURE 5.17 A selection is created that fits the width of the Zone I box.

FIGURE 5.19 Selections from the photograph are pasted beneath the zone scale to showcase grayscale tones.

FIGURE 5.20 The stacking order of the Layers panel can be modified by clicking and dragging a layer to a new position above or beneath a different layer.

FIGURE 5.21 Rename a layer by double-clicking on the layer name.

SELECT, COPY, AND PASTE

Remember that to copy part of an image, you must first select it. To select part of an image, you must identify and select the appropriate layer. It's very common for new learners to forget to click on the layer first and then select the image. If you see a warning that "No pixels were selected," check to see which layer is currently active.

12. Press ⌘-C to copy this part of the image and ⌘-V to paste it. Click the Move tool and move the new, pasted image to the bottom of the composition along the Zone Scale (FIGURE 5.19).

13. Eek! You might be pasting your images beneath **Layer 1** (which contains the Zone System scale). If this is a problem for you, click and drag **Layer 1** in the Layers panel so it's just above the **Background** layer (FIGURE 5.20). You can adjust the layer stacking order by dragging layers above or below one another. This will in turn adjust how the viewer understands which image is "on top of" another or closer to her eye. While you're making Layers panel adjustments, rename **Layer 1** to remind yourself that it's the layer containing the zone system scale. Double-click on the word "Layer 1" in the Layers panel and type "Zone Scale" when the field turns blue (FIGURE 5.21).

14. Continue repeating Steps 10 through 12 to find as many parts of the zone system as you can in this digital photograph. I placed image swatches near Zones 0 through V.

15. Rename your layers to match the zones you placed them in (FIGURE 5.23).

TIP FOR SELECTION CONSISTENCY

If you want to keep your selection boxes the same size, you can use a key command to select the first image portion you pasted and then use that selection to copy a new area of the image. In the Layers panel, simply press the Command key and click on the Layer thumbnail to make a selection around items on that layer (FIGURE 5.22). Once the layer is selected, use a selection tool (such as the Rectangular Marquee tool) to move the selection to an area of the digital photograph you want to copy. Then be sure to activate the **Background** layer before pressing ⌘-C to copy.

FIGURE 5.22 Command-click on a layer's thumbnail icon to select everything on the layer.

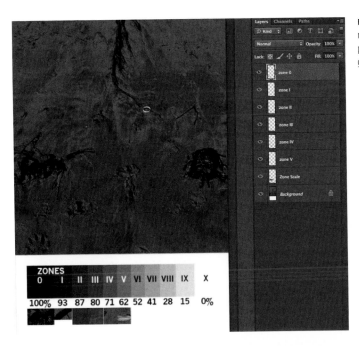

FIGURE 5.23 The Layers panel displaying renamed layers to fit the zone for copy and pasted selections from the original background layer.

MODIFY THE TONAL RANGE WITH A LEVELS ADJUSTMENT LAYER

You may have noticed that the tonal range of your digital photograph is clustered into the first four or five zones. The reason that the image contains such dark values is that it was exposed not for the mid-tone values, but for the highlights. Why? Photoshop does a decent job of recovering shadow details, but it's impossible to recover a burned-out highlight. So now that you have an image exposed for the highlight areas, you need to level the tonal range.

CROP TOOL To make a freestyle crop, make sure that "Unconstrained" is selected from the top-left pull-down menu in the Options panel.

1. Select the Crop tool (the fifth down in the Tools panel). Crop the image to include the photograph and delete the zone system scale by dragging the bottom, middle crop anchor to the bottom edge of the photograph (**FIGURE 5.24**).

FIGURE 5.24 Drag the anchors at the edges of the Crop tool selection to frame the new crop of the document.

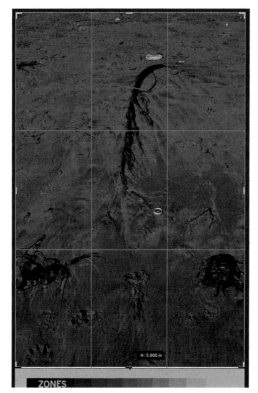

FIGURE 5.25 Click the checkmark in the Options panel to commit to the crop.

FIGURE 5.26 The Histogram graphs the amount of information in each of the 255 gray tones in a bitmap image. The left side of the graph maps the shadow areas (Zone 0, for instance), and the right side maps the highlights (Zone X).

2. Confirm the crop by pressing the checkmark icon in the top-right area of the Options panel (**FIGURE 5.25**). You can always start anew by pressing the Escape key on the keypad or pressing the No icon in the Options panel.

3. Click on any other tool to hide the crop edges from your view. (I usually click on a selection tool when I'm not working with a particular tool.) Also, click on **Layer 0** or the **Background** layer, as you'll work on or above the digital photo in the next steps.

4. You've already seen the range of gray values within this photograph. Now it's time to visualize that same range as a graph called a *histogram*. Choose the Window menu > Histogram. The histogram graph represents how many pixels exist at each gray value within the image. Typically, you'll be dealing with 8-bit images that have a tonal range of 256 gray values from black (0) to white (255). This accounts for all of the continuous tones that happen throughout the zone system. The human eye requires only 200 shades of gray to perceive a continuous tone.

Notice that the Histogram panel (**FIGURE 5.26**) displays the most information on the left side of the graph. The taller the vertical bar, the more information there is at any particular value. The values start at 0 on the left side of

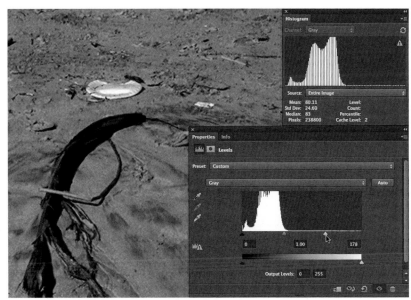

FIGURE 5.27 With **Layer 0** selected as the active layer, click on the adjustment layer icon for Levels.

FIGURE 5.28 Modify the Levels by dragging the slider on the right to reposition the highlights in an area of the image where pixel content exists.

the x-axis (black) and increase to 255 (white) on the right side of the x-axis. This histogram tells us what we already know: most of the image information is compacted in the darker ranges of the composition. There's hardly any information beyond Zone IV and only a little bit of information in what we might consider middle gray or (approximately) Zone V.

5. In the Adjustments panel, click on the second icon (its icon looks like a bar graph) to add an adjustment layer for Levels (**FIGURE 5.27**). Levels will open in the Properties panel. If you don't see the Adjustments panel, choose the Window menu > Adjustments. All panels can be accessed from the Windows menu.

6. The Levels dialog box will resemble the histogram you just studied in Step 4. The difference is that you're able to push the highlights or shadows, resulting in a reorganization of the tonal range. Since the image was exposed for the highlights, in effect, this stage lets you process for the shadows. The slider on the left side relates to the shadow areas of the image, the slider in the middle relates to the mid-tones, and the slider on the right side relates to the highlights. Push the right slider (the highlights) toward the middle of the graph. How far should you push the slider? This will depend on your aesthetic choices. I pushed the highlight slider until it reached the new level, 178 (**FIGURE 5.28**). You could press the Auto button

and then decide whether you want to use what Photoshop provides as the best adjustment. I zoomed in on the image, and kept an eye on the highlight areas (in this case, the plate at the top of the photo). When I pressed the Auto button, I didn't like seeing the highlights on the plate falling into Zone X. (In others words, the plate became "too hot.")

7. Look at the histogram now—it should show a new graph representing the changes you made with the Levels adjustment layer.

8. When you're happy with your adjustment, simply close the Properties panel (**FIGURE 5.29**). The beauty of an adjustment layer is that you can access and modify it at any time. The changes to the tonal range you implemented in Step 6 can be removed or modified because they're contained on their own layer. So if you printed this image and realized that you pushed the highlights too far toward the shadows (or not far enough), you could always open the adjustment layer and alter its settings. To open the Levels adjustment layer, double-click its Layer thumbnail icon in the Layers panel.

9. Save your file as **chapter05-levels.psd**.

 ## LAB CHALLENGE

While visualizing the values in the zone system, take a series of photographs making use of different lighting situations in which you expose the image for the highlight areas. Bracket these exposures so that you can then open the images and create a Levels adjustment layer to recover the shadows and expand the tonal range.

CHAPTER 6
COLOR MODELS

THE EXERCISES IN this chapter will encourage you to consider color as a relational element in your compositions. Just as values relate to one another—one can't be considered lighter without being lighter than another—color is dependent on its surrounding context. Color can be studied in vector graphics or bitmap art. Since adjusting color in a digital photograph is more complex than adjusting color in a flat graphic, you'll learn about color through the lens of photo editing (forgive the pun). You'll use adjustment layers and explore the Gradient and Transparency panels while learning the basic tenets of color theory.

Color is really a combination of three properties: hue, saturation, and luminosity (HSL). *Hue* specifies what we typically think of as the color, such as blueness or redness. *Saturation* refers to the grayscale value or chroma. *Luminosity* refers to the degree of brightness, referred to in Adobe applications as *lightness*.

FIGURE 6.1 Johannes Itten, *Farbkreis* (Color Wheel), 1961.

HSB OR HSL?

Hue, saturation, and brightness or lightness are often included in color editing tools common to most software applications where selecting or modifying color is an option. You may see HSB (hue-saturation-brightness) or HSL (hue-saturation-lightness) in reference to the relationship between these three components of color editing. In Adobe Photoshop, the Hue/Saturation adjustment tool, which you'll use in Exercise 1, refers to the third component as *lightness*, so we will use the language Adobe uses: HSL.

SUBTRACTIVE PROCESSES

In an elementary art course, you may have learned about the relationships between primary and secondary hues using an RYB (red-yellow-blue) color model (**FIGURE 6.1**) to predict the result of mixing paints. You might have tried to mix equal portions of red, yellow, and blue to produce a rich brown. My failed attempts always resulted in a murky gray.

This subtractive process involves two players: the surface on which the paint is applied and the pigment. In this case, the surface reflects the light that's transmitted to your eye. Let's assume the surface is white. A white surface will reflect all colors of light in approximately equal proportion. When red paint is applied to the surface, you may think that the color red is being "added" to the white surface. However, all the colors of the spectrum are present, and the white surface is reflecting back to your eye all colors except those that are subtracted by the particular pigment. A more precise translation of this experience is that the red pigment absorbs the other hues that are already present. So the red pigment subtracts those hues from your visual experience.

I've always found the subtractive process hard to wrap my head around and the paint and brush ridiculously difficult to control. So I'm grateful that computer graphics are made up of light and no pigments are involved.

ADDITIVE PROCESSES

Since the computer screen projects light to your eye, the process of combining hues to create color is an additive process, whereby color is a result of mixing projected light. When there's no light, you are in darkness. Any color at all is produced by adding light.

RGB

The primary hues for this additive process are red, green, and blue (**FIGURE 6.2**). These hues of light exist at specific wavelengths and cannot be created by mixing any other lights together. When all three hues are present in equal amounts, the result is light with no hue in a range from dark gray to white. (This might remind you of the zone system.) When none of the hues are present, there is no light. The obvious result is black.

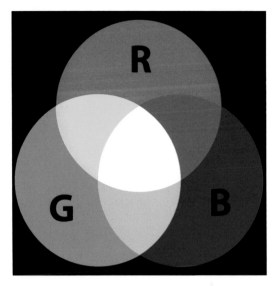

FIGURE 6.2 Additive RGB color diagram. Original version by Mike Horvath (2006); new version by jacobolus (2007). Courtesy of Wikimedia Commons.

Since red, green, and blue are the primary hues in the additive process, any image that you open in Photoshop from your digital camera (or that you scan) will automatically be set in RGB color mode. If you're preparing images or graphics for presentation on a screen (for instance, the web, a video monitor, or a kiosk), you'll most likely continue working in RGB mode. The final viewing location will use the RGB spectrum, so it makes sense to prepare images for RGB display.

A RETURN TO HISTOGRAM VALUES

Remember viewing the tonal scale in Photoshop's Histogram panel (or even in the Levels dialog) in the Chapter 5 exercises? The tonal range was computed from the number 0 to 255, as there are 256 possible shades of gray present in any 8-bit graphic. Now that you know more about the additive process, think more deeply about this concept: when the gray value is 0, you should see black. That's why the 0 value on the left side of the chart is indicative of the shadow areas in a bitmap image. The value 255 is essentially white light. This is when the light is on full-blast.

The complementary hues for each primary hue are as follows:

• Red is the complement for cyan.

• Green is the complement for magenta.

• Blue is the complement for yellow.

This is illustrated by the hues' positions on the RGB "wheel." (This isn't a terribly accurate term, but these are the hues you'll find when the primary hues overlap.) You'll experience this in Exercise 2.

There are other color modes that you can choose while working on your files. In Chapter 5, you converted the original colored image to grayscale by changing the mode to grayscale.

CMYK

If you're preparing images for commercial printing (meaning that you're sending the file to an offset or digital printer), set the image to CMYK color mode. (Choose Image menu > Mode > CMYK.) In this printing process, the file contains four color channels that each store the separate values for the primary pigments: cyan, magenta, yellow, and black.

FIGURE 6.3 Vincent van Gogh, *Irises*, 1890. The blue flowers are in extreme contrast with the yellow in the background, as these complementary colors are opposites on the color wheel.

The aim of this book is to guide you through basic exercises relating to design principles and theories. Offset printing is slightly outside the scope of this text, but a good rule to follow is to always communicate with the printer. She will tell you what the specifications are for printing on her press and may even provide directions for converting RGB images to CMYK mode.

PRIMARY AND COMPLEMENTARY COLOR RELATIONSHIPS

The strongest contrast is created when the primary hues are placed near their secondary hue counterparts (FIGURE 6.3). Traditionally, secondary or complementary hues directly oppose the primaries on the color wheel. In the RGB model, the complementary hues are a mixture of two of the pure primary light hues. (In other words, mix red at a level of 255 with green at a level of 255, and you'll arrive at yellow, the complement to blue.) Another way of explaining this is when one of the three RGB hues is set to zero and the other two are fully present, the result is the complement of the absent RGB primary (FIGURE 6.4).

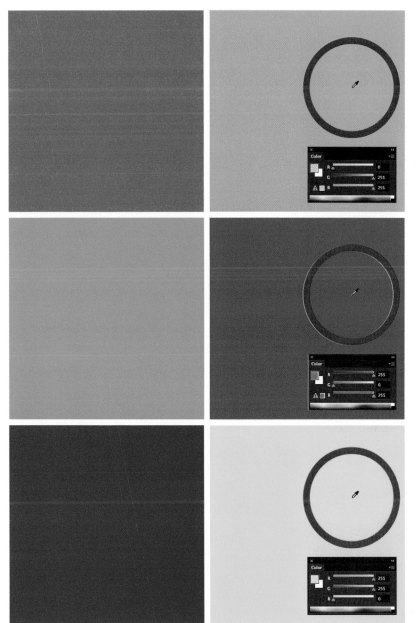

FIGURE 6.4 Red, green, and blue (the left column) are the primary colors in the additive process. To the right of each color is its complement: cyan, magenta, and yellow. Notice the Color panel atop each complementary color. The missing hue is the primary to its left. For instance, cyan is created by mixing two of the three primaries (green and blue) and leaving the red value at zero.

When Josef Albers created his *Homage to the Square* paintings, his presentation was more meaningful than you might expect. His placement of colored paint as the subject of the painting, rather than the tool for expression, transformed how artists experimented with the boundaries between media and subject, or process and expression. This emphasis on formal properties such as color as the subject of a work of art has been further explored in new media works of the late 20th and early 21st centuries.

In Brian Piana's online project *Tweeting Colors*, Twitter messages are transformed into a collection of colors (**FIGURE 6.5**).

Jack Hughes's *Colour Clock* (**FIGURE 6.6**) also transforms information into colors. The browser or screen application converts hours, minutes, and seconds into hexadecimal values relating to the red, green, and blue values that can be displayed online.

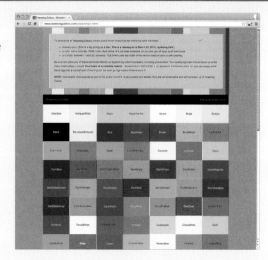

FIGURE 6.5 Brian Piana, *Tweeting Colors*, 2010. Screenshot courtesy of the artist.

FIGURE 6.6 Jack Hughes, *Colour Clock*. Screenshot courtesy of the artist.

WARM AND COOL

Hue can also be used to dictate how the viewer perceives the depth of an image. Warm hues appear closer to the viewer, while cool hues tend to recede into the background. This phenomena is demonstrated in Tiffini Myers' abstract photograph: the warm hues in the center float to the foreground as the cool blue tones at the edges fade to the background (**FIGURE 6.7**). In the RGB model, when the image is more blue than red, the hue will be cooler. When images contain more red than blue, the hue will be warmer. The green value will influence the degree of warmth or coolness and, of course, the hue itself.

Additive and subtractive processes do not affect the warmness or coolness of a hue.

SIMULTANEOUS CONTRAST

Bauhaus teachers Josef Albers and Johannes Itten developed color studies and theories that influenced abstract, op (short for "optical"), and conceptual artists' perception of color and its role throughout the mid-20th century. Albers's *Homage to the Square* series, consisting of hundreds of paintings of nested squares, illustrates his idea of halation, sometimes referred to as *simultaneous contrast* (**FIGURE 6.8**). You'll learn more about halation in Exercise 2.

LINK See Richard Nelson's *Albers Homage to the Square: An Explanation* on Vimeo at www.vimeo.com/25215702.

In the exercises in this chapter, you'll create various color studies using the selection tools and adjustment layers.

FIGURE 6.7 Photo by Tiffini Myers © 2013.

FIGURE 6.8 Screenshot of Richard Nelson's *Albers Homage to the Square: An Explanation* on Vimeo.

WHAT YOU'LL NEED

Download the following source materials to complete the exercises in this chapter:

✔ The **chapter6-start** folder from the Chapter 6 downloads area on the companion website.

You could also use your own digital photographs, although your settings will undoubtedly differ from mine.

WHAT YOU'LL MAKE

In the exercises in this chapter, you'll create both harmony and simultaneous contrast using Hue adjustment layers (**FIGURE 6.9**). You'll also learn to use the Levels and Hue adjustment layers to color correct a photograph. You'll see how to apply color to a black-and-white photograph in Photoshop in the Screencast.

FIGURE 6.9 The results of the exercises in this chapter include a study of harmony (top left), contrast (top right), and color corrections ("before" on the bottom left and "after" on the bottom right).

EXERCISE 1 HARMONY IN RECTANGLES

Harmony is achieved when colors near one another on the color wheel or within the color model are juxtaposed in the image. The starting file is a black-and-white image. In the following exercise, you'll convert the image to RGB mode and then apply two Hue adjustment layers to create color harmony within the image.

1. Open **harmony.psd** from the **chapter6-start** folder. This may look familiar, as it's one of the images you used in the Bridge exercises in Chapter 4.

SELECTION TOOL

The Rectangular Marquee tool is sometimes referred to as the Rectangle selection tool because all of the marquee tools are used to select parts of a bitmap image.

2. Choose the Rectangular Marquee tool and try to draw a rectangle that follows the white frame surrounding the photograph. You'll notice that it isn't possible because the frame is on a slight tilt (**FIGURE 6.10**).

3. Deselect this area by clicking anywhere outside the selection or by pressing **Command(⌘)-D**.

4. Redraw the selection using the Polygonal Lasso tool—choose it from the Tools panel (**FIGURE 6.11**). To use this tool, click just once inside one of the four corners of the frame. Release the mouse. Drag the mouse to the next corner of the frame (move in a clockwise or counterclockwise direction)

FIGURE 6.10 The Rectangular Marquee tool creates square and rectangular selections. Since the frame of the image is slightly tilted, the selection does not fit the frame.

FIGURE 6.11 The Polygonal Lasso tool is grouped with the Lasso and Magnetic Lasso tools in the selection area of the Tools panel.

FIGURE 6.12 End the Polygonal Lasso selection by clicking on the location where you started the selection.

ZOOM ZOOM

To zoom in or out easily, you can use the key commands ⌘-+ (zoom in) or ⌘-– (zoom out). You can also press **Space bar-⌘** (zoom in) or **Space bar-⌘-Option** (zoom out). Using the **Space bar-⌘** shortcut loads the Zoom tool, so you can click exactly on the area you want to magnify. ⌘-+ (or -) simply enlarges the magnification while leaving the center of the image in your viewing area.

WATCH OUT! If you thought you were creating a selection with the Polygonal Selection tool but received the message "No pixels were selected," then you probably didn't close the selection. Be mindful while making that last click. Or you may have double-clicked in the process of selecting. This tool is a bit finicky.

and click once. Release the mouse. Repeat this until you've clicked on three of the four corners. To return to the fourth corner, zoom in and be sure to click the Polygonal Lasso tool in the same location where you began this selection. You'll see a small circle next to the bottom of the tool icon, indicating that you're closing the selection (FIGURE 6.12).

5. To add the first wash of color to the image, use the Hue adjustment layer. If you try to click the icon to add an adjustment layer for hue, you'll notice that it's unavailable (FIGURE 6.13). You can't add color to the image until you're working in a color mode that supports color information. Choose the Image menu > Mode > RGB Color to convert the bitmap image from Grayscale mode to RGB.

FIGURE 6.13 The Hue adjustment starts the second row in the Adjustments panel.

FIGURE 6.14 The Colorize button applies a wash of color to parts of the image affected by the Hue/Saturation adjustment layer.

FIGURE 6.15 Press the Command key (Mac) or Control key (PC) while clicking on the mask icon of the Hue/Saturation adjustment layer to create a selection based on the mask.

6. Now press the Hue adjustment layer icon. Inside the Properties dialog, you can adjust the hue, saturation, and lightness of the selected area of the image. Notice that your selected edges have disappeared. Press the Colorize button toward the bottom of the Hue/Saturation window and drag the Hue slider toward a warm orangish-yellow (FIGURE 6.14).

You'll learn to use layer masks in Chapter 8, *Select, Copy, Paste, Collage.*

7. The Hue/Saturation adjustment layer is saved in the Layers panel. Notice that the adjustment layer has two thumbnail icons on it: the layer thumbnail and the layer mask thumbnail. The mask is where the original selection you made in Step 4 has been saved. The adjustment for hue and saturation has been applied only to that area. Press the Command key while clicking once on the layer mask thumbnail (FIGURE 6.15). The Properties panel changes to display the mask properties, and the selection is loaded in the document.

8. Choose the Select menu > Transform Selection. Now you'll scale the selection edges. This won't scale or transform the image, just the selection. Press the Shift key and hold it while you drag one of the selection edges in toward the image to decrease the size of the selection (FIGURE 6.16). Press the Commit Transform button on the top right of the Options panel when you're satisfied with the new selection.

9. When any of the selection tools are loaded, you can move a selection around the image without transforming the image or the selection size by clicking and dragging from within the selection—the selection tool will transform to a white arrow with a small selection marquee to its bottom right. Click and drag the selection so it's centered in the image space (FIGURE 6.17).

10. Return to the Adjustments panel and add a new Hue/Saturation adjustment layer. Press the Colorize button and drag the Hue slider to the left of the warm yellow to add an orange hue to the selected area (FIGURE 6.18). You may need to increase the saturation.

FIGURE 6.16 The Photoshop interface for transforming a selection looks similar to the interface for transforming a layer or image. Notice that the selection, represented by the "marching ants" or dashes, has decreased in scale while the image remains the same size.

FIGURE 6.17 Move a selection by clicking and dragging it with any selection tool.

11. Repeat Steps 7 through 10 to make a third rectangle inside the second one. Adjust the selection to include a deep magenta wash of color using another Hue/Saturation adjustment layer (FIGURE 6.19).

12. Save your final file as **harmony-final.psd**.

FIGURE 6.18 A second Hue/Saturation adjustment layer is added on top of the first within a smaller selection area.

FIGURE 6.19 A third Hue/Saturation adjustment layer is added on top of the first within a smaller selection area.

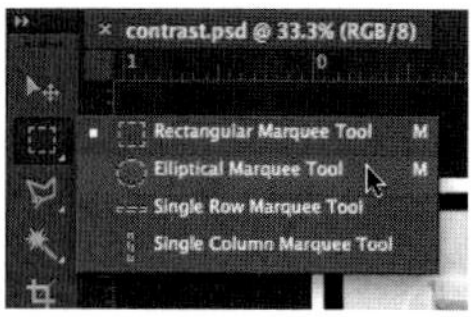

FIGURE 6.20 The Elliptical Marquee tool is grouped with the Rectangular and Row Marquee tools in the selection area of the Tools panel.

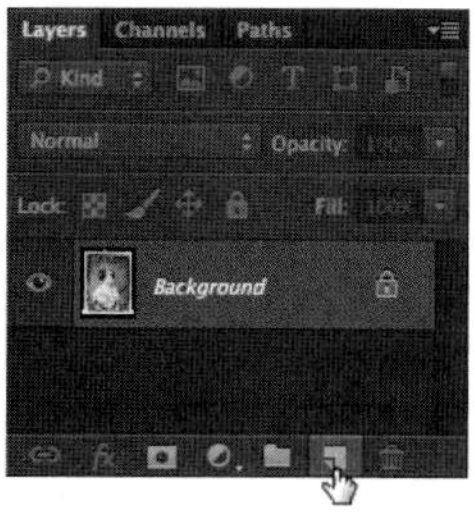

FIGURE 6.21 Add a new layer by clicking on the icon next to the Trash icon in the Layers panel.

YIKES! If you double-click the layer outside the layer's name, you'll open the Layer Style dialog. Close it and try to rename the layer again. You have to double-click right on the name to do this.

EXERCISE 2 SIMULTANEOUS CONTRAST IN CIRCLES

Simultaneous contrast or *halation* is achieved when complementary colors are juxtaposed within an image. In this exercise, you'll convert the starting file to RGB mode and then apply a primary hue and its complement within "parent" and "children" circles using the Layers panel and the Color blending mode.

1. Open **harmony.psd**, the same file you started with in Exercise 1. Convert the mode to RGB Color (see Step 5 of Exercise 1) and then choose File > Save As and save the file as **contrast.psd**.
2. Choose the Elliptical Marquee tool from the Tools panel—it's nested in the same set of selection tools containing the Rectangular Marquee tool, so press your mouse on one scroll to load the other if you need to (**FIGURE 6.20**).
3. Click and drag to create a circular selection while pressing the Shift key. The Shift key constrains the proportions, so the ellipse will become a circle. Try to fill as much of the frame as you can.
4. Press the new layer icon in the bottom of the Layers panel (**FIGURE 6.21**). Rename Layer 1 by double-clicking on the name **Layer 1** and entering a new name. I named my layer **blue**.
5. Double-click the Foreground color chip at the bottom of the Tools panel. The Color Picker dialog is open. Use the slider on the thin rainbow of hues to zoom in on a blue hue. The box on the left side of the window shows you what that hue looks like as it increases in value from top to bottom. (Notice pure white in the top-left corner and black in the lower-right corner.) It also shows the hue with a gradation of saturation from the top-right corner

WHILE YOU'RE DRAGGING SELECTIONS

All the selection tools follow a similar working methodology:

- When you press the Shift key while dragging your selection, the rectangle or ellipse will conform to a perfect square or circle. **Release the mouse before you release the Shift key.**
- When you press the Option key before you begin dragging the mouse, you can "draw" the selection from its midpoint outward. (Yes, you can combine the Shift and Option keys if you want to, as well.)
- While you're dragging the mouse to draw the selection, press the space bar to move the position of the selection around the image. I find this especially useful when I'm trying to align a selection with a specific part of an image.

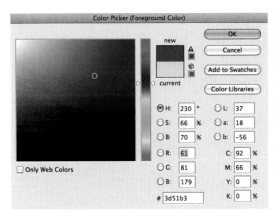

Color Picker (Foreground Color)

OK
Cancel
Add to Swatches
Color Libraries

new
current

◉ H: 230 °   ○ L: 37
○ S: 66 %   ○ a: 18
○ B: 70 %   ○ b: -56
○ R: 61   C: 92 %
○ G: 81   M: 66 %
○ B: 179   Y: 0 %
3d51b3   K: 0 %

☐ Only Web Colors

FIGURE 6.22 The Color Picker displays a range of chroma values for a selected hue from the top right of the window to the bottom left (in this case, blue from highly chromatic or saturated in the top-right corner to desaturated gray in the bottom-left corner). The hue shifts in value from top to bottom (from white/light at the top to dark/black at the bottom). Choose a hue by dragging the slider in the rainbow strip of colors.

new
current

FIGURE 6.23 Warning icons in the Color Picker window let you modify color choices based on your final output. The top warning is for the printing gamut: click the square below the exclamation point to select a similar color that can be printed. The bottom warning is about colors available on the web.

where it's most heavily saturated to the lower-left corner where it's desaturated. As you move the circular color selection icon around this box, your new foreground color loads in the New color field (**FIGURE 6.22**). There are two icons to keep an eye on next to the New color field in this dialog. One is an exclamation point in a triangle, which gives you information about colors that are out of the printing gamut (will not print). The other is a cube, which lets you modify your color selection so that it's part of the web-safe palette. You needn't be concerned with web-safe colors now, but get in the habit of clicking on the blue color swatch below the out-of-gamut warning as a best practice (**FIGURE 6.23**). Press the OK button to exit the dialog.

FIGURE 6.24 Drag a layer to the Create a new layer icon to duplicate it in the Layers panel.

6. Before filling the circle with blue, check on two items: you should still see your selection edges because you haven't yet deselected the circle, and the layer named **blue** should be active (highlighted) in the Layers panel. If both of these are true, choose the Edit menu > Fill. Contents should be set to Foreground Color, and the Blending Mode should be Normal at 100% Opacity. Press OK.

7. Deselect the circle by pressing ⌘-D on the keypad.

8. Drag the **blue** layer to the Create a new layer icon (**FIGURE 6.24**). Rename the resulting **blue copy** layer to **orange**. Two blue layers are in the same location, one on top of the other. It seems as though there's only one, but you'll modify the image in the next steps and see that there are two.

9. While the **orange** layer is active, press ⌘-I on your keypad to invert the color of items on the layer. The blue circle will become orange.

10. This time, instead of transforming the selection, you'll transform the orange shape. Choose the Edit menu > Free Transform. Press the Shift key as you drag one of the corners toward the middle of the shape to reduce its size (**FIGURE 6.25**). Press the Enter key on your keypad to confirm the transformation or use the Commit Transform checkmark in the Options panel.

KEY COMMAND Instead of Edit > Fill, I use **Option-Delete** to fill with the foreground color. Press ⌘-**Delete** to fill with the background color.

FIGURE 6.26 Lock the transparency of a layer by clicking on the Transparency Lock icon in the Layers panel.

FIGURE 6.25 Press and hold the Shift key while transforming a shape to maintain its proportions.

11. Use the Move tool to move the orange circle so that it's positioned in the middle of the blue circle.

12. Repeat Steps 8 through 11 to create a new layer named *cyan* with one exception: instead of pressing ⌘-I (which would simply load the same blue as the outer circle), you'll need to change the hue to cyan using a different method. Press the Lock icon in the Layers panel to lock the transparent parts of the **cyan** layer (**FIGURE 6.26**). Then load cyan into the Foreground color chip using the Color Picker or the Colors panel and apply it to the circle with the key commands (see the note near Step 6).

13. The grand finale: you'll now apply these colors to the photograph by changing their blending modes. One at a time, set each of the circle layers to the Color blending mode (**FIGURE 6.27**). The total effect won't be visible until all three are set on Color mode. Layer blending modes are used to determine how each layer interacts with the ones beneath it in the stacking order of the Layers panel. The Color blending mode transforms filled color areas into a wash of color applied to the texture of the bitmapped image.

14. Save the file as **contrast-final.psd**.

 COLOR COMPARISON

Open the two final files, **harmony-final.psd** and **contrast-final.psd**, to view them side by side. If you open both files in Photoshop (with nothing else open), choose Window > Arrange > Tile All Vertically (**FIGURE 6.28**). Can you see how the image containing contrasting colors has a tension and feels smaller, while the image where the hues create harmony seems bigger? The circles recede into space, whereas the rectangles make the woman's face pop out toward the viewer. The way that colors relate to one another will affect the viewer's perception. When you're finished studying the results of these two exercises, close both files.

Normal
Dissolve

Darken
Multiply
Color Burn
Linear Burn
Darker Color

Lighten
Screen
Color Dodge
Linear Dodge (Add)
Lighter Color

Overlay
Soft Light
Hard Light
Vivid Light
Linear Light
Pin Light
Hard Mix

Difference
Exclusion
Subtract
Divide

Hue
Saturation
✓ Color
Luminosity

cyan

orange

blue

Background

FIGURE 6.27 Color is one of many blending modes you can select from the Blending Mode pull-down menu in the Layers panel.

FIGURE 6.28 A side-by-side comparison of the final harmony and contrast files.

EXERCISE 4 COLOR CORRECTION

Color photographs, whether they're captured digitally or on film, often require some degree of color correction in the printing or production process. In this exercise, you'll alter the color in the photograph **correction-start.psd** using the Levels and Hue adjustment layers.

1. Open the file **correction-start.psd**. This is purposefully a not-so-great photograph. Do the best you can to crop the composition and correct its color. You may be surprised at your ability to make something decent out of something terrible.

2. Crop the photograph using the rule of thirds (see Exercise 5 in Chapter 4) as a guide to set the beach debris along the left vertical line (**FIGURE 6.29**).

3. Begin by adjusting the tonal range. Since this is a color photograph, you'll adjust each color channel within the Levels dialog. Click the Levels icon in the Adjustments panel.

4. Don't adjust the tonal range on the RGB composite. Instead, use the pull-down menu to select the Red channel and adjust the tonal range just for the red parts of the image (**FIGURE 6.30**). Remember that the complement of red in an RGB image is cyan. So you'll not only place the shadows into a position where there's image information (move the left slider toward where information begins on the histogram), but also adjust the midtone slider slightly to see a slight intensity in the red areas of the image.

BE CAREFUL!
Your adjustments should be minor, not major deviations. You should just barely be able to see the changes you're making to the image. Instead of pushing or pulling the midtone sliders, I usually place my cursor in the midtone box and use the Up Arrow and Down Arrow keys to adjust this part of the tonal range in increments of one.

FIGURE 6.29 A tighter crop of the original photograph.

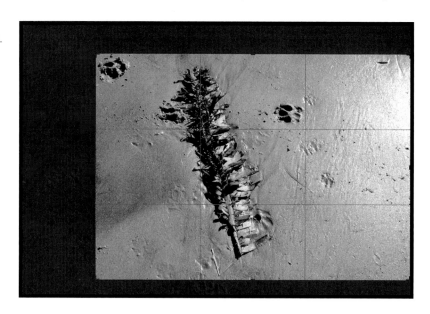

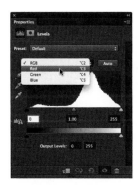

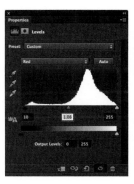

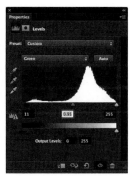

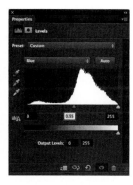

FIGURE 6.30 The Levels Property panel displays levels for each separation of colors. In an RGB image, you'll see the RGB composite histogram, as well as one for each color: red, green, and blue.

FIGURE 6.31 Set the midtones in the red channel of the Levels adjustment layer.

FIGURE 6.32 Set the midtones in the green channel of the Levels adjustment layer.

FIGURE 6.33 Set the midtones in the blue channel of the Levels adjustment layer.

This will also be seen as a reduction in cyan throughout the midtones (**FIGURE 6.31**).

5. Use the pull-down menu to adjust the green channel. Set the shadows; then adjust the midtone slider. For a quick visual reminder, push the slider all the way toward the shadows and then push it all the way toward the highlights. Return the midtone number to "1" and make a slight adjustment (**FIGURE 6.32**).

6. Use the pull-down menu to adjust the blue channel as you did the red and green channels (**FIGURE 6.33**). Close the Properties dialog when you're done. You can always reenter the Levels adjustment layer by double-clicking the layer thumbnail in the Layers panel.

7. Add a Curves adjustment layer by pressing its icon in the Adjustments panel. (It's just to the right of the Levels icon.)

8. Curves are often used to increase the overall contrast in an image. The icon presents a graph with an S-shaped curve on it. This S-curve is a popular format for increasing contrast in the Curves dialog. In the Curves dialog, add an anchor point where the information dips the most in the shadow areas and pull the anchor point slightly down and away from the middle line. Repeat this action in the highlight area, but pull the anchor up and away from the line (**FIGURE 6.34**). Be gentle: you don't want to push your shadows or highlights to the point that there's no image information available in those areas. Close the Properties dialog when you're done.

9. Save the file as **correction-final.psd**.

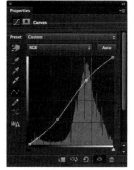

FIGURE 6.34 Apply an S-shaped Curve adjustment to increase contrast.

10. Finally, preview your before-and-after color correction by hiding and showing the adjustment layers in the Layer panel. Click both of the eyeball icons to the left of each layer to hide the adjustments (**FIGURE 6.35**); then click in that part of the Layers panel again to show each layer (**FIGURE 6.36**). Alternatively, leave the layers showing and open the start file. View the files side by side as you did in Exercise 3 (**FIGURE 6.37**) and pat yourself on the back.

FIGURES 6.35 AND 6.36 View the document with and without the adjustment layers by toggling the eyeball icons on layers in the Layers panel.

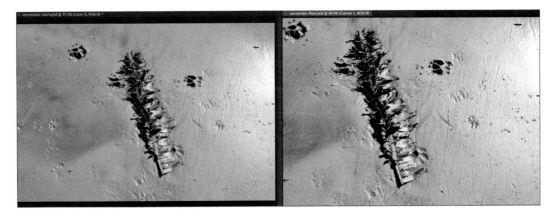

FIGURE 6.37 A side-by-side view of the original photograph and the cropped and adjusted image. The modified image is warmer than the original, suggesting the warmth of the beach. Its cropping also leads the eye into the frame by eliminating passive negative space between the top edge and the left paw print. Image elements are aligned via the rule of thirds.

SCREENCAST 6-1 APPLYING COLOR TO A BLACK-AND-WHITE PHOTOGRAPH

You can apply color to a black-and-white photograph using the skills you learned in Exercises 1 through 4, with a few minor variations. View the screencast to learn more.

All screencasts are available on the companion website, www.digitalart-design.com, or on the YouTube playlist, www.youtube.com/playlist?list=PLAy6P5IoEjy2v3kZKCt8spqJ50nLb2XQI.

 # LAB CHALLENGE

Use Photoshop or Adobe Illustrator to design a mock-up for an online project at the intersection of color relationships and social media.

FIGURE S3.1 Nicéphore Niépce, *View from the Window at Le Gras*, 1825–27. This printed photograph, taken with a camera obscura, shows a view of the roof and surrounding area of Niépce's estate during an eight-hour exposure. Unless it is traveling, you can view the original image at the Harry Ransom Center on the campus of the University of Texas at Austin.

DIGITAL MANIPULATION AND ~~FREE~~ FAIR USE

DIGITAL MANIPULATION of images is rooted in the art of photo manipulation, and photo manipulation is nearly as old as the advent of printed photographs. Nicéphore Niépce created one of the earliest known photographs in 1825 and then produced the infamous *View from the Window at Le Gras* photograph (made with a camera obscura) sometime between 1825 and 1827 (FIGURE S3.1). The 1830s through 1850s were a time of advancement in photographic and printing technologies, including the daguerreotype process (1837), which made possible the fixed development of printed images; Alexander Wolcott's first American patent for a camera (1840); William Henry Fox Talbot's calotype process (1841), which permitted multiple prints to be made from one negative; and Frederick Scott Archer's collodion process (1851), which lessened the time of image exposure to just two to three seconds. While the technology of the art form grew, artists and experimenters also pushed the boundaries of photography's aesthetic possibilities.

LINK Explore the Metropolitan Museum of Art's microsite about *Faking It*, the first major exhibition devoted to the history of manipulated photography before the digital age, at http://www.metmuseum.org/exhibitions/listings/2012/faking-it.

REFERENCE [1] Dawn Ades, *Photomontage* (London: Thames and Hudson, 1976) pg. 9.

REFERENCE [2] For more on the Hurricane Sandy viral photograph, see the Snopes article, The Imperfect Storm, at www.snopes.com/photos/natural/nystorm.asp.

In the 1830s, Talbot and Anna Atkins made cyanotype prints of found objects on paper (refer back to Figure 5.2). In her book *Photomontage*, Dawn Ades considers these a type of photographic manipulation that predates and inspires the photogram (or Rayogram or Schadograph) works by Man Ray, Christian Schad, and László Moholy-Nagy in the 1920s. By the 1850s, Hippolyte Bayard, Henry Peach Robinson, and Oscar Gustav Rejlander had developed combination printing as a pictorial approach to photography in which the medium was used for storytelling, as opposed to documenting. Bayard relied primarily on the combination technique to create separate exposures for different parts of the image. (Ansel Adams's zone system had not yet been conceived.) Robinson and Rejlander created combination prints to bring multiple images into one frame, expanding the narrative of the photograph by way of juxtaposition (FIGURE S3.2). Many thought these images were deceitful, as photography was considered to be a scientific process that captured the truth of a moment. Ades writes, "The members of the Photographic Society in France were banned from exhibiting composite works" [1]. In the age of Adobe Photoshop, I probably don't have to convince you that the photographic image can tell multiple truths, and it can create a deceptive illusion at the whim of the photographer. Photographic hoaxes brought nor'easter storm clouds both to Henry Peach Robinson's 1890 photograph (*Nor'Easter*) and the viral image of the Statue of Liberty following Hurricane Sandy in October 2012 [2].

FIGURE S3.2 Henry Peach Robinson, *Fading Away*, 1858. The artist used five different negatives to create this combination albumen print.

In the exercises in Chapter 7, *Repairs and Hoaxes*, you'll learn to perform digital photographic repairs and create a simple hoax in Photoshop using the Spot Healing Brush tool, selection tools, Clone Stamp tool, Burning and Dodging tools, and Layers panel.

While photographs were manipulated throughout the late 1800s, the Russian Constructivists (the Soviet group of photo collage artists) and Dadaists of the 1920s assembled works of photomontage that are remembered today for their political and disruptive anti-art aesthetics.

The truthfulness of the photographic image is a subject that has a rich textual history. See especially the first essay in Susan Sontag's *On Photography* and Roland Barthes's *Camera Lucida*.

PHOTOMONTAGE AND COLLAGE

During the 1910s and 1920s, there were multiple ways of conceptualizing the collage or photomontage. Soviet Russian architect El Lissitzky "renounced self-expression in art, along with easel painting" [3]. His use of photography and collage demonstrated his belief that artists should be grounded in the technological processes relating to industry. His contemporary Aleksander Aleksandr supported the concept of *faktura*. In relationship to photography and collage, faktura was a theoretical belief in discovering a "medium's distinctive capabilities by experimenting with its inherent qualities" [4]. Rodchenko, Lissitzky, and other Russian Constructivists used the manipulation of photographs through juxtaposition to experiment with the medium and combine images of man, science, industry, and the future with typography, lines, and basic shapes. These works were largely utilized for political propaganda.

REFERENCE [3] Mary Warner Marien, *Photography: A Cultural History* (Upper Saddle River, NJ: Prentice Hall, 2002). pg. 244.

REFERENCE [4] Ibid., pg. 245.

During the same time period, the Dada art movement spread throughout Europe and to New York. Dada artists also utilized collage and juxtaposition to create works of anti-art. Though factions of the Dadaists had their differences, the work of the avant-garde was largely created in reaction to the political interests leading to World War I and the art historical subjectivism inherent to the Expressionist movement. While the Dadaists rejected logic, capitalism, and rules, they embraced the technology that the Expressionists were responding to with their moody, human, nonrealistic paintings. The anti-logic of Dada is articulated in one of Tristan Tzara's *Dada Manifesto* of 1918 [5]:

REFERENCE [5]: See Tristan Tzara's *Dada Manifesto of 1918* at www.391.org/manifestos/19180323 tristantzara_dadamanifesto.htm.

> I am writing a manifesto and there's nothing I want, and yet I'm saying certain things, and in principle I am against manifestos, as I am against principles.

You can easily find this and other manifestos online.

The Berlin Dadaists agreed that the term *photomontage* best described their efforts, as the word "monteur" translates from German to "mechanic" and from French to "assembly." Much of the photomontage or collage work created in this time period has an edgy, aesthetic quality: words and images overlap, chaos is preferred to logic, and dynamic movements are prevalent. Photographs are cut and pasted together from preprinted or found source materials,

LINK See a gallery of Dada photomontages at www.CutandPaste.info.

MARCEL DUCHAMP'S FOUNTAIN

In 1917, French artist Marcel Duchamp (who was affiliated with the New York Dadaists) entered his *Fountain*, a urinal he had signed with the pseudonym R. Mutt, in the Society of Independent Artists exhibition (**FIGURE S3.3**). The work was rejected from the show, but it had far-reaching implications for generations of artists that followed. Duchamp challenged the role of the artist: he selected an everyday object (what he called a "readymade"), positioned it as a work of art (by entering it into a fine arts exhibition), and treated it as the maker of an art piece would by adding his signature. While the Society of Independent Artists did not appreciate Duchamp's mind game in 1917, *Fountain* would go on to become one of the most celebrated works of conceptual art of the 20th century.

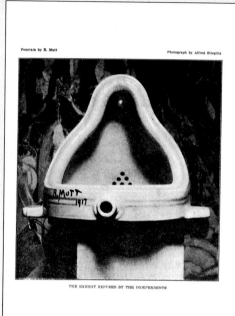

FIGURE S3.3 Marcel Duchamp, *Fountain, 1917.* Photograph by Alfred Stieglitz for *The Blind Man No. 2*, edited by Henri-Pierre Roche, Beatrice Wood, and Marcel Duchamp (New York, May 1917). pg. 4.

such as newspapers and magazines. Instead of painting a blank canvas, the role of the artist was transformed into that of a collector of raw data and an assembler of new messages using materials of mass communication. These images are not meant to deceive the viewer into believing an alternate reality. Instead, they're meant to demonstrate a quality of rebellion or disobedience and co-optive authorship. The edges of the cut-and-pasted images are apparent. Outlines around separate images are unworthy of blending, as their separateness is central to understanding the politicized message.

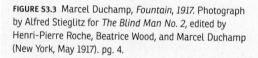

PRECURSOR TO PUNK

While you may have never heard of the Dadaists before, the works of George Grosz, John Heartfield, Hannah Höch, El Lissitzky, Aleksandr Rodchenko, Kurt Schwitters, and others might remind you of the punk movement that began in the 1970s. A similar attitude and aesthetic lineage can be traced from the latter to the Dadaists and Russian Constructivists and even to the Italian Futurists who came before them.

Of course, the collage style seen in Dadaist works has been used by artists and designers throughout the 20th and 21st centuries. The opening title of *Monty Python's Flying Circus* showcases Terry Gilliam's detailed animation collages that draw visual parallels to works by Hannah Höch [6]. The deconstruction movement in typographical layout of the 1990s also takes its cue from the perspective of Dada disorder.

REFERENCE [6] View the opening credits to Monty Python's Flying Circus at http://youtu.be/49c-_YOkmMU.

SURREALISM

The first of two Surrealist manifestos was written in 1924 by French artist André Breton. The Surrealists were less politically charged than the Dadaists and more interested in exploring the unconscious. If the Dadaists wanted to instigate social change of the outer world, the Surrealists aimed to develop human consciousness through an examination of perception in the inner mind. The movement spread through diverse forms of production to include photography, painting, film, acting, musical composition, and writing.

Un Chien Andalou (*An Andalusian Dog*) was written and directed by Luis Buñuel and Salvador Dalí in 1929 [7]. The silent film is more of a dreamscape than a narrative, often demonstrating a double-exposure where film clips are montaged.

REFERENCE [7] You can often find the full version of *Un Chien Andalou* on YouTube.

During the same time period, Russian filmmaker Sergei Eisenstein developed montage-editing techniques that he wrote about in articles and books. Dubbed the "father of montage," Eisenstein used repetition, symbolism, juxtaposition, rhythm, and double-exposure in his films. Similar to the Constructivists who used photo collage for propaganda purposes, Eisenstein was a Bolshevik artist who utilized new filmmaking techniques for political purposes [8].

REFERENCE [8] You can see the first part of Sergei Eisenstein's *Strike* (1925) on YouTube at http://youtu.be/VtjKauYAqMM. Notice the transformation from the man to the owl near the end of the clip.

Of course, just as photo manipulations occurred long before the avant-garde movements of the 20th century, *A Trip to the Moon* (1902) by Georges Méliès predates the Surrealists and films by the Soviet father of montage by more than 20 years. The silent 14-minute science fiction fantasy is loosely based on Jules Verne's novel *From the Earth to the Moon* and H. G. Wells's *The First Men in the Moon.*

In the exercises in Chapter 8, *Select, Copy, Paste, Collage,* you'll learn to create a cut-and-paste style photo collage with selection tools, the Pen tool, the Magic Wand tool, and the Layers panel in Photoshop. Later, in Section 4, *Typography,* you'll use Adobe Illustrator to add text to this collage. The subject of the collage is the film *Un Chien Andalou.*

DIGITAL MANIPULATION

In the exercises in Chapter 9, you'll use gradients on a layer mask to blend two photographs as a proof of concept for a faux iPad app. The layer mask's tonal range is used to gradually shift a layer from being hidden to viewable.

Of course, manipulation doesn't start and end with the Dadaists and the Surrealists. The advent of the networked society calls for new tools for interacting with our various linked screens. User interface (UI) designs for interactive media can be created with pixels or with vector art (see Section 1, *Bits, Pixels, Vectors, and Design*). For this reason, many UI designs are developed in Photoshop. Over the years, Photoshop has expanded its primary function as a bitmap application to include a strong collection of vector shape tools. These tools are often used for digital creation and image manipulation (by way of juxtaposition and/or masking). In Chapter 9, *Blended Realities*, you'll learn the basic ideas to keep in mind while developing an application ("app") for an iPad or other touch-screen device.

FAIR USE AND APPROPRIATION

Not all visual works are protected by copyright laws. In your collages and photo manipulations, you're free to use images that are in the public domain. These include official media created by the U.S. government, much of the content in the Library of Congress (LOC), and works that have an expired copyright (the death of the author plus 70 years for U.S. authors). Online collections including the LOC website and its Flickr stream, NASA's image gallery, as well as Wikimedia Commons are excellent resources for finding and downloading these types of images or media, although it is always your responsibility to determine the copyright.

In addition to the public domain and expired copyrights, some artists actively contribute to a growing collection of media licensed with alternative mechanisms to the traditional U.S. copyright. GNU and Creative Commons licenses allow artists to set specific guidelines in regard to how their work can be shared, transformed, or redistributed, both commercially and noncommercially.

FAIR USE

The fair use doctrine is important for media makers because it's the part of the U.S. copyright law that permits the use of previously published materials, provided that a particular set of conditions are met. When you use previously published work in your new creation, it's considered to be a *derivative* of the original. Here are the four criteria that a judge or jury would use to determine if your use is legitimately fair:

1. *The purpose of the derivative work.* For instance, a collage made by an instructor that will not be sold or distributed beyond the classroom is probably fair, while one inserted into a commercial publication is likely to be ruled in violation.

2. *The nature of the content of the original.* Factual content can legitimately be reused, whereas creative content is considered to be intellectual property.

3. *How much of the original work is used in the derivative.* For visual works, there is no set guideline for how much you are allowed to use. But, if the transformative quality (not quantity) of the new work is hard to recognize, your work may be so similar to the original that it seems to use "too much" of it.

4. *The effect of the new work on the actual or potential market value of the original.* If the new work defames the original or lessens the value of the original work, the use would not be considered fair.

Commercial artists and designers must be very careful in regard to using prior published works. As a general rule, you should always seek permission from the author, even if the work is licensed in a way that suggests redistribution is permissible. Some of the images you will use in the following chapters may appear to be licensed relatively freely. Nonetheless, I contacted all authors to ensure that we have permission to use the media included in this text.

APPROPRIATION

Appropriation is a conceptually rich practice of borrowing, reclaiming, and transforming an original work of culture that informs and inspires artists who express their ideas in a variety of media formats. Though appropriation can be found in visual culture throughout recorded history, many artists learn of the concept through early 20th century art: Pablo Picasso and Georges Braque's mixed-media Cubist collages and Marcel Duchamp's readymades (see the sidebar on Duchamp's *Fountain*), or mid-century works such as Andy Warhol's *Campbell's Soup Cans*. The intentional act of appropriation as a means of creating transformative visual culture has become even more prevalent in the age of digital media.

You'll download and use images that are licensed with a "copy left" (Creative Commons or GNU license) or are in the public domain in the first two chapters of this section.

Artists and designers often borrow images, media, formats, or ideas from prior recognizable works in visual culture. The word "appropriation," however, means more than just the simple action of borrowing. To appropriate is to borrow *and* to transform. In this way, appropriation (when successful or obvious) will help your work meet the third criterion in the fair use test.

REMINDER If you're creating appropriated work for commercial purposes, be sure that you have permission to modify the original work.

VERISIMILITUDE

REFERENCE [9] Unilever, *Dove Evolution of Beauty* (video), 2006. http://youtu.be/iYhCnOjf46U.

REFERENCE [10] Simon Willows, *Slob Evolution*, 2006. http://youtu.be/lV8JardV74w.

Verisimilitude is a scientific, theoretical term that is generally used in the arts to allude to a quality of truthlikeness. If your aesthetic intent is to trick a viewer into believing in an alternate reality, then the quality of verisimilitude is present. Layering, blending, and matching lighting sources and tonal differences will be key aesthetic players in your process of assembling the image. Almost any advertisement in any medium—print, web, video, and so on—relies on these techniques. Dove created a campaign deconstructing this process in their series of *Evolution of Beauty* commercials [9]. The Dove campaign deconstructed the advertising industry's use of verisimilitude to sell a particular "truthfulness of beauty" to their female demographic. In 2006, Simon Willows's parody, *Slob Evolution*, was nominated for a Daytime Emmy Award [10]. Willows's work appropriates Dove's style and format while inverting the message. This YouTube video is an example of verisimilitude (the truthlikeness of the video as an advertising campaign with a production quality similar to Dove's original) and appropriation (the act of both borrowing the visual culture reference and transforming the message to invert the meaning).

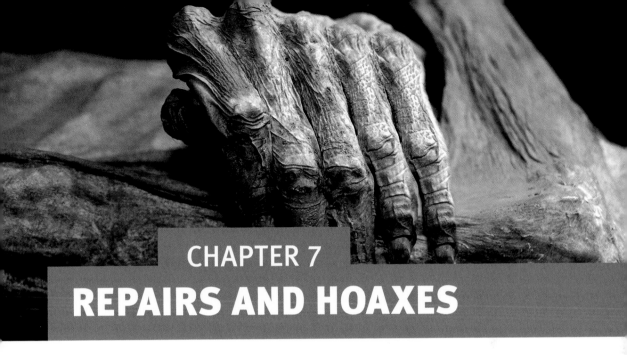

CHAPTER 7
REPAIRS AND HOAXES

THE EXERCISES IN this chapter will provide technical lessons and teach you to match textures and values to create photographic illusions in two compositions. You'll explore various tools for *healing* and *cloning* parts of an image, and add a simple layer mask to blend image features for a quality of verisimilitude.

DIGITAL REPAIRS

LINK For more information on the repair tools in Photoshop, see the Adobe Photoshop help page: http://helpx.adobe.com/photoshop/using/retouching-repairing-images.html

The repair tools are grouped together in the Photoshop Tools panel—all of them hide behind the Spot Healing Brush tool. The tools I use most often to make repairs are the Spot Healing Brush tool and the Clone Stamp tool. The Patch tool can be hard to control or predict, and the Red Eye tool does what you think it does. (It's certainly useful in those situations.)

The Spot Healing Brush tool functions as a fix-it paintbrush. You simply click on any part of the image, and the brush attempts to *repair* (or correct uneven tones in) the area based on a sample of nearby pixels. Of course, it's never a good idea to modify your original image. So when using these tools, I recommend copying the background layer to preserve the original file. You'll learn more about *non destructive* editing in Chapter 8, *Select, Copy, Paste, Collage*.

HEALING BRUSH This third tool is essentially a combination of the Spot Healing Brush tool and the Clone Stamp tool: it lets you sample a source and tries to even tones and blemishes based on nearby pixel information.

The Clone Stamp tool is also a brush. Cloning is a two-step operation: Photoshop needs to understand what you're cloning and where the clone should be applied. So you'll need to sample an original source (the *what* part of the question) and then brush the sample into a new location (the *where* part). The sampling part of the Clone Stamp operation can sometimes be tricky to learn, but once you master the tool you'll be able to repair just about anything.

Before Photoshop, artists manipulated images during the photo shoot, in the darkroom, or on the print, for instance, with SpotTone to correct for dust spots. This seems like a lost art now that basic photo repairs can be made so quickly using software. However, manipulating photographic imagery has ethical implications for photojournalists and media contributors in the digital age. For instance, the National Press Photographers Association (NPPA) Code of Ethics includes the following statement:

REFERENCE [1] See www.nppa.org/code_of_ethics

> Editing should maintain the integrity of the photographic images' content and context. Do not manipulate images or add or alter sound in any way that can mislead viewers or misrepresent subjects [1].

WHAT IS ETHICAL IN REGARDS TO DIGITAL MANIPULATION?

In the "Changes to Photographs" section of the *NPPA Special Report: Ethics in the Age of Digital Photography*, Rev. Don Doll, S.J. is credited for the following ideas: "There are technical changes that deal only with the aspects of photography that make the photo more readable, such as a little dodging and burning, global color correction, and contrast control. These are all part of the grammar of photography, just as there is a grammar associated with words (sentence structure, capital letters, paragraphs) that make it possible to read a story, so there is a grammar of photography that allows us to read a photograph. These changes (like their darkroom counterparts) are neither ethical nor unethical—they are merely technical." (See www.nppa.org/node/5127 for more information.)

Instances of photo manipulation to "get a better shot" have led to firings (for instance, Bryan Patrick from the *Sacramento Bee*) and loss of credibility (the infamous *National Geographic* cover of the Egyptian pyramids in 1982 where a horizontal image was smooshed into a vertical cover space). They've also led to increased criticism within the field. Take a look at two shots of O. J. Simpson published in June 1994 by *Newsweek* and *Time* magazines: the *Time* photograph was manipulated to make Simpson's skin appear darker than it actually is.

You can see both images of O. J. Simpson on the cover of the two magazines side by side on the "O.J. Simpson murder case" Wikipedia page.

CREATING A HOAX

While visual reporters need to handle digital manipulations with caution and care, artists often use these tools to create commentary on popular media and historic subject matter. For instance, Josh Azzarella's still and video works use manipulation to revise historic events by way of deletion. In his still image, *Untitled #15 (Tank Man)*, Azzarella re-creates the scene from Tiananmen Square, originally photographed by Associated Press photographer Jeff Widener. In Widener's image, the man is face-to-face with several Type 59 tanks during the Tiananmen Square protests of 1989. However, in Azzarella's image, the tanks are removed, and the man is left isolated in the middle of the street, seemingly out of the way of danger (FIGURE 7.1). Similarly, *Untitled #7 (16mm)* is an 11-second loop showing President John F. Kennedy driving near the grassy knoll but never experiencing the fatal bullet wound. The footage of JFK riding in the car is haunting for contemporary viewers who know where the drive leads, even though it never quite gets there [2]. While these examples of revision and manipulation aren't meant to hoax or deceive the viewer (after all, we know what the artist is up to), the strategies for image manipulation are the same as those used to create a photographic hoax, which you'll do in Exercises 4 and 5.

REFERENCE [2] See Josh Azzarella's videos on his website: www.joshazzarella.com/videoworks2004/videoworks2004.html.

FIGURE 7.1 Josh Azzarella, *Untitled #15 (Tank Man)*. This image is a single frame in Azzarella's video. Image appears courtesy of the artist.

FIGURE 7.2 A portrait of President John F. Kennedy before and after digital repairs.

WHAT YOU'LL NEED

Download the following source materials to complete the exercises in this chapter:

✔ The **chapter7-start** folder from the Chapter 7 downloads area on the companion website includes **repair-start.psd** and **hoax-start.psd**.

I found these two starting photographs on the Library of Congress website and Wikimedia Commons. You can download the photographs from the companion website or use the source materials from the web (see the sidebar).

You'll benefit from the ability to see changes in values and textures across all areas of the image.

WHAT YOU'LL MAKE

In the exercises in this chapter, you'll repair a dusty portrait of JFK (FIGURE 7.2) and create an "extra finger" mummy hoax (FIGURE 7.3). The repairs and hoax share the aesthetic quality of verisimilitude—they deceive the viewer into believing your manipulated version of reality.

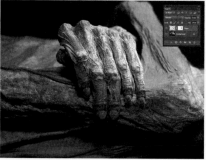

FIGURE 7.3 A mummy hoax includes an extra finger.

DOWNLOADING HIGH-RESOLUTION IMAGES FROM THE LIBRARY OF CONGRESS WEBSITE AND WIKIMEDIA COMMONS

1. The photograph of President John F. Kennedy is available on the Library of Congress website. Beneath the thumbnail of the image on the left side of the page, you'll see a link to download the 32.1 MB TIFF file of the image. This is the largest image available, and it's the one you should download, because you can always scale down but you can't add pixels. 32 MB is a large black-and-white file! It's approximately 17 by 21 inches at 300 DPI. I downloaded this image and then scaled it down to 9 inches vertically at 300 DPI for the **repair-start.psd** file that I've included in the files on the companion site. If you want your brush sizes to match mine during the exercises, do the same or use the files on the companion site.

2. The file **GuanajuatoMummy03.jpg** is available from Wikimedia Commons. The highest resolution file can be downloaded by clicking the "Full resolution" link that appears beneath the image on the file page. If you click directly on the image itself, you'll also be able to view the largest image and then use Control-click or the contextual (right-click) menu to save the image.

IMAGE CREDITS FOR THE SOURCE PHOTOGRAPHS
President John F. Kennedy, head-and-shoulders portrait, facing front (1961) appears and is used in this chapter courtesy of the Library of Congress [LC-USZ62-117124]. Hand of Guanajuato Mummy appears and is used in this chapter courtesy of Tomás Castelazo.

EXERCISE 1 REMOVE DUST AND HEAL JFK'S BLEMISHES

1. Download the two photographs you'll need for this chapter and save them in a folder named **chapter07**. Use the downloads from the companion website or find the JFK photo at www.loc.gov/pictures/item/96523447. The mummy photo is on Wikimedia Commons. Go to http://commons.wikimedia.org and search the term "mummy" to find it. If you're accessing the source files (that is, you're not using the companion website downloads), be sure to download the full resolution or largest images; then save the JFK file as **repair-start.psd** and the mummy file as **hoax-start.psd**.

PUBLIC DOMAIN AND CREATIVE COMMONS LICENSED IMAGES

To begin the exercises in this chapter, you'll use two images that are, for different reasons, free to you. The portrait of JFK has two listings that let me judge that the image is in the public domain:

- Rights Advisory: No known restrictions on publication.

- Notes: U.S. Navy photo.

Since there are no known restrictions and this was a U.S. Navy photo (and government media is typically in the public domain), I have assessed that the image is fair to use. Also notice that the Library of Congress includes the following in red letters: Rights assessment is your responsibility.

The mummy image is licensed under the Creative Commons Attribution-Share Alike 2.5 Generic license. Since the image has a Share-Alike component (and this book is not licensed with a CC-BY-SA license, as it would be written in shorthand), I contacted the author for permission to use the image.

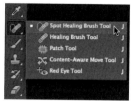

FIGURE 7.4 Duplicate the **Background** layer by dragging it to the Create a New Layer icon at the bottom of the Layers panel.

FIGURE 7.5 The Spot Healing Brush tool is grouped with other repair tools.

FIGURE 7.6 When the **spot healing** layer is active, it's highlighted, and there's a frame around the layer thumbnail icon.

2. Open the JFK portrait, **repair-start.psd**, in Photoshop. Set the workspace to Essentials.

3. In the Layers panel, drag the **background** layer to the Create a new layer icon (FIGURE 7.4).

4. Rename the **background** layer *original* and rename the layer copy **spot healing**. Begin with the Spot Healing Brush tool on this layer.

Keep a copy of the original file in the Layers panel when working on repairs. Naming your files as you work will keep the panel organized and help you work efficiently as the size of the list increases.

5. Choose the Spot Healing Brush tool from the Tools panel (FIGURE 7.5). This tool is simple to use as it functions as a brush. Be sure the **spot healing** layer is active—if it's not, click on it so the layer is highlighted in the Layers panel (FIGURE 7.6).

6. Always peek at the tool options, especially before using a new tool. For the Spot Healing Brush tool, you can change the brush size and hardness (or softness) level, the mode (leave that on normal), and the type. Click on the pull-down menu next to the set brush size and make sure that the Hardness level is set to zero, as you'll want to use a soft brush for this procedure. Further to the right on the Options panel, click the Content Aware radio button so the Spot Healing Brush tool will use image data in areas near where you click to try to match image details, and check the Sample All Layers box (FIGURE 7.7).

FIGURE 7.7 The Options panel for the Spot Healing Brush tool is set to Content Aware and Sample All Layers.

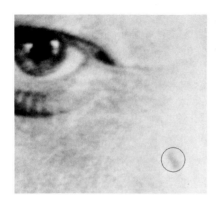

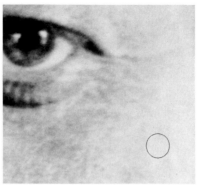

7. Place the Spot Healing Brush tool on or near the blemish on JFK's right cheek. (Don't click yet.) Zoom in a lot! I viewed the image at 300% before making the first repair. The brush size is easily changed while you're working by pressing the hot keys, open bracket ([) to reduce the brush size and close bracket (]) to enlarge the brush size. Use the key commands to make the brush size just larger than the blemish. Then click one time (**FIGURE 7.8** and **FIGURE 7.9**). The Spot Healing Brush tool should replace the blemish with even skin tones in one simple click. Again, double-check that you're working on the **spot healing** layer!

CURSOR ICONS If you don't see a circle representing the size of the brush in Photoshop, check your Photoshop preferences. The brush cursor should be set in the Photoshop menu > Preferences > Cursors. Choose Normal Brush Tip and make sure you didn't leave the Caps Lock key depressed.

HISTORY IS FULL OF REVISIONS

Repairs will inevitably leave you clicking on the Photoshop file hundreds of times. It's easy to become click-crazy in the process. Familiarize yourself with the History panel, as you'll come to rely on this handy Photoshop archive. There are three things you need to know about using the History panel:

- Access the History panel from Windows > History or the History icon along the strip of panels on the right side of the Application window.

- By default, Photoshop may save only 20 of your previous clicks or steps. You'll want to increase this when doing this type of work. Choose the Photoshop menu > Preferences > Performance. On the right side of the dialog, enter 99 in the History States text field. The more clicks or previous states you save, the more RAM you'll use. If your computer is slow or you're lacking RAM, you may want to skip this step.

- To go back a step or two, or five, click once on the name of each of the previous steps in the History panel until your file appears in the state that you want to begin working on anew. There's nothing else you need to click. Simply begin working again, and the History panel will create new steps, overwriting the grayed-out step or steps that you're leaving out of your process.

ZOOM TOOL You can easily access the Zoom (in) tool while working with most other tools by pressing the **Space bar-Command(⌘)** keys. Click in the area you want to enlarge. To zoom out, press **Space bar-⌘-Option** (on a PC: **Space bar-Control** or **Space bar-Control-Alt**).

8. While you have an enlarged view of the image, you'll notice dust in his dark jacket and also on the negative in the area surrounding his head. You may also find other minor blemishes on his skin tones. Repair all of this slowly. Use just one click at a time for each spot. Don't click and drag. Change the brush size according to the size of the blemish so that the brush is just barely larger than it. Finally, be sure you're doing all of this on the **spot healing** layer! Save your work as **repair-end.psd** when you're happy with the repairs you've made so far. You'll continue to save on top of **repair-end.psd** to update it as you work through the next two exercises.

9. Always review your modifications at a zoom level of 100% (or actual size). Click the Eyeball icon next to the **spot healing** layer in the Layers panel to hide and show the layer. You should see your repairs disappear (showing the original image with all its imperfections) and also see the repaired image while toggling between hiding and showing the layer (**FIGURE 7.10**).

FIGURE 7.10 The **spot healing** layer is invisible (left side) and visible (right side) in order to preview repairs. You can easily see your repairs by clicking the Eyeball icon on and off in the Layers panel.

EXERCISE 2 JFK'S EYES: TONAL REPAIRS WITH DODGE AND BURN

Now you'll focus on repairing the eye area. Since you've already done a once-over with the Spot Healing Brush tool for dust, scratches, and major blemish repairs, you'll do this additional, localized work on a separate layer. In this exercise, you'll place a copy of JFK's eyes on a new layer that you'll modify with the Dodge and Burn tools. If you've never printed a negative in the darkroom, the analogy between this tool and common darkroom practices might be vague. When dodging an area of the sensitized paper during an exposure to light in a black-and-white wet lab, for instance, a common exposure time for the adjustment might be about 10 percent of the total exposure. So, you might start with the Exposure Value set at 10% in the Dodge tool options. Of course, this value varies from negative to negative (or print to print), so it's common to make a best guess when using this tool in combination with ⌘-Z.

1. Choose the Lasso tool from the Tools panel (**FIGURE 7.11**). This tool lets you make a free-form selection around any part of the image. It's not a good tool to use when you need to perform a precise selection, but it's perfect for quickly isolating a general area of the image.

2. Draw a loose circle all the way around the left eye area, including a bit above the eyebrows. Be sure to begin and end the selection at the same point so that Photoshop knows the complete area of the selection. You'll see flickering dashed lines surrounding the selected area, often referred to as "marching ants." Now you'll add a selected area around the right eye to the current selection. Press and hold the Shift key while drawing a circular shape around the right eye area with the Lasso tool—you might notice an additional, tiny plus sign near the bottom of the tool icon. You should have two sets of marching ants on the image, one surrounding each eye (**FIGURE 7.12**).

FIGURE 7.11 The Lasso tool is grouped with other selection tools.

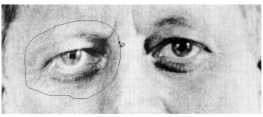 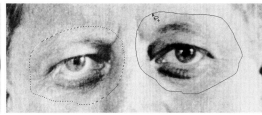

FIGURE 7.12 Start and end the selection with the Lasso tool at the same location in the image. Press and hold the Shift key to add to an active selection. The "marching ants" show a selection around the eye.

You can add to any selection using one of the Photoshop selection tools by pressing the Shift key. If you want to add extra area to an existing selection, you'll have to begin the "new" part of the selected area from within the existing selection. If you want to subtract part of an existing selection, press and hold the Option key while starting the "deleted" area of the selection from outside the existing selection. This is much more easily demonstrated than understood by reading text. To see a demonstration, view the screencast for this chapter.

All screencasts are available on the companion website, www.digitalart-design.com or on the YouTube playlist, www.youtube.com/playlist?list=PLAy6P5loEjy2v3kZKCt8spqJ50nLb2XQI.

KEY COMMANDS When copy and pasting from one layer to another, an alternative to ⌘-C/⌘-V is to use the single command ⌘-J to "float" the selected area to a new layer.

Why not use the Spot Healing Brush tool here? You could work with the Spot Healing Brush tool to correct the eye bags, but the truth is that there should be a little shadow beneath the eyes in this photograph. In this situation, correcting the tones by burning and dodging will maintain the integrity of the image.

3. Look in the Layers panel and make sure that the **spot healing** layer is active. Copy and paste the selection by pressing ⌘-C to copy it, followed by ⌘-V to paste it. You copied the selection from the repaired layer so you won't have to re-repair any parts of the selection that have already been healed.

4. In the Layers panel, rename the new layer **eyes**.

5. JFK's wrinkles aren't too extreme, so leave those alone in this image. However, his eye bags are a bit dense. In opposition to this, his eyebrows (especially his left brow) are so light they barely register. Use the Dodge tool and the Burn tool to lighten the shadow areas beneath the eyes and darken the brows. Begin with the Dodge tool, located a couple of tools above the Type tool in the Tools panel (FIGURE 7.13).

6. Glance at the Layers panel. Nothing should have changed there—you should be working on the **eyes** layer. (Click it to make it active if you noticed that another layer is active.) Now check out the Options for the Dodge tool. Again, you'll want to use a soft brush, so set the brush Hardness value to zero if the brush isn't already soft. Select Shadows from the Range pull-down menu, as the eye bags are shadows you'll want to lighten. Now you need to estimate a reasonable dodging exposure value. The general rule is that you can always

FIGURE 7.13 The Dodge tool is grouped with the Burn and Sponge tools. These tools alter the values and intensity of the hue in an image.

COPYING IMAGE PARTS

Be extra attentive to the Layers panel when copying selected parts of an image. It's common for a new user to attempt to copy part of the image that she can see, but that isn't actually on the selected layer. If you do this, you might get an error message stating "Could not complete the copy command because the selected area is empty." This happens to everyone at some point during image manipulations. Simply press OK to exit the warning dialog and then activate the appropriate layer before attempting to copy again.

brush the Dodge tool over an area more than once, so it's better to err on the side of a lower value. I tried a few smaller values before realizing that if I set the Exposure Value to about 15% on this image, I could quickly brush over the eye bags one time to produce a decent result. Remember to zoom in and set the brush size so it's just about the same size or larger than the shadow area you're targeting (use the [and] hot keys) and then play with the exposure value and ⌘-Z or the History panel. Zoom out to 100% to evaluate your results. The modification should not be extreme. Modifying the photograph in this way will make the president appear slightly less tired. Your modification should be believable!

7. While still working on the **eyes** layer, switch to the Burn tool. Choose Highlights from the Range pull-down menu in the Options panel. Play with the exposure value (I ended up using 10%) and make a quick brushstroke over JFK's left eyebrow to darken it.

8. Review your modifications at actual size. Click the eyeball icon next to the **eyes** layer in the Layers panel to hide and show the layer (FIGURE 7.14). Save your work.

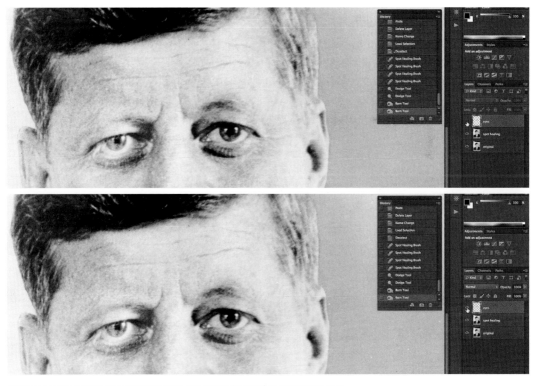

FIGURE 7.14 The *eyes* layer is invisible (top) and visible (bottom) to preview repairs.

REDUCING WRINKLES

You'll use the Spot Healing Brush tool again, but this time a minor adjustment to the layer will help the change seem believable.

1. Draw a loose selection around the forehead with the Lasso tool, making sure to avoid the eye area you just modified. However, you'll want to include the area between the eyes in your selection (**FIGURE 7.15**). Activate the **spot healing** layer. (Remember: this part of the image doesn't exist on the **eyes** layer that you were just working on, and to copy it you need to activate the layer where the pixels are saved.)

2. Copy and paste the forehead from the *spot healing* layer to a new layer. Rename the layer **forehead**.

3. The new layer will paste directly above the active layer in the Layers panel. Move the **forehead** layer above the **eyes** layer in the panel—this is called rearranging the stacking order of the layers (**FIGURE 7.16**). Any modifications you make on this layer should be visible in the event that there's overlap

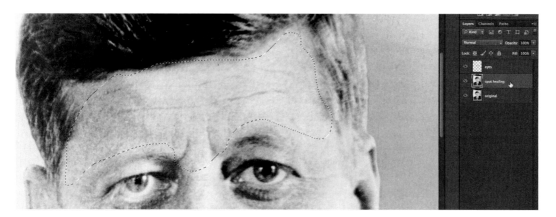

FIGURE 7.15 The forehead area is selected with the Lasso tool on the *spot healing* layer.

FIGURE 7.16 Rearrange the stacking order by dragging layers in the Layers panel.

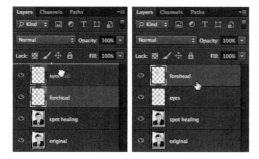

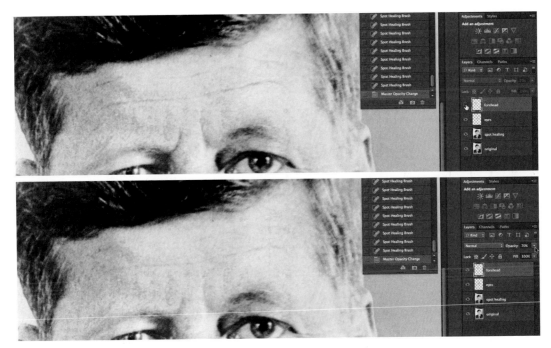

FIGURE 7.17 The **forehead** layer is invisible (top) and visible (bottom) to preview repairs.

with the eyes when selecting the forehead. Toggle the **forehead** layer on and off (use the Eyeball icon) to make sure that the eyes retain their adjustments.

4. Repair the **forehead** layer moderately with the Spot Healing Brush tool. Don't make it perfect—JFK's facial age should be close to the reality of his wrinkles. When you're finished, reducing the layer opacity (I set mine to 70%) will bring some of the wrinkles back without emphasizing them in that area of the image. Review your modifications at actual size and save your work (**FIGURE 7.17**).

EXERCISE 4 — IT'S A HOAX! ADDING AN EXTRA MUMMY FINGER

In this exercise, you'll add an extra mummy finger using the Clone Stamp tool. This tool functions similarly to the Spot Healing Brush tool, but you're responsible for the location of the source and the repair area. You'll work with a hard-edged and soft-edged brush in this exercise. In the next exercise, you'll clean your work with a layer mask.

1. Open **hoax-start.psd** in Photoshop. Set the workspace to Essentials.

FIGURE 7.18 The Clone Stamp tool is grouped with the Pattern Stamp tool in the Tools panel.

FIGURE 7.19 Brush settings are in the Options panel. The brush hardness is set to 85%.

2. In the Layers panel, press the Create a new layer icon. Unless you pressed the icon more than once, the layer's default name is **Layer 1**. Rename it **finger**. You now have an empty layer named **finger** above the locked **Background** layer in the Layers panel.

3. Choose the Clone Stamp tool from the Tools panel (**FIGURE 7.18**). View the Options panel. I set my brush to 250 pixels and changed the Hardness value to 85%. Since you'll be copying pixels with this tool, you'll want to use a brush that isn't too soft. The soft edges often blur the pixel information, which you want to keep sharp, at least during the copying portion of this process. Keep the Mode set to Normal and the Opacity and Flow at 100% and check the Aligned Sample box. Remember, you'll sample first with this tool and then clone. If you check the Align box, you're telling Photoshop to keep the sample area aligned with the cloning area. You'll see that it makes sense to keep the source and clone aligned. Finally, choose All Layers from the pull-down menu (**FIGURE 7.19**).

4. Zoom in. Make sure the **finger** layer is active—this is where you want to place your cloned finger. Place the Clone Stamp tool (which basically functions as a brush with an extra sampling step) on top of the last knuckle. Press the Option key and click just once in this location (**FIGURE 7.20**). Don't drag the mouse. You just told Photoshop that this is the area that you want to sample as you clone the new finger.

5. Move the mouse to the right of the last knuckle and down a little bit to align it with a plausible location for a new knuckle (**FIGURE 7.21**). The Clone Stamp tool provides a preview of what the cloned image will look like in your composition so you can get the alignment just right before committing to a click. Click and drag downward, tracing the finger, until you reach the end of the fingernail (**FIGURE 7.22**). Save the file as **hoax-end.psd**, which you'll save and update at the end of the next exercise.

Congratulations! You just added a sixth finger to a mummy. In the next exercise, you'll clean the cloned image data to make the new finger blend with the rest of the composition.

FIGURE 7.20 Sample from the mummy's knuckle with the Clone Stamp tool.

FIGURE 7.21 Paint a new finger using the Clone Stamp tool aligned next to the sampled finger.

FIGURE 7.22 The new finger in position. The brush hardness ensures that pixels are sampled accurately.

EXERCISE 5 · SOFTENING CLONED EDGES

Since fingers don't stay the same size from the knuckle to the nail, there are extra parts of the cloned finger that obstruct the view of the original composition through which the viewer can tell that the image has been manipulated. In this exercise, you'll use a layer mask to hide extra parts surrounding the cloned finger. Consider this exercise to be a brief introduction to the layer mask. You'll learn more about layer masks in the next two chapters.

DEFAULT COLORS KEY COMMAND Since you'll always work with white and black on Photoshop layer masks, you should know the hot keys to load these default colors. Press the letter D on your keypad to load the default colors and press the letter X to switch the foreground and background colors.

1. In the Layers panel, activate the **finger** layer and then press the Add Layer Mask button (**FIGURE 7.23**). You'll see a new icon in the Layers panel—a white square next to the layer icon of the finger.

2. The layer mask is used to hide or show parts of a layer. Since the **finger** layer contains only the extra, cloned finger, the mask will affect only this image data. You could work with the Eraser tool to delete image data, but instead I want you to work in a nondestructive way to simply hide (rather than delete) pixels. Layer masks operate in white (show the layer content), black (hide the layer content), and shades of gray (make the layer content partially hidden). Choose the Brush tool and load black into the foreground color chip (**FIGURE 7.24**).

FIGURE 7.23 While the **finger** layer is active, the Add Layer Mask icon is pressed.

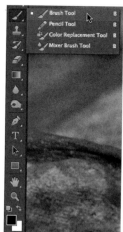

FIGURE 7.24 The Brush tool is selected with black loaded into the foreground color chip.

3. View the Brush tool options. Set the Hardness value to 0, as you'll want to use a soft-edged brush. Leave the Mode set to Normal and the Opacity and Flow at 100%.

4. Before you add black paint, softly, to the layer mask (which will indicate which parts of the **finger** layer should be hidden), make sure that the mask is active in the Layers panel. You can click once on the Layer icon or on the mask. Notice that whichever is activated has white edges around its icon. When you're sure that the mask is active, paint black using your soft brush around the edges of the finger where you want to hide the extra image details (FIGURE 7.25).

5. Notice that the layer mask now contains an abstract black painting on its white background. Option-click on the layer mask icon in the Layers panel to show just the mask in your composition—you may notice that the name of the file indicates that you're viewing the Layer Mask in the title area (FIGURE 7.26). The black areas of the composition are hidden. The white areas are revealed. Look for gaps between the black and white areas.

FIGURE 7.25 Extra image details are hidden by the mask as you paint on it with black.

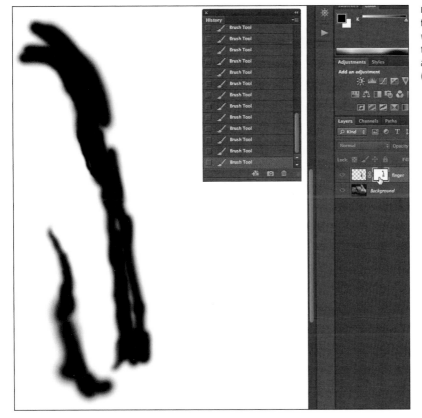

FIGURE 7.26 A view of the **finger** layer mask. The white areas are visible in the document. The black areas are hidden from view (or masked).

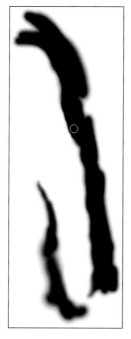

FIGURE 7.27 The layer mask is cleaned as gaps are filled in with black.

FIGURE 7.28 The mummy finger hoax is complete and visible in normal editing mode.

You may want to review those parts of the composition and add more black or white paint to fill in the gaps (FIGURE 7.27). This is an easy way to clean the mask because you can really see how the image details are being treated. Option-click on the Mask icon in the Layers panel again to resume the normal working mode and continue to modify the layer mask (FIGURE 7.28).

6. Remember to view the document at actual size and then save the file.

LAB CHALLENGE

Create a hoax! Modify a current news story by using the repair and clone tools you learned about in this chapter on a fictitious news image. In news photography, the caption is important, too. Don't forget to write a caption to accompany your newsworthy image.

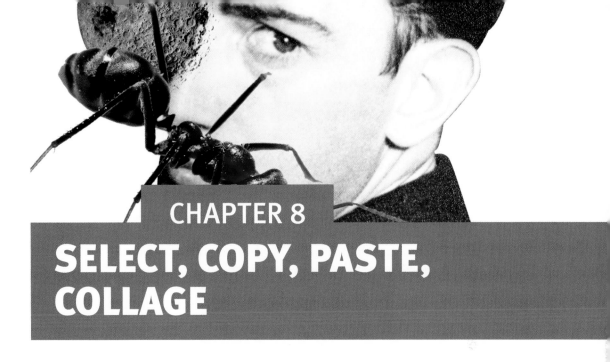

CHAPTER 8

SELECT, COPY, PASTE, COLLAGE

THE EXERCISES IN this chapter will provide technical lessons in photographic collage and teach you about juxtaposition. You'll use the Dada style of photomontage (in which source materials are often made visually apparent) to create a collage that could be used to promote the 1929 Surrealist film *Un Chien Andalou*. You'll explore various tools for precision selecting, copying, and pasting parts of an image. In Chapter 10, *Type and Image*, you'll revisit this collage that was created in Adobe Illustrator and add typography on top of the photomontage.

PRECISION SELECTING WITH THE PEN TOOL

To make your cutout precise, you'll need a perfectly sharp selection. In most cases, the Pen tool provides the best method for creating this type of selection. Unfortunately, I've found it to be one of the hardest tools in the Adobe Creative Cloud to teach to new students. Part of the problem is the name: this tool does not, despite its name, act like a pen. You won't click and drag your mouse around a contour to trace it with the Pen tool. However, when the tool is used properly, the result is a perfect tracing of the contour of an image with a path comprising multiple anchor points. The Pen tool is used in Adobe Photoshop and Illustrator (and other Adobe applications). Bundled with the Pen tool are the Add Anchor Point, Delete Anchor Point, and Convert Anchor Point tools. I find it more accurate to think of the Pen tool as a "drop anchors" tool rather than a pen.

The second challenge of learning the Pen tool is that you have to predict where the path is going before it gets there. People who excel at using the Pen tool are typically adept at drawing. They can intuit where the contour of the resulting path is headed, which enables them to plot anchor points in just the right places. If drawing isn't your best talent, consider this an opportunity to learn how to see and predict the contour of a shape.

It's important to understand the fundamentals of working with the Pen tool, as follows:

- To add an anchor point, click just once. Then release pressure and move the mouse. Don't click and drag; instead, click, release, and reposition.

- Click again to add the next anchor point, which creates a path between the two points.

- To create a curved path, click and drag ever so slightly while plotting the anchor point. You'll see resulting *Bézier handles*, which look like tiny paths with their own anchors originating at your point.

- During the contour tracing, you may need to Option-click directly on an anchor point to access the Convert Anchor Point tool. This changes the anchor point from a place where two straight, angular lines meet to one that supports a curve with its Bézier handles. (Or the reverse—Option-click on an anchor point to change what would be a curve to a straight line.)

- Curves can be difficult to understand at first. The Pen tool will create an anchor point at the apex of the curve and two Bézier handles that you can use to determine the direction and intensity (hardness or softness) of the curve.

Of course, the advantages of the Pen tool far outweigh the growing pains of mastering it. You'll be able to make crisp paths around image parts, which can then be converted to a selection that you'll eventually use to create a layer mask. For some projects, there's simply no better way to go about masking an image than to start with the Pen tool and convert its resulting path to a mask. This is the first process you'll learn in the following exercises.

MEMBERS SPEAK FOR THEMSELVES

Mark Edwards designed a smartphone/QR code campaign for AIGA (American Institute of Graphic Arts) in 2011. The phone displays video of a designer's talking mouth, which completes its associated postcard (**FIGURE 8.1**). This interactive campaign is an example of a collage where the precision of the mouth or dissonance of the mouth to face scale (as you move the phone near or far from the printed piece) is part of Edwards's play with juxtaposition.

FIGURE 8.1 Design and concept by Mark Edwards, *Members Speak for Themselves, 2012.* Postcard series for the AIGA Orange County Chapter in California.

NONDESTRUCTIVE EDITING

This section could also be called, "Why You Should Use a Mask Instead of the Eraser Tool." I'm so adamant that you should never delete pixels that I won't even demonstrate the Eraser tool. You should, instead, always retain your pixels. Your goal is always to preserve the original image file and edit bitmap graphics on separate masks, adjustment layers, or layer copies. It's not too difficult to stay true to this credo with simple tonal repairs, but when juxtaposing image parts, you'll eventually want to delete part of the image. This is where the layer mask is a necessary part of your arsenal: it is a weapon of massive nondestruction!

The fundamentals of working with layer masks include the following:

- A layer mask can be applied to an unlocked layer. If you want to add a mask to a digital photograph opened directly from your camera, double-click on the name *Background* to rename and unlock that layer in the Layers panel.

- When a layer mask is applied, it's linked to the layer thumbnail (or content) by default.

- If you create a selection on a layer and then add the mask, the mask will automatically show the selected area and hide everything else.

- If you add a layer mask to a layer with no selection in place, the mask will show everything on the layer.

- On the layer mask itself, white is used to show or reveal layer contents, while black is used to hide parts of the layer. Gray is used as a blending tool because it acts as a trigger for levels of transparency.

- Edits can be made to a layer mask with the Brush tool, Pencil tool, Fill command (from the Edit menu), or Gradient tool.

- When working with layer masks, you'll need to be aware not only of what layer you're editing, but also of whether you're editing the layer content or the layer mask.

- You can see and edit just the mask in grayscale mode. You can also disable the mask to see all of the layer content.

- A layer mask can be deleted. At the time of deletion, you'll have to choose whether to press the Apply button, which applies the mask to the layer before deleting the mask (it's safest to do this if you've saved a copy of the layer with the mask intact), or the Delete button (if you want to start anew).

While a student at the University of California, Irvine, Jonathan Cairns created *Filthy*, a digital collage from appropriated materials (**FIGURE 8.2**). The comic panels, pixelated photo of Lonelygirl15 (search for her on YouTube if you don't know the reference), and scans or screenshots of news articles juxtaposed in the background represent digital and analog sources of information and entertainment for the bull-headed, hybrid figures wandering in the foreground.

FIGURE 8.2 Jonathan Cairns, *Filthy*, 2006. Digital collage, 24 x 30 inches.

WHAT YOU'LL NEED

Download the following source materials to complete the exercises in this chapter:

✔ The **chapter8-start** folder from the Chapter 8 downloads area on the companion website includes four photographs: an image of a hand I created for this exercise and others from online sources.

You can download the photographs from the companion website or use the source materials. In these exercises, you'll learn how to see image relationships through juxtaposition.

WHAT YOU'LL MAKE

In the exercises in this chapter, you'll create a cut-and-paste style collage in which the edges of the images are visible, solid lines (**FIGURE 8.3**).

FIGURE 8.3 The final collage created in the Chapter 8 exercises.

IMAGE CREDITS Portrait of Salvador Dalí appears courtesy of the Library of Congress, Prints & Photographs Division, Carl Van Vechten Collection, [LC-USZ62-116608]. The photograph of the meat-eating ant feeding on honey is courtesy of Flagstaffotos.com.au. Earth's Moon captured by the Apollo 16 metric camera in 1972 is in the public domain.

Did I mention that the Pen tool can be hard to teach to new users? Well, this chapter contains a double-whammy. Layer masks are also difficult for those new to Photoshop. Remember, you have to start somewhere. It's OK to mess up while working on these exercises: that's the point of practice. When it's time to implement these ideas in your own work, however, you'll be ready to combine the precision of the Pen tool with the intelligence of the layer mask. I've included extra online video material to support this chapter because it can be much easier to understand these processes by watching rather than reading.

 EXERCISE 1

SET UP THE COLLAGE WORKSPACE

The final collage will fit a workspace of 5.5 by 7 inches at 300 dots per inch (DPI), so keep this final target in mind while viewing the largest image component. Coincidentally, the first image you'll place in the document, the photograph of Salvador Dalí, is the largest. You'll use a cutout around his bust as a visual anchor for other juxtaposed images.

1. Open Photoshop and choose File > New Document. Set up the document to be 5.5 by 7 inches, 300 DPI, RGB color mode, and Transparent in the background contents area.

2. Download the large TIFF image of Salvador Dalí from the Library of Congress (LOC) website (**FIGURE 8.4**) or open it from the **chapter8-start** folder. If you're working with the original download from the LOC website, rename the file **dali.tif** and place it in a folder on your Desktop named **chapter08**.

   You can download the portrait of Dalí from www.loc.gov/pictures/item/2004662765.

3. Open **dali.tif**. Crop the photo so that only his head is in the frame (**FIGURE 8.5**). This will give you a more accurate understanding of the size of the part of the file that you'll use in the collage.

   REMINDER Did you forget how to use the Crop tool? See Chapter 4, Exercise 5.

4. View the document's resolution by choosing the Image menu > Image Size dialog box. Notice that the image was saved at 400 DPI. *Safely* (meaning, do not add pixels to the document) change the resolution to 300 DPI. Make sure that the Resample Image box is not checked before you make this change (**FIGURE 8.6**).

FIGURE 8.4 Download the largest available file from the Library of Congress website.

FIGURE 8.5 The Dalí image is cropped to include only his head.

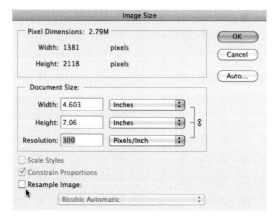

FIGURE 8.6 Uncheck the Resample Image check box in the Image Size dialog box to redistribute pixels.

FIGURE 8.7 You'll see selection edges around the Dalí image as a result of choosing Select > All. When the image is selected, copy it before clicking on the tab to the new document where you'll paste the selection.

5. Dalí's head is nearly as large as the new document, so you now can be assured that the image will be large enough to meet your specifications. Press OK to exit the Image Size dialog box if you haven't done so already. Press **Command(⌘)-A** to select all of the image on the active layer. Press ⌘-C to copy the selection. Click on the tab of the untitled (new) document (**FIGURE 8.7**). Press ⌘-V to paste the image of Dalí into the empty document. Rename the layer **dali**. Choose File > Save As and save the working collage document as **chapter08.psd**.

6. Close **dali.tif**. You don't need to save changes you made to the document.

TRACE AN IMAGE CONTOUR WITH THE PEN TOOL

In this exercise, you'll trace the contour of Dalí's head and shoulders with the Pen tool by placing anchor points in key locations on the perimeter of the shape. The anchor points should be set in places where the path of the line changes or is about to change. The Pen tool will make a path, not a selection. Your goal is to create a closed path outlining Dalí's bust. A closed path is a complete shape—the starting and ending anchor points are the same. Ultimately, you'll save the path in the Paths panel.

FIGURE 8.8 The Pen tool grouped with other related tools.

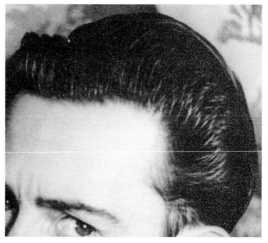

FIGURE 8.9 Begin a path with the Pen tool and notice that the anchor points that are created on the image.

ZOOM IN When you're creating a path or a selection or making any type of image manipulation, you really want to see what you're doing in a close view.

1. Choose the Pen tool from the Tools panel (**FIGURE 8.8**).

2. You can start anywhere to begin creating your path. I clicked the Pen tool once on the dent in Dalí's hair to begin my path (**FIGURE 8.9**).

3. Release the mouse. My second anchor point is just over the first curve of his hair. If you click once past that curve, you'll notice that the path created by two clicks is a straight line (**FIGURE 8.10**). Since you want the path to curve at this point, press ⌘-Z to undo the last step. Instead of a single click, position the mouse in the same location, but this time when you click, add a minor mouse drag in a downward direction. You'll see the curve begin to form. Drag the mouse until the curve traces the contour of his hairline (**FIGURE 8.11**).

REMINDER You must start and end the path on the same anchor point to close the path.

FIGURE 8.10 A straight path is created by two clicks with the Pen tool.

FIGURE 8.11 Notice the resulting Bézier handles on either side of the anchor point. These let you control the curve. While drawing the path, you can ignore the handles. After the path has been made, you may want to use the Direct Selection tool to modify anchor point positions or Bézier handles.

FIGURE 8.12 Click and drag the Bézier handle to alter the shape of the curve.

FIGURE 8.13 Option-click on an anchor to lose a Bézier handle. This enables you to change the direction of the path.

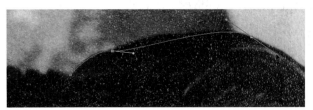

4. The next place you want to click is toward the top back of Dalí's head. I've purposefully clicked and dragged to try to make the path fit my contour in the way that I watch new students do this (FIGURE 8.12). Notice that the last part of the path starts to meet my needs, while the first part deviates from my intentions. When you create a curve, the next anchor point will be drawn in the direction of the previous curve. In this case, the direction of the previous curve is essentially the opposite of the direction that my path should be taking. Again, press ⌘-Z to undo this error. You need to make one crucial move before drawing this path in the next step.

5. Since the curve changes the direction of the path, and since the contour does not follow what the Pen tool is set to do, tell the anchor point to lose the Bézier handle directing the curve. Accomplish this by pressing the Option key while clicking on the anchor point (FIGURE 8.13). Now one of the handles is missing, but as you plot your next anchor point, you'll notice that you can control the curve to fit the needs of your path.

6. Now plot the point you tried in Step 4 at the top of Dalí's head. Click and drag slightly downward so the path matches the contour of his head (FIGURE 8.14). The curve of the path aligns beautifully with the shape of his head.

7. You may need to zoom out slightly before plotting the next anchor. I clicked and dragged downward near the lower-bottom of Dalí's head to fit my path around the shape (FIGURE 8.15). My anchor point is purposefully above the area where the curve changes again to move back inward.

8. Option-click on the anchor point, again, to lose one of the Bézier handles and allow the path to change directions. Click and drag on the portion of his hairline that turns inward before the last part of hair that meets the ear (FIGURE 8.16).

FIGURE 8.14 Click and drag the Bézier handle to match the path to the contour of the image.

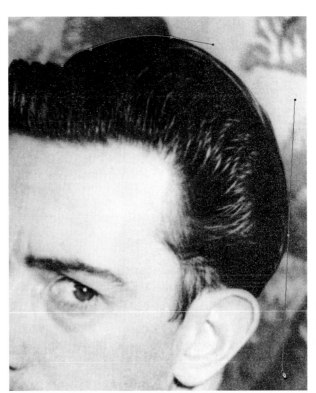

FIGURE 8.15 Fit anchor points to modify the path. It should match the contour of the image.

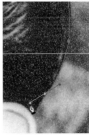

FIGURE 8.16 Remove a Bézier handle to change the direction of the path.

9. Keep working in this fashion around the perimeter of Dalí's head. If you're not sure when to Option-click on the anchor point, you can always try to make the next move and see if the path is following the contour. If it doesn't, press ⌘-Z (Undo) and delete a Bézier handle. It's OK to work in a way that includes an element of experimentation and best-guessing until you understand the tools. When you get to the bottom part of the bust, you can make a large, sweeping curve that excludes the furry element near his jacket (FIGURE 8.17).

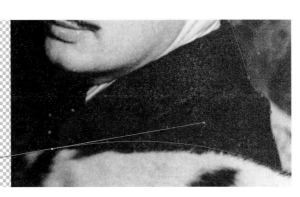

FIGURE 8.17 A large curve at the bottom of the image excludes the furry element.

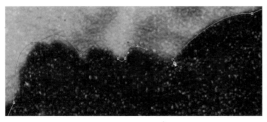
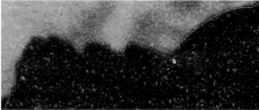

FIGURE 8.18 A small circle near the Pen tool indicates that the path is about to be closed.

FIGURE 8.19 Double-click the work path to name and save it.

PEN TOOL If the path is not closed, you won't be able to convert the path to a selection (which is, in this case, the purpose of creating the path).

THE PATHS PANEL is located in a tab next to Layers and Channels. If you don't see it, you can choose Window > Paths to open the panel.

If you use the Direct Selection tool to move the path in one area, be mindful of how the rest of the path may change. Sometimes this isn't the best solution because the change in one location disrupts the path everywhere else. Keep reading: one of the next steps might be a better solution for your situation.

10. You must complete or "close" the path by making your last click meet up with your first anchor point. Notice that the Pen tool displays a circle icon near the bottom of the tool to indicate that the click you're about to make will close the path (FIGURE 8.18).

11. Save the path in the Paths panel by double-clicking on the work path. Name the path **dali-head** and then save the file by pressing ⌘-S (FIGURE 8.19). Now the path is saved with the file.

 ## EXERCISE 3 MODIFY PATHS

The path that you create with the Pen tool doesn't need to be perfect after your first effort at tracing the contour. You'll almost always have to make modifications to the path once it's closed. In this exercise, you'll modify the path so it fits the contour of Dalí's bust. I deliberately run into pitfalls in the next several steps to demonstrate how to make modifications to a path. Your process may not follow these steps exactly, but you should be able to learn how to modify your path by viewing this series of exercise steps.

1. Zoom in to about 200% by pressing the Command and the = key. Inspect your path—you can start anywhere. I'll begin in the same area where I started plotting my anchor points. I'm looking for any place where the path doesn't fit the contour of my shape.

2. Choose the Direct Selection tool from the Tools panel (FIGURE 8.20). This tool is used to modify the path. The first modification I'll make is in a place on the back of Dalí's head where the path includes a little bit of the background. I'll simply click on the path and move it inward so the contour of the path is on the outline of his dark hair (FIGURE 8.21).

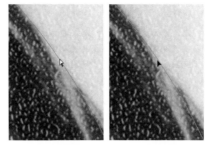

FIGURE 8.20 The Direct Selection tool is used to modify paths and anchor points.

FIGURE 8.21 Click and drag the path with the Direct Selection tool to move it closer to the contour of the image.

 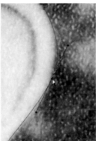  

FIGURE 8.22 Click and drag Bézier handles to modify curves for the best fit around image edges.

3. I've noticed that my path is also slightly askew near Dalí's ear. In this situation, the curve doesn't match the contour. I can control this by modifying the Bézier handle. First, I'll click on the anchor point with the Direct Selection tool in order to see its Bézier handles. Then I'll click and drag on one of the handles to see how that modifies the curve (**FIGURE 8.22**). Click anywhere outside the path to deactivate it when the modification is complete.

4. In some cases, you may need to move the anchor point and modify the Bézier handle (**FIGURE 8.23**).

 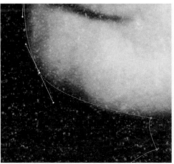 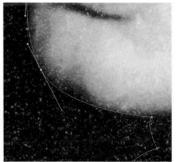

FIGURE 8.23 Move anchor points and modify Bézier handles around the contour of the image.

FIGURE 8.24 Use the Add Anchor Point tool to create new anchor points on a path.

5. You also might need to add an anchor point and then modify it. To add an anchor point, click directly on the path with the Add Anchor Point tool (FIGURE 8.24). Then use the Direct Selection tool to make modifications (FIGURE 8.25).

6. Finally, you may need to convert an anchor point from one that indicates a straight, angular connection of lines to one that supports a curve. The Convert Anchor Point tool (FIGURE 8.26) is used for this purpose. With it, you can click on any anchor point to change it from anchoring a straight line to a curve. I have a section of hair dips that are repeatedly drawn with straight edges. Somehow, one of my last dips took on a curved shape. I've used the Convert Anchor Point tool to change that anchor point from curvy to straight and modify the end of my path (FIGURE 8.27).

7. I'm still not happy with that last hair area. What I'm noticing there is an extra anchor point. Too many anchor points will make your path bumpy or inconsistent. When using the Pen tool, the dictum "less is more" couldn't be more appropriate. I used the Delete Anchor Point tool (FIGURE 8.28) to eliminate one of the anchor points and then the Direct Selection tool to reposition the path (FIGURE 8.29).

8. Press ⌘-S to save your work.

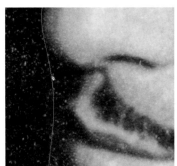
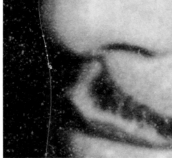
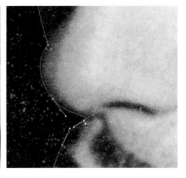

FIGURE 8.25 I added an additional anchor point near the curve of Dalí's nose. Then I used the Direct Select tool to modify the anchor point and its Bézier handles, changing the shape of the path to fit the curve beneath the nose.

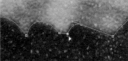

FIGURE 8.26 Use the Convert Point tool to change an anchor from a curve to a straight edge (or vice versa).

FIGURE 8.27 Convert anchor points to support a hard angle, rather than a curve.

FIGURE 8.28 Use the Delete Anchor Point tool to simplify a path by eliminating anchors.

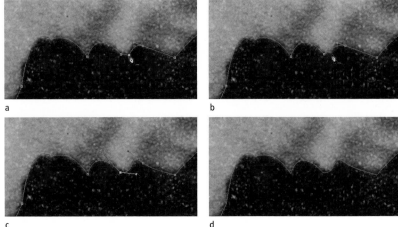

a

b

c

d

FIGURE 8.29 Clockwise from top left: a. Click on an extra anchor point with the Delete Anchor Point tool. b. The resulting path has one less anchor point. c. Drag a Bézier handle to modify a curve. d. The resulting path outlines the contour of the image.

EXERCISE 4 CONVERT A PATH TO A SELECTION TO A LAYER MASK

This exercise may seem short, but it can be extremely helpful. You'll need to memorize these steps to convert a path to a pixel-based mask. Now that the path is saved in the Paths panel (Exercise 2, Step 11) and you've modified it to best reflect the contour of your image (Exercise 3), it can easily be transformed into a selection. You'll use the selection to create a layer mask, hiding the background imagery surrounding Dalí's bust.

VECTOR MASKS AND PIXEL MASKS

In this exercise, you'll make a pixel-based mask for the photographic collage. Since you used the Pen tool to create a vector path surrounding Dalí's bust, the alternative would be to apply a vector mask to the layer. This can be done by pressing Command and clicking the Add Layer Mask icon at the bottom of the Layers or Paths panel while the path is active. The benefit of a vector mask is that the mask can be modified at any time by modifying the path. However, further blending with pixel tools such as the Brush tool can't be accomplished on a vector mask. (You'd have to create an additional pixel layer mask.) Since you'll work with vector tools in Photoshop in Chapter 9, *Blended Realities*, I thought it best to show you this process of converting a vector path to a pixel mask here. You should use whichever method seems appropriate in your own work.

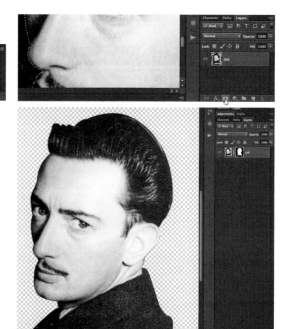

FIGURE 8.30 Load a path as a selection from the Paths panel and notice the marching ants around the selection edges in your document.

FIGURE 8.31 When you add a layer mask, the Mask icon appears on that layer in the Layers panel. The black parts of the mask indicate areas that are invisible (or masked), while the white parts of the mask indicate visible areas.

1. In the Paths panel, activate the path by clicking on it once (it will appear blue); then press the Load Path as Selection icon (**FIGURE 8.30**).

2. Look at the Layers panel. Only one layer, **dali**, should be active. (Click it once if it somehow became inactive.) Press the Add Layer Mask icon at the bottom of the Layers panel (**FIGURE 8.31**). The marching ants surrounding your selection are translated on the layer mask as a black-and-white representation of the areas hidden (not selected) and shown (selected). Press ⌘-**S** to save your work.

LAYER MASK START-UP: TO SELECT OR NOT TO SELECT

You can add a layer mask to an image layer at any time. You can begin with a path, convert it to a selection, and then add the mask (a perfect way to work when you want a crisp edge around the image area). You can make a basic selection with the Lasso tool or one of the Marquee tools and then add a mask. Or you can skip selecting entirely and just add a layer mask to edit with black, white, or gray paint.

FIGURE 8.32 The layer thumbnail of the Dalí layer is active.

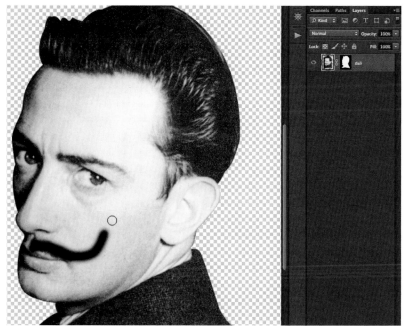

FIGURE 8.33 The active part of the layer will be modified—in this case, black paint is applied to the content of the layer, not the mask. So a black line is drawn on the layer.

3. Inspect the **dali** layer. The layer has two icons. On the far left is the layer thumbnail. I like to think of this as the content icon because you can see the actual content of the layer represented by its icon. Click once on this to make it active—you'll see four white corners surrounding the layer thumbnail (**FIGURE 8.32**). When the layer thumbnail is active, any action will modify the layer itself. For instance, painting with black paint on the image while the layer thumbnail is active will literally add black paint to the image (**FIGURE 8.33**). (If you followed my drawing activity in Figure 8.33, press ⌘-Z to undo the brushwork.)

4. Continue to inspect the **dali** layer. To the right of the layer thumbnail is the layer mask thumbnail. The icon is a black-and-white representation showing which parts of the layer are hidden (the black background areas) and which parts are on display (the white bust). Click once on this icon to activate it—again, you'll see four white corners surrounding the layer mask thumbnail (**FIGURE 8.34**). When the layer mask thumbnail is active, you'll be modifying the mask, not the content. This is typically achieved with white, black, or shades of gray using the Brush, Pencil, or Gradient tools. You can also select an area and fill it with white, black, or gray on the mask. If I painted with black paint on the image while the layer mask thumbnail was

FIGURE 8.34 The layer mask is active, and its thumbnail is highlighted.

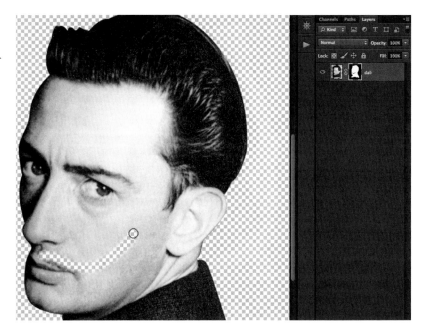

FIGURE 8.35 The active part of the layer will be modified—in this case, black paint is applied to the layer mask. Since a black line is drawn on the mask, pixels in that area of the image are hidden.

active, I would be adding black paint to the mask. This is different than adding color to the pixels of the bitmap image. Here, I'm telling the mask where to hide pixels. Black indicates hidden pixels, so my same mustache-inspired swoop of black renders part of Dalí's face transparent as I add it to the layer mask (**FIGURE 8.35**). (If you followed my drawing activity in Figure 8.35, press ⌘-Z to undo the brushwork.)

 ### EXERCISE 5 SCALE, ADJUST, AND ORGANIZE

You can see a video demonstrating how to use the Rectangular Marquee selection tool to measure the space precisely when numbers aren't your best friend on the Foundations of Digital Art and Design YouTube playlist (linked from the companion website).

By default, a layer mask is linked to its layer thumbnail. This means that when you move or scale the contents of the layer, the mask will reposition or scale accordingly. In this exercise, you'll make minor modifications to the layer content—so be sure that the layer thumbnail is active before you begin.

1. Press ⌘-R to show the rulers; then drag a guide from the left ruler to about one-third of the distance across the document space.

2. In this step, you'll decrease the scale of Dalí's torso. Remember to activate the layer thumbnail first! Click on it so you're not modifying the mask. Then press ⌘-T (Edit menu > Free Transform) to make your transformation. Always press the Shift key while scaling an image so it doesn't skew disproportionately. Shift-click on the top-left transformation box and drag

it downward and to the right until Dalí's nose is in line with the guide you created (FIGURE 8.36). Press the Return key to commit to the transformation. Use the Move tool if you need to adjust the vertical position of the **dali** layer. Again, press the Shift key while dragging to constrain the movement along the guide.

3. Add a Hue/Saturation adjustment layer to create a monotone cyan wash on the bust of Dalí—remember to press the Colorize button.

4. Finally, organize the Layers panel by grouping the two layers. Assuming that the adjustment layer is active, Shift-click on the **dali** layer so that both layers appear active. Click on the hard-to-see and unlabeled pull-down menu at the top right of the Layers panel to see a list of Layers panel options. Select New Group from Layers and then release the mouse (FIGURE 8.37). Name the group **dali** and click OK. The two layers are now organized into a single group. You can click the sideways arrow to expand or minimize layers contained in the **dali** group. Press ⌘-S to save your work.

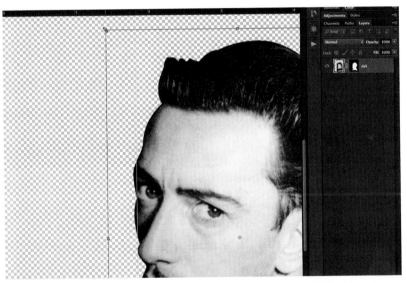

FIGURE 8.36 When the Layer Content and Mask icons are linked in the Layers panel, they will be transformed together. In this image, Dalí's torso and the mask used to control its hidden parts are scaled.

FIGURE 8.37 Select layers to organize and then choose New Group from Layers from the Layers panel menu.

COPY A LAYER TO AN OPEN DOCUMENT

Starting with the release of Photoshop CS4 (2008), new documents open in tabs. Copying a layer from one open document to another is not terribly intuitive with this feature. You'll accomplish that task in this exercise.

1. Open **hand.psd**, an image I created for use in this collage. (It's saved in the **chapter8-start** folder on the companion website.) Notice that the document contains a layer group named *hand*. In it is a layer containing a photo of a hand and a levels adjustment layer.

2. Minimize the layer group and click on the folder so the entire group is active. Choose the Move tool from the Tools panel. Click anywhere on the image of the hand in the application window (not in the Layers panel) and drag the mouse over the tab of **dali.psd** (FIGURE 8.38). The composite document will come to the foreground of the open documents. At this point, you need to continue to drag the mouse down from the tab into the Dalí image document (FIGURE 8.39). Release the mouse. If it didn't work for you on the first attempt, try it again. (It took me three or four tries the first time I learned to do this with tabbed documents.)

3. With the entire **hand** group active, use the Move tool to position the hand in the composite. Then press ⌘-T to access Free Transform. Rotate the hand and press the Return key to commit to the transformation. Set the hand in place—consult the final image file for positioning—and save your work. You can close the **hand.psd** document now that it's part of the composite image, **dali.psd**.

FIGURE 8.38 Copy a layer or layer group to an open file, Part A: Activate the layer or layer group, position the Move tool in the application window (anywhere on the image), and then click and drag the mouse to the tab of the opened document. Keep the mouse depressed as you move on to Part B (Figure 8.39).

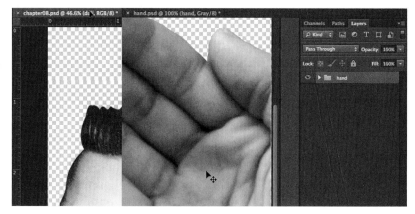

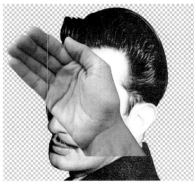

FIGURE 8.39 Copy a layer or layer group to an open file, Part B: Move the mouse from the open tab down into the application window and release the mouse. View the Layers panel—the layer or layer group will join the stacking order.

EXERCISE 7 THE MAGIC WAND

Once in a while, the Magic Wand tool can truly produce desired results nearly effortlessly. When you click on part of an image with the Magic Wand tool, it selects pixels near the location you clicked as determined by color. It *attempts* to select like-colored pixels. From experience, I know that it's not always successful. You'll soon understand when you'll be able to work magically with the wand and when you'll have to spend time with the Pen tool. You can adjust this tool like all others using the Options panel.

1. Download the moon image from the companion site or the National Space Science Data Center. (Use the high-resolution TIFF and rename the file **moon.tif**.) Open the **moon.tif** document in Photoshop.

2. With the **moon.tif** document open in Photoshop, press ⌘-A to select the entire image area and then press ⌘-C to copy the image. Click the **chapter08.psd** tab to activate the collage composition. Press ⌘-V to paste the moon from its home document to the collage. You can close **moon.tif** when you see the moon pasted into the Dalí collage image.

IMAGE CREDIT Earth's Moon captured by the Apollo 16 metric camera in 1972 is available at http://nssdc.gsfc.nasa.gov/imgcat/html/object_page/a16_m_3021.html.

It's very common to go through the ⌘-A, ⌘-C, tab, ⌘-V steps and see nothing pasted into a new document. If this happens to you, check which layer was active in the starting document. Usually, the problem is that you started on an empty layer or an adjustment layer and, therefore, copied no pixel data.

NASA IMAGES IN THE PUBLIC DOMAIN

Photographs taken by astronauts, photographers, or mechanical cameras for NASA are part of the public domain because they were commissioned by the U.S. government. An excellent database of images is located at nasaimages.org, and, of course, you can browse nasa.gov. I found the moon photograph by doing a Google image search for the word "moon," knowing that I wanted to click through to a page that looked like it might be hosted by NASA or the U.S. government. Another option is NASA on the Commons, a Flickr photostream that's easy to search and includes public domain photographs.

FIGURE 8.40 The Magic Wand tool is used to select like pixels in a bitmap image.

FIGURE 8.41 The selection edges around the moon's contour.

WATCH OUT! Did the Magic Wand tool select something entirely different than what you expected? Make sure that the moon layer is active before selecting the moon image! You'll always have to watch out for activating the layer that you intend to work on.

FREE TRANSFORM TOOL You can rotate and scale an image within the Free Transform tool. To rotate, put your cursor just outside one of the four corner anchor points and then click and drag.

3. Rename the new layer **moon**. Choose the Magic Wand tool from the Tools panel (**FIGURE 8.40**). In the Options panel, set the Tolerance level to 18 (meaning, select like-colored pixels within a radius of 18 pixels, as far as those like colors seem to exist). Check the Anti-alias and Contiguous buttons to make the edges of the pixel selection crisp and to create a selection based on image areas that touch one another. Make sure that the Sample All Layers box is not checked, as you want to sample and select only pixels on the moon layer. Click once anywhere in the black image space surrounding the moon. You'll see a selection around the contour of the moon and into its crevices on the right side (**FIGURE 8.41**).

4. Add a layer mask to the **moon** layer (**FIGURE 8.42**). Surprise! It's the opposite of what you wanted. If you selected the area that you wanted to remove and then added a mask, don't worry. The good news is that it's simple to invert your layer mask. Make sure the layer mask is active and then choose Image > Adjustments > Invert. Or press ⌘-I, a good key command to know if you, like me, will repeatedly find yourself flip-flopping the selected area (**FIGURE 8.43**).

5. Click on the layer thumbnail to make the content of the layer active. Position, scale, and rotate the moon so it seems to be popping out of where Dalí's eye should be. Use the Move tool followed by Edit > Free Transform again, as you did in Exercise 6.

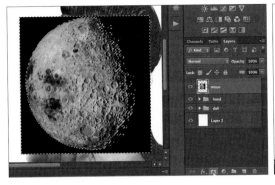

FIGURE 8.42 When you add a layer mask, the selected pixels will be visible. In this case, the selected pixels are the parts that you intend to hide.

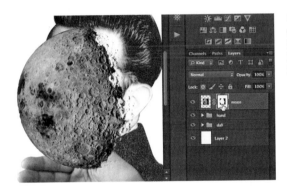

FIGURE 8.43 When the colors on the layer mask are inverted, the hidden pixels become visible, and the visible pixels become hidden.

6. Did you notice a thin, gray line creating a rectangle around the edges of where the moon background once was? The initial selection must not have included all of the black background. You'll need to modify the layer mask to eliminate the unwanted line from the collage:

   A. Click on the *moon* layer mask thumbnail to activate it.

   B. Choose the Brush tool from the Tools panel. In the Options panel, make sure that the Opacity and Flow are set at 100% and the Mode is Normal.

   C. Make sure that black is loaded into the Foreground color chip. (You'll use black paint to hide this part of the layer.)

   D. Reduce or increase the size of the brush so it just covers the width of the line. The key command is the open and close brackets, [and].

   E. Click just one time at one of the four corners of the black line (the starting point for one of the lines if you think of them as four separate lines). Don't click and drag (FIGURE 8.44).

DEFAULT COLORS KEY COMMAND Press the letter D on the keyboard to load the default foreground and background colors (black and white). Press the letter X on the keyboard to swap the foreground and background colors.

FIGURE 8.44 Click once on the beginning of a line with black paint on the layer mask.

FIGURE 8.45 Reposition the mouse and Shift-click to draw a straight line on the mask, eliminating unwanted visible lines on the layer.

F. Reposition the mouse to the end of the first line. Press the Shift key and click once (**FIGURE 8.45**). The drawing and painting tools will create a straight line if you click once; then move the mouse, press Shift, and click again (in most Adobe applications).

G. Repeat steps D, E, and F to hide the remaining three black lines.

EXERCISE 8 · SELECT, COPY, PASTE, REPEAT

Repetition is the best way to learn new techniques in Photoshop. Most of the steps in this exercise will be similar to those you've experienced in previous exercises. When images are juxtaposed to create a collage, repetition and contrast are two forces that help the viewer understand the visual message. In the final collage file (mine is saved as **chapter08.psd**), the large, dominant ant contrasts in size with the repeated smaller ants crawling on the palm of the hand (a memorable scene in *Un Chien Andalou*, a Surrealist film directed by Dalí and Luis Buñuel). The large ant also makes contrast in direction with the vertical plane anchored by Dalí's bust. Another way of stating this is that the large ant is a dynamic visual force, while the bust of Dalí is static. The repetition of the yellow hue on the moon (another reference from the film—it's easily forgotten as a metaphor for its more shocking visual counterpart, a sliced eyeball) and hand.

IMAGE CREDIT The ant file by Flagstaf Foto is available at http://commons.wikimedia.org/wiki/File:Meat_eater_ant_feeding_on_honey02.jpg.

1. Download the ant image from the companion website or the largest image from its source page on Wikimedia Commons. Rename the image **ant.jpg** if you need to and place it in your **chapter08** folder.

2. Open **ant.jpg** in Photoshop; then copy and paste it to the **chapter08.psd** collage file (see Exercise 7, Step 2). Close **ant.jpg**.

3. Name the new layer *ant* and attempt to select the white background surrounding the ant with the Magic Wand tool. You'll find that increasing the

FIGURE 8.46 Left image: Hover the Magic Wand tool over an area where you want to add (use the Shift key) or subtract (use the Option key) from the current selection. Right image: Press the appropriate key command (in this instance, the Shift key was used to add to the selection) and click once. The selection is modified.

Tolerance to about 32 will be helpful. When you have much of the background selected, but not all of it, you can add to your Magic Wand selection by pressing the Shift key while clicking again in an unselected area (**FIGURE 8.46**). Repeat this until you have a selection that's close to fitting the contour of the ant.

4. Clean the layer mask on the **ant** layer. You may need to slightly brush in a leg or two using white paint. (Remember that white paint will make those layer parts visible.)

5. Make the layer thumbnail active; then move, scale, and rotate the ant using the Free Transform tool (⌘-T).

6. Add a yellow monotone hue to the hand and moon images. You can use a Hue/Saturation Adjustment layer, or you can do this in the blue area of a Levels adjustment. Since the *hand* layer group already includes a Levels adjustment, I modified the midtone blue levels (**FIGURE 8.47**) and repeated this for the **moon** layer.

7. Did you notice that as you add adjustments above each layer, they affect the whole document? The image of Dalí became much less cyan because these adjustments for yellow (or away from blue) were made to the **hand** and **moon** layers. Coincidentally, those two layers appear above the **dali** layer in the stacking order of the Layers panel. In this step, you'll *clip* the adjustment

CLIPPING LAYERS
Option-clicking between layers will clip the top layer to the layer beneath it. You can use this to keep an adjustment layer tied directly to layers positioned beneath it. You can also clip layers to create a mask. Option-click between layers a second time to separate the clipping group.

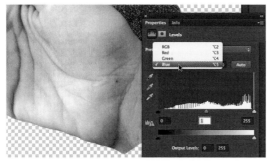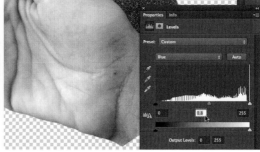

FIGURE 8.47 Adjust the blue levels to add a monotone yellow hue.

FIGURE 8.48 Create a clipping layer between the **Levels** and **hand photo** layers.

FIGURE 8.49 Duplicate the **ant** layer with the command from the Layers panel.

layer to the one layer it should affect. Press the Option key while clicking between the adjustment layer and the image layer beneath it; then repeat this on the second pair of adjustment and image layers (**FIGURE 8.48**).

8. Organize your Layers panel with a new layer group, **moon**.

9. Finally, duplicate the **ant** layer, scale and rotate it, and then duplicate the smaller ant and repeat to create the ants in the palm of the hand (**FIGURE 8.49**). I added a small shadow on a copy of the **hand** layer beneath each ant using the Burn tool (set to Midtones, 10%) to make them appear more connected to the hand ("floating" images are often easily grounded with a small shadow). When you're done, organize the duplicate ant layers into their own layer group. Clip a Black & White adjustment layer to the group. You can view my process in the *Screencast: Duplicate, Transform, Burn, Organize, and Adjust—Ants in the Hand* video.

SCREENCAST 8-2 DUPLICATE, TRANSFORM, BURN, ORGANIZE, AND ADJUST—ANTS IN THE HAND

Readers who enjoy experimentation will likely be able to transform and place the ants without much guidance. However, in this video demonstration I complete Step 9 of Exercise 8 for those who want to see my step-by-step process.

All screencasts are available on the companion website, www.digitalart-design.com, or on the YouTube playlist, www.youtube.com/playlist?list=PLAy6P5loEjy2v3kZKCt8spqJ50nLb2XQI.

 LAB CHALLENGE

Create a Dada-style collage in which the edges of the contours are visible to suggest the conceptual tension between the juxtaposition of visual elements. This requires a tension between at least two separate ideas. Use layer masks, selection tools, and adjustment layers when necessary and don't forget to organize the Layers panel as you work.

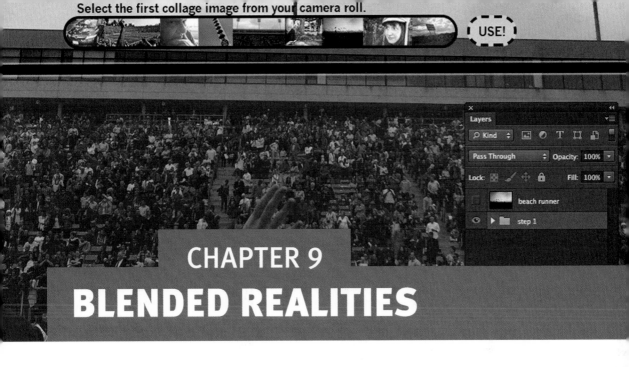

CHAPTER 9
BLENDED REALITIES

THE EXERCISES IN this chapter will provide technical lessons in blending images for a truth-like visual result. Following the Surrealist style of altered realities, you'll collapse the source materials into a final composition in which it's hard to tell where one image ends and another begins. You'll mock up an Adobe Photoshop document as a design concept for an augmented reality experience. And you'll continue to use tools learned throughout chapters in this section, with an emphasis on Photoshop's shape and masking tools using both vector and pixel-based masks.

BLENDED REALITIES IN NETWORKED SPACES

LINK For more on the notion of the digital realm as a performance arena, read or listen to Terry Gross's 2012 interview with Sherry Turkle on Fresh Air at www.npr. org/2012/10/18/163098594/ in-constant-digital-contact-we-feel-alone-together.

Networked technologies connect virtual hubs and provide social, scientific, and entertainment frameworks for blended virtual and analog environments. Common to the blended space are anonymity, virtual augmentations of physical spaces, and the ability to assume alternate identities (for instance, on Facebook, in chat rooms, on Second Life, and so on). Digital and electronic media, including sensors and programming languages, allow artists, designers, and developers to anthropomorphize virtual, seemingly sentient objects. These objects take common forms such as the voices of the iPhone's Siri (4s and later) or your GPS car navigation tool. However, sentient objects are also points of exploration for digital artists such as Kelly Dobson, who created *Blendie* (FIGURE 9.1), or more recently, objects that blog or tweet. (Search online for "blogjects" or "tweetjects" for examples.)

REFERENCE [1] Read Cory Doctorow's complete summary of *Shaping Things* by Bruce Sterling at http:// boingboing.net/2005/10/26/ bruce-sterlings-desi.html or see the primary source. Bruce Sterling, *Shaping Things* (Cambridge: MIT Media Press, 2005).

Before blogjects and tweetjects, Bruce Sterling predicted "spimes" in his 2005 book *Shaping Things*. Cory Doctorow summarizes Sterling's notion of a spime as a "location-aware, environment-aware, self-logging, self-documenting, uniquely identified object that flings off data about itself and its environment in great quantities" [1]. While the word *spime* isn't as popular today as a *blogject* or *tweetject* (names specific to the medium in which the self-logged or documented information is presented), Sterling's understanding of how blended realities would shape objects holds up well. *Botanicalls* is a collaborative project that started in 2006 and has since been updated. The developers' goal was to foster interspecies communication between plants and humans using sensory and telecommunications technologies (FIGURES 9.2 AND 9.3).

FIGURE 9.1 Kelly Dobson's *Blendie* (2003-4) is a 1950s Osterizer blender altered with custom-made hardware and software for sound analysis and motor control. For a finer appreciation of this work, visit http://web.media.mit. edu/~monster/blendie/dob-son_blendie_small.mov or find Blendie on YouTube.

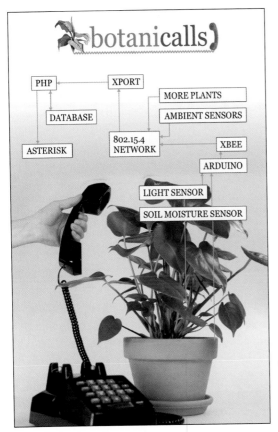

FIGURES 9.2 AND 9.3 Postcard for Botanicalls created by Sai Sriskandarajah (CC-by-nc-sa). The Botanicalls project by Rob Faludi, Kate Hartman, and Kati London began in 2006. "Botanicalls opens a new channel of communication between plants and humans, in an effort to promote successful inter-species understanding" (botanicalls.com/about). You can also see Botanicalls at the Maker Faire in Texas (2007) on the PBS show *Design Squad* at http://youtu.be/9u5wOqpdFfc.

LINK For more on blended realities, see the Blended Reality SlideShare presentation by the Technology Horizons Program, Institute for the Future (2009) at www.slideshare.net/ seanness/blended-reality.

REFERENCE [2] See http:// invaders.soulbit7.com for more information about AR Invaders.

Botanicalls plants are equipped with sensors to mine plant-life data, and plant owners can hear the "voice" of the plant via phone calls or (in later versions of the Botanicalls kits) Twitter feeds sharing information about the plant's development and needs, such as plant history, watering and fertilization needs, soil conditions, and so on.

The term *augmented reality* has become popular as mobile devices and tablets have become able to run apps in which physical spaces are blended with text, graphics, videos, or location information. The devices are a portal to the augmented space. *Oyster City*, for example, is an augmented reality educational experience (refer back to the introduction of Section 1). Augmented experiences can be informational, entertainment-based, or consumer-driven (find the nearest hotel or restaurant). Soulbit 7's *AR Invaders* is an iPhone app that brings a Space Invaders–style game to your physical surroundings. Instead of shooting aliens, your targets are alien ships that appear to be flying in your actual surroundings as you view them through the game's interface (**FIGURE 9.4**). As Soulbit 7's press kit states, "Space invaders was never this real" [2].

In the exercises in this chapter, you won't be programming or retooling sensors or electronic devices, but you will showcase your design—a concept for an augmented reality application that lets a user collage two photographs saved on her iPad. To produce the final composition, you'll add a couple of new technical skills to your practice and review many of the skills you've learned in previous chapters, such as working with vector shapes in Photoshop and applying a gradient to a layer mask.

FIGURE 9.4 *AR Invaders.* Photos © Soulbit7.

SCREEN RESOLUTION

Chapter 5, *Resolution and Value*, briefly touched on screen resolution. However, for this chapter you'll create a design with a screen purpose in mind: an *app* (application). Let's make this easy and suppose that the app design is to be created for a standard iPad3. One of the challenges of designing for networked devices is that you never know the resolution of your end user's viewport—the specific screen area in which the user experiences networked digital content. In a browser, there are many possibilities. However, a standard iPad is always set to a specific screen resolution. By limiting yourself to this device, you know the size of the viewport and the screen resolution to use. For the same reason, you'll force the user to view the app in landscape mode.

The standard iPad screen resolution is 1024 by 768 pixels in landscape mode. Apple recommends designing the app at 1024 by 748 pixels to account for the 20 pixels of space allotted to the iPad status bar. (The same would be true if you flipped modes, although the 20 pixels would be deducted from the larger side.) The resolution of the standard iPad is 132 pixels per inch (ppi). For reasons that are beyond the scope of this text, the preferred method of developing apps is to use vector graphics for the user interface. You'll begin the exercises in this chapter with a start file, **chapter09-start.psd**, set to 1024 by 748 pixels at 132 ppi.

Vector images are preferred in application development as they can be exported at twice their size (or more, or less) without concern for bitmapped pixilation or blurriness for viewers using high-resolution devices.

VECTOR SHAPES IN PHOTOSHOP

Many apps are essentially a set of tools represented by graphic icons that overlay the camera view, accessible in the tablet or mobile device. Since the size of the viewport can vary greatly, working with scalable vector graphics is more logical than developing two (or more) sets of pixel graphics for each possible resolution. For these exercises, you'll spend most of your time developing vector graphics using Photoshop's vector shape tools. Although Photoshop is primarily thought of as a bitmap or pixel-based application, it's also commonly used to create user interface (UI) designs with vector shapes. You'll notice that a slightly different icon appears in the Layers panel when the layer contains vector elements.

APPLYING GRADIENTS
TO LAYER MASKS

The Layers panel is often used to store graphics in groups representing steps of an activity or frames of an animation. In the following exercises, you'll develop four steps that a user of the app would encounter. You'll present them in four separate layer groups. If you wanted to share this with others, you would export each layer group as a single image file.

In Chapter 7, *Repairs and Hoaxes,* and Chapter 8, *Select, Copy, Paste, Collage,* you learned to create a layer mask. You started with either a selection or created a layer mask:

- If you started with a selection, the mask was a representation of the selection where white covered the inside of the selected shape and black filled the nonselected areas.

- If you created a layer mask with no selection as a starting point, the white mask showed everything, and you applied some black paint to the mask in order to brush a level of transparency on your layered content.

In this chapter, you'll continue to explore masking. It takes about three chapters (or three classes or learning modules) for my students to grasp the depth of creativity and expression that masks afford the savvy digital image manipulator. You should have mastered the nondestructive editing concepts presented in the introduction to Chapter 8; otherwise, consider a review before proceeding.

In addition, there are a few new masking concepts and techniques you should understand:

You can toggle between seeing the effects of a layer mask and hiding the mask by pressing Shift and clicking directly on the mask of any layer. You'll see a red slash through the mask when it's invisible (**FIGURE 9.5**).

- A layer mask is also called an *alpha channel.* Alpha channels are black, white, and gray representations of transparencies associated with specific media content (such as a layer). Alpha channels are saved in the Photoshop document and can be exported when the file is used in another application.

- A mask can be a pixel-based layer mask (created by clicking once on the Add Layer Mask icon in the Layers panel) or a vector-based mask (created by Command-clicking on the Add Layer Mask icon in the Layers panel).

FIGURE 9.5 View your file with and without a layer mask by pressing the Shift key while clicking once on the layer mask icon in the Layers panel. Shift-click to disable and enable the mask.

If you're primarily working with vector shapes, it makes sense to also use a vector-based mask. If you were to export the mask as an alpha channel, for instance, and the mask would be scaled (as it would for interactive media like the app concept you're developing in this chapter), you'd want it to be rendered as a vector graphic. You'll apply a vector-based mask in Exercise 4.

- Finally, you can add a gradient to a layer mask to smoothly transition one photograph from fully visible (opaque) to transparent. You'll apply a gradient to a pixel-based layer mask in Exercise 7.

KEY COMMAND
You can view the mask in your document window by Option-clicking on a layer mask. This is especially helpful for understanding the relationship between the transparent and nontransparent areas of the image content on the layer.

WHAT YOU'LL NEED

Download the following source materials to complete the exercises in this chapter:

✔ The **chapter9-start** folder from the Chapter 9 downloads area on the companion website includes **chapter09-start.psd** and **camera-roll.psd**.

You'll learn to see how blended images are layered visual messages. The blended images in these exercises include graphic elements (tools) floating atop a camera view and a transition between two images where the seam is impossible to locate.

WHAT YOU'LL MAKE

In the exercises in this chapter, you'll create a sketch of a concept design in Photoshop using vector-based shape tools and vector- and pixel-based layer masks. Four layer groups will separate each of the steps you'll showcase as the interface design (FIGURE 9.6).

FIGURE 9.6 The resulting file for the exercises in Chapter 9 will include four layer groups—one for each demo step of the user experience.

ARTICULATE THE DESIGN CHALLENGE

You'll develop a conceptual mock-up for a faux iPad application in the following exercises. Although you're doing this for educational purposes, you should be able to articulate your visual solution when developing a design that demonstrates a process. The fake app is a tool that generates collaged photographs. When launched, it opens a view of the user's saved photographs accessible through the native camera app. (I'll call this the "camera roll" because this is the language Apple developed.) There are four distinct steps the user takes when building her collage, so you'll create a simulated screenshot of each of these steps to present your concept in a rudimentary demonstration. The four demo steps correspond to four layer groups you'll create in these exercises. As you read each step, view **FIGURE 9.6** to see the concept demonstrated, as well as a view of the Layers panel.

Refer to these steps while you're working through the following exercises whenever you need a reminder of the design goals.

1. **Demo step 1:** The user selects the first photograph, a graduation ceremony. The app lets her crop part of a photograph to use in her final collage. So, in your mock-up, you'll need to give the impression of a cropping tool in action on the first photograph. Selecting and cropping an image requires feedback to the app when the crop is complete. You'll design a simple "USE!" button for the user to click when she's satisfied with her crop.

2. **Demo step 2:** The user selects the second photograph. To show this, you'll simply create a duplicate layer group with a new photograph in place and a different cropped area. However, you now want to show what happens after cropping is complete and the user wants to create her environment. The same tools should be viewable, but with a twist. A "MAKE!" button replaces the "USE!" button to tell the app to begin the processing phase. Assume that the viewer can simply click on a different photo to start this step anew.

3. **Demo step 3:** The user controls the process of blending the images, such as positioning the two images in one composition and directing the blend line where the photos transition from one to the next. In the mock-up, you'll show this in simplified form, where the photographs and blend lines appear as if they're being positioned. (If I were really trying to sell this idea to someone, I would probably create more than one frame showcasing this process.) Again, the app needs feedback from the user. The user has made her decisions about the collage, and next she'll want to save her result to the camera roll. So the action that the button produces for this step is "SAVE!"

4. **Demo step 4:** The user admires her final composition. The final view shows the collaged image as if it were saved as a new photograph. No application tools are visible because the user would now be in the iPad camera application—the camera roll—viewing a saved image.

COMBINE VECTOR SHAPES IN PHOTOSHOP

EXERCISE 2

While Photoshop is primarily used for editing bitmap graphics, there are also vector-based tools in the Tools panel. These include the vector shape tools, the Pen tools (if the path is converted to a shape), and the Type tool. In this exercise, you'll start by creating a vector shape using the Rectangle tool and then modify the resulting rectangle with two new rectangle vector shapes.

Each time you use a vector tool, there are two significant pull-down menus you should review in the Options panel. The first is the Pick tool mode with the Shape, Path, or Pixels options—you'll use the Shape mode for all the exercises in this chapter. The second is the Path operations menu, which controls how the resulting shape will or will not be combined with the previous shape. The Shape mode is intuitive, but the Path operations can be a bit tricky. You'll work with Path operations in Steps 5 and 6.

1. Open the **chapter09-start.psd** file. Review the image size and resolution specified in the Image Size dialog (press **Command(⌘)-Option-I** and press OK to exit). You may also want to view the **chapter09-final.psd** file to see how the layer groups relate to each of the steps outlined in Exercise 1.

2. Click the Eyeball icon in the Layers panel next to the **beach runner** layer to make it invisible because the graduation photo will be the first selected image.

3. Choose the Rectangle tool from the Tools panel (**FIGURE 9.7**). Set the tool to Shape mode using the pull-down menu in the Options panel (**FIGURE 9.8**). Also, set the Fill to none, the Stroke to black at 3 points, use the default, solid line, and check the Align Edges box.

4. Call the first user tool you'll draw the *crop edges* tool; it will be available only when the user has made a photo selection. Click and drag to draw a rectangle across the lower portion of the photograph. The rectangle has been saved as a vector layer in the Layers panel. (Notice that the Layer thumbnail icon looks different than a Pixel Layer thumbnail icon.) Modify the shape by increasing the Stroke value to 5 points (**FIGURE 9.9**).

FIGURE 9.7 The Rectangle tool is a shape tool. Avoid confusion by understanding the differences between the shape and selection tools.

FIGURE 9.8 Select Shape mode from the Options panel. When drawing with shape tools, you can create shapes, paths, or pixels.

FIGURE 9.9 The Stroke value is 5 points on the **Rectangle 1** layer. Notice the different icons on the shape and pixel layers.

FIGURE 9.10 When the shape tools are active, use the Options panel to modify shapes.

5. So far, you've made a rectangle. What you want to create is a set of four crop corners with lines extending along the top and bottom portions of the crop area (see demo step 1 in Figure 9.6). This means that you want to lose the middle parts of the rectangles on the left and right sides. (This should remind you of working with the Pathfinder panel in Adobe Illustrator, as discussed in Chapter 3, *Modify Basic Shapes*.) Choose Subtract Front Shape from the Path operations pull-down menu in the Options area (FIGURE 9.10). Press ⌘-R to view the rulers. Drag and drop a horizontal guide 50 pixels down from the top of the rectangle. Add another guide 50 pixels above the bottom of the rectangle. Starting outside the document area, draw a box using the Rectangle tool. (You may need to expand the application frame until you see some gray space outside the document.) Your box should be positioned on top of the outline of the rectangle on the left side between the two guides; then repeat the drawing on the right side (FIGURE 9.11).

FIGURE 9.11 It may be difficult to see in this screenshot, but when you're subtracting a shape, the Shape tool will show a small minus sign (-) in its lower-right corner.

6. The two rectangles have been subtracted from the large rectangle—notice that this is all being saved on one vector layer in the Layers panel. However, the design isn't quite what it should be (to my mind). Now you need to subtract everything from the middle of the rectangle. Be sure the Subtract Front Shape operation is still active and zoom in. (I viewed the document at 400% while working on this step.) Draw another rectangle to exclude the mid-space. Start the drawing at the top-left inner corner of the frame and then click and drag to the lower-right corner (**FIGURE 9.12**). Be careful not to exclude portions of the corner lines.

7. Inspect your work. Does it look like a tool you'd use to crop images? Toggle a view of your work without (and with) the edges of the paths by pressing ⌘-**Option-H** a few times. Press ⌘-; (semicolon) to hide and show guides. Use the Direct Selection tool to modify anchors of the path as you learned to do in earlier chapters (Chapter 3 using Illustrator, Chapter 8 using Photoshop).

8. Rename the **Rectangle 1** layer **crop area**. Save your work as **chapter09.psd**.

Unfortunately, the Photoshop and Illustrator interfaces are not identical, even when it comes to accomplishing the same goal. You'll have to learn a slightly new interface to combine vector shapes in Photoshop because there's no Pathfinder tool. For this reason, many people design user interface components in Illustrator. You can work in whichever application you prefer.

FIGURE 9.12 Subtract the middle part of the rectangle.

EXERCISE 3 LAYER EFFECTS

Layer effects can tend to look canned, so use them sparingly. In my opinion, filters or layer effects are rarely the solution to photographic- or image-based design challenges. However, they are convenient for creating lines, highlights, or shadows on vector shapes, and thus have become popular when designing user interface elements. There is an appropriate context for everything (except the font Comic Sans, which you'll learn about in the next section).

1. Use a layer effect on the **crop area** layer to add a highlight to the edges of the frame you constructed in Exercise 2. Click the **crop area** layer if it's not active already. Press the *fx* icon at the bottom of the Layers panel and choose Outer Glow from the list of layer effects (**FIGURE 9.13**).

2. When I did this, I basically left the default settings in place, but changed the opacity to 60% and selected Cone contour mapping in the Quality area of the dialog box because I preferred the way the glow appeared with this setting (**FIGURE 9.14**). You can click through the various settings to see the visual results they produce. Once you're happy with how it looks, press OK to exit the Layer Style dialog.

Toggle the visibility of particular effects by clicking their associated Eyeball icons in the Layers panel.

3. Notice that the Layers panel now includes Effects as an indented part of the **crop area** layer. You can toggle any effect on or off (visible/invisible) by clicking the Eyeball icon next to it.

4. Vector layers can be modified using the Direct Select or other path-oriented tools. After reviewing my work, I decided to double the value of the outline. With the **crop area** layer active, change the Stroke value to 10 points.

FIGURE 9.13 Layer effects, such as Outer Glow, are accessible from a pull-down menu in the bottom of the Layers panel.

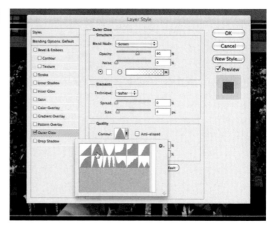

FIGURE 9.14 Layer style settings can be modified, including the blending mode, opacity, contour, and more. Be sure to check the Preview box in order to see your changes.

Did you notice that it seemed like nothing happened? You have to modify the path that's subtracting the front shape to show the change you made to the Stroke value:

A. Zoom in.

B. Click the inside anchor of the top-left corner with the Direct Selection tool.

C. Hold the Shift key as you click once to add the inside anchor at the top-right corner to your active selection. Both should appear as filled-in squares or anchors.

D. Press the Down Arrow key five times to nudge the anchors 5 pixels down from their starting position (**FIGURE 9.15**). This enables a Stroke value of 10 pixels to appear in view.

E. Click anywhere outside the path with the Direct Selection tool to deselect the anchor points.

F. Repeat this process with the two anchor points on the right side, the bottom, and the left side of the inner rectangle stroke.

5. Choose the Rectangle tool and set its options to create a new shape layer. Then select Shape from the tool mode menu and New Layer from the Path operations menu in the Options panel. Zoom in to see the intersection at the inner corner of the rectangle; then click and drag to create the highlight area across the inside of the crop marks. Change the Fill value to yellow (RGB 255, 255, 0) and the Stroke value to none (**FIGURE 9.16**).

FIGURE 9.15 Left: A close-up view of one of the selected anchor points. Right: The lower image shows the increase in border size after the anchor points have been moved down by 5 pixels. Compare this thickness with the border seen in the top image.

FIGURE 9.16 A shape layer with a yellow fill.

FIGURE 9.17 A view of the Layers panel with the **highlight crop** layer stacked between the **graduation** and **crop area** layers.

6. In the Layers panel, rename **Rectangle 1** to **highlight crop**. Set the Fill slider to 20% and drag the layer so it's stacked between the **graduation** and **crop area** layers (FIGURE 9.17). Save your work—so far you've created about half of the first demo step.

EXERCISE 4 ADD A VECTOR MASK

You'll begin this exercise by opening the **camera-roll.psd** file. (Download it from the companion site if you haven't done so already.) You may notice that the set of camera roll images are not uniform in shape. In this exercise, you'll use the vector mask to fit a layer group containing disparately sized images into a neat, elliptical shape.

1. Open the file **camera-roll.psd**. Drag the layer group **camera-roll** to the **chapter09.psd** tab. When your work in progress is in view, move the cursor to the document window to drop the layer group into this document.

2. Add a vertical guide to the center of the document (512 pixels).

You can also add a vector mask by activating the layer and choosing the Layer menu > Vector Mask > Reveal All. When you hover your mouse over the mask, it should say *vector mask*, not *layer mask*.

3. Choose the Rounded Rectangle tool and drag to create a new shape layer approximately the size of the row of images—the elongated ellipse should fit inside the images so that when you use this shape to mask the photos, there won't be dead space. Choose a gray Fill value and set the Stroke value to 2 points (FIGURE 9.18).

4. Rename the new layer **roll ui**.

5. Click on the **camera roll** layer group to activate it. Command-click on the Add Layer Mask icon to add a vector mask to this layer.

You'll see a difference between clicking on the Add Layer Mask icon (which results in a pixel-based layer mask) and Command-clicking on the Add Layer Mask icon (which results in a vector-based mask).

6. Click on the **roll ui** layer, press ⌘-A to select all. and then press ⌘-C to copy the shape layer. Click the Eyeball icon to make the layer invisible.

7. Click once on the vector mask of the **camera roll** layer group to activate it; then press ⌘-V to paste the shape layer you made to demonstrate the user interface (FIGURE 9.19). Press ⌘-D to deselect it. The group of images now fits into the elongated elliptical shape.

8. Click on the Eyeball icon next to the **roll ui** layer. Set the fill to transparent. You should have a black outline around your masked images.

FIGURE 9.18 A rounded rectangle created with the Rectangle Shape tool has a gray fill and a black stroke. It's in front of a row of thumbnail images, which extend beyond its borders.

FIGURE 9.19 Paste the shape layer into the **camera roll** vector mask.

CREATE A BUTTON

Buttons are commonly expressed by simple graphic shapes with shadows, outlines, glows, or background colors. There are loads of free buttons you can download from the web that may be timesavers for future projects. In this exercise, you'll create a simple button and explore Shape tool options.

In web or mobile media development, it's common to use an image as a background element. Files are referenced in code as bg, shorthand for "background." You can learn more about this online in Section 5, *The Web*.

1. Choose the Rounded Rectangle tool and draw a new shape layer to create a basic button.

2. Fill the button with gray and set the Stroke value to 2 points and black. Click the Set Stroke type pull-down menu and choose More Options. Select the dashed line preset and then modify the preset for a 3:2 ratio between dashes and gaps (**FIGURE 9.20**).

FIGURE 9.20 Customize the stroke settings to create a dashed outline around the shape.

3. Rename the new layer **button bg**.

4. Choose the Type tool (the T in the Tools panel) and add the word "USE!" to the button in black, sans serif type. I used the typeface News Gothic set in bold at 9 points. Use the Move tool and the Arrow keys on your keyboard to nudge the word into the center of the button.

5. Create a new layer group from the four layers: **roll ui**, **USE!**, **button bg**, and **camera-roll**. Name the new group **camera roll ui**.

6. Move the group so it's centered on the page about 20 pixels above the crop area. If you choose the Move tool, you can click the Show Transform Controls button in the Options panel to easily locate the center of the group. Use this to align the group center to the guide you drew in Exercise 4, Step 2 (**FIGURE 9.21**).

7. Create a new type layer with directions to the user: "Select the first collage image from your camera roll." Use the same type settings you used for the button and align it to the left, top of the camera roll interface. I nudged my line of type about 5 pixels above the top outline. Move the type layer into the **camera roll ui** layer group (**FIGURE 9.22**).

8. Create a new layer group for all layers except **beach runner** and name the group **step 1**. This layer group lets you easily hide or show the first demo step when presenting the four-step user interaction (**FIGURE 9.23**).

FIGURE 9.21 Centering content is made simple when you check the Move tool's Show Transform Controls button in the Options panel.

FIGURE 9.22 A type layer is aligned and stored in the **camera roll ui** layer group.

FIGURE 9.23 Group all layers except **beach runner** into a layer named **Step 1**.

EXERCISE 6 — COMPLETE LAYER GROUPS FOR STEPS 2 AND 3

Now it's your turn to create the visuals for demo step 2 and the tool set for demo step 3. You'll copy and paste many of the layers and layer groups, utilize the **beach runner** layer, and make minor modifications to create demo step 2. Then you'll make a simple circle with the Ellipse tool, a dashed-line with the Line tool, a yellow fill using the Rectangle tool (keep using paths, not pixels), and a new Type tool layer to complete step 3 (**FIGURE 9.24**). I've recorded this exercise as this chapter's Screencast in case you need help. You'll blend the two images together in the next exercise to finish the **step 3** layer and create the **step 4** layer.

SCREENCAST 9-1 CREATING LAYER GROUPS

You can watch how I completed the steps for Exercise 6, creating layer groups for the steps 2 and 3 of the demo.

All screencasts are available on the companion website, www.digitalart-design.com, or on the YouTube playlist, www.youtube.com/playlist?list=PLAy6P5IoEjy2v3kZKCt8spqJ50nLb2XQI.

FIGURE 9.24 A final view of the document and Layers panel with Exercise 6 complete. The image opacities are set at 70% to make the blend and crop guides visible, and a white background is added behind the images. All of these changes are documented in the screencast.

GRADIENTS AND LAYER MASKS

To create the representation of the final result (demo step 4), turn off the **crop area** layers, set the opacity of the two photos back to 100% (I had them set at 70% opacity in the **step 3** layer group to show how they might blend and where the crop areas were indicated), and then add a gradient to a layer mask on the top photograph (**beach runner**) in the Layers panel stacking order. In this app mock-up, since the user would have pressed the Save button upon leaving demo step 3, the resulting image is a blended collage saved to the camera roll. No tools are necessarily viewable since the device moves the image to the camera roll.

1. Duplicate the **step 3** layer group and rename it **step 4**.

2. Delete the white background layer you might have made at the bottom of the stacking order. Delete all the tool layers (including the **crop area** layers, as you no longer need to see which parts of the images are cropped). The **step 4** layer group will simply contain the two photographs. If you added a mask to the **beach runner** layer, you could either leave it in place and overwrite what was there, or you could delete it (do not apply it) and start anew. I deleted the layer mask I had on the **beach runner** layer to show the next step from a more accurate starting point that could be applied to other visual challenges.

3. Add a layer mask to the **beach runner** layer—not a vector mask, as camera images will be made of pixels. This should be the top layer in the stacking order. Since nothing was initially selected, the beach image will be visible with a white mask (showing all parts of the layer). The graduation photograph will not be visible yet.

4. Choose the Gradient tool (**FIGURE 9.25**). From the Gradient picker pull-down menu in the Options panel, choose the first icon to draw the gradient from the foreground color to the background color. Make sure that the Mode is set to Normal and Opacity is 100%.

5. Set the default foreground and background colors to white and black. Now the gradient will be drawn from white to black (visible to invisible on the mask).

6. Click and drag a straight line from near the runner's head to the graduate's hand. Don't forget to hold the Shift key while dragging the tool to create a straight line. In the Layers panel, you'll see a gradient from white (at the top of the document) to black (at the bottom), indicating that the transparency of the top image fades out (**FIGURE 9.26**).

FIGURE 9.25 The Gradient tool in the Tools panel.

FIGURE 9.26 A gradient drawn on the **beach runner** layer mask blends the image from visible (top area) to invisible (bottom area), indicated by the transition from white (top area) to black (bottom area) on the mask.

Toggle the Eyeball icon next to each layer group in the Layers panel to review the demo steps.

7. As always, the layer mask is locked by default with the layer thumbnail. Click the Lock icon to unlock the layer mask, which will enable you to move the mask separately from the layer content. If the blend between the top and bottom image didn't happen in just the right way, you can redraw the gradient line or simply reposition the mask with the Move tool (**FIGURE 9.27**).

FIGURE 9.27 I wanted to see the blend take place a little lower in the document. Here you can see that I unlocked the mask from the layer thumbnail, made sure that I was editing the mask, and used the Move tool to slightly reposition the mask straight down the page.

 ## LAB CHALLENGE

AR Invaders (refer to Figure 9.4) is a play on the classic video game *Space Invaders*. Design a set of vector shape tools and a proof of concept for an augmented reality game in response to AR Invaders. While brainstorming your concept, answer the following questions: Who is invading the viewer's space? How will you represent him/her/them? What tool or tools does the user need to destroy the invaders? Can your user transform her invaders without relying on destruction as the ultimate goal? What are the necessary steps for playing the game?

FIGURE S4.1 A Pueblo petroglyph (a rock carving, as opposed to a rock painting which would be referred to as a *pictograph*) in Boca Negra Canyon at Petroglyph National Monument in New Mexico. Likely carved by ancestors of today's Pueblo Indians, Puebloans had lived in the Rio Grande Valley since before 500 CE.

SECTION 4
TYPOGRAPHY

TYPOGRAPHY IS the visual design of language. It's an essential component of any media presentation that includes words. As mentioned in the introduction, readers and students of this book are enrolled in a wide variety of academic programs. The communications department I teach in doesn't require students to complete a course in typography. Graphic design students, obviously, will take several typography classes. The exclusion of typography from any program that's even a bit visually oriented is hard for me to understand (although I'm certain it has to do with the number of course units available, a bias toward nonvisual classes, and faculty who aren't aware of typography in their everyday lives).

So this is what I tell all my students: *take at least one typography class.* Go to a junior college or community college, sit in on a university class for no credit, do whatever you have to do to take at least one course in type. Without a knowledge of typography, you'll be left with a basic visual vocabulary for images but not for the

There are many resources for learning typography. My favorite books include Ellen Lupton's *Thinking with Type*, which is accompanied by an outstanding website full of tools for students and educators alike; John Kane's *A Type Primer*; Erik Spiekermann's *Stop Stealing Sheep & Find Out How Type Works*; and Emil Ruder's *Typographie: A Manual of Design*.

design of words. Imagine a day in your life where you never see a printed word (on a screen, on paper, on the highway, on a billboard, or on informational signage). Life as we know it would be drastically different and wholly uninformed without the written word. Surely, we would rely on pictographs, petroglyphs (**FIGURE S4.1**), or design some other means of communicating ideas, but isn't it convenient that in the English language we only have to consider 26 letterforms? This section focuses on the intelligent consideration of the design of letterforms with regard to how they appear when printed or on the screen, how the display of text is best planned for the human eye, and how type relates to other design elements.

LETTERFORMS

Letterforms are designed by typographers who manipulate the shapes of common glyphs (letterforms, numbers, and other communicative symbols). Typographers place a special emphasis on the relationships between thin and thick lines, positive and negative space, the space that a glyph occupies, and more. While you won't be designing new letters in the exercises in this section, you'll begin to notice the differences among typefaces. Each font has its own personality. Your choice of a typeface for a project should be informed by its style and the message you intend to communicate in your project. Toward this end, you'll learn some basic anatomical definitions and historical classifications that will help you make informed decisions.

LINK See the Library of Congress's interactive *Gutenberg Bible* exhibit at http://myloc.gov/ Exhibitions/Bibles/ Interactives/html/ gutenberg/index.html.

The movable type developed by the German blacksmith Johannes Gutenberg revolutionized European cultures in the 15th century (**FIGURE S4.2**). Ideas could be transmitted via printed matter with a new ease, much as the invention of the internet transformed communication in the latter part of the 20th century. The way in which type is disseminated, however, has changed in the last 500 years. Glyphs were once physical objects, carved into metal or wood, and then inked and pressed onto paper, vellum, or other materials. Printers in the predigital era faced the same design issues (such as alignment and spacing) that you'll tackle with digital tools. Just as Photoshop's Burn and Dodge tools are direct descendants of darkroom techniques (discussed in Chapter 7), the leading and kerning you'll learn about in this section are descendants of movable type.

FIGURE S4.3 A diagram showing selected elements of a letterform. Serifs are rendered in magenta. For a more robust directory, visit the Letter Anatomy page on Ellen Lupton's *Thinking with Type* website at http://thinkingwithtype.com/contents/letter/#Anatomy.

WHAT'S IN A LETTER?

A traditional typography course would cover the many parts of a letter in depth. I've limited the following list of definitions to those you'll need for a basic conversation about type in a work of design or digital art. **FIGURE S4.3** showcases a letter's baseline, x-height, cap height, serif, ascender, and descender. The baseline is the invisible line that a letter, word, or sentence sits on: it's the implied line that keeps typography moving in one direction. The x-height is the distance from the baseline to the top part of a lowercase letter in any font, while the cap height is the distance from the baseline to the top of an uppercase letter. Since typefaces can have enormous or tiny x-heights, the size of this part of the letterform influences the amount of space the letter takes up in a composition and the viewer's perception of the size of the type. The serif is a small detail that hangs off the end of some of the strokes defining a letterform. Ascenders and descenders are parts of the letter that escape above the x-height or below the baseline, respectively.

CLASSIFICATIONS OF TYPE

John Kane identifies classes of type on a historic timeline in his book *A Type Primer* in **TABLE 7.1**.

REFERENCE [1] See www.scalafont.com/story to read more about Majoor's Nexus Principle.

Though developed as a new classification of type, italic is now a common style addition to typeface families (**FIGURE S4.4**). Kane suggests that square serifs, for instance, were a response to the advertising industry's need for bold, heavy, commercial type (**FIGURE S4.5**). Martin Majoor (designer of the Scala and Nexus typefaces, among others) coined the Nexus Principle [1], whereby multiple typefaces including both sans serif and serif letters are created based on one form.

> *Although it's not a good idea to set too much body copy in italic, you will notice the shortened line length when letterforms are slanted with decreased kerning.*
>
> Although it's not a good idea to set too much body copy in italic, you will notice the shortened line length when letterforms are slanted with decreased kerning.

FIGURE S4.4 Italic is now a common type style or variation. The same sentence appears here in Calson 10/12 point (read as "10 over 12 points," meaning the size of the font is 10 points and the leading, or space between the lines, is 12 points). The top sentence is rendered in italic, and the bottom is in regular style. Notice how the italic style occupies less space on the page than the regular variation of the same typeface.

FIGURE S4.5 *An American Time Capsule: Three Centuries of Broadsides and Other Printed Ephemera*, the fourth of six advertisements of Boston Printing, 1860. Library of Congress, Rare Book and Special Collections Division. In this advertisement: bold, commercial type includes serifs, sans serifs, slabs, and more!

HISTORIC TIMELINE OF CLASSES OF TYPE

CLASS/DATE	EXAMPLE	
Blackletter 1450	$\mathfrak{X}$	Designed to emulate handwriting styles of monks and scribes in northern Europe
Oldstyle 1475	X	Oldstyle was "based upon the lowercase forms used by Italian humanist scholars for book copying (themselves based upon the ninth-century Caroline miniscule)" [47].
Italic 1500	*X*	Although developed as a new classification of type, italic is now a common style addition to typeface families.
Script 1550	*𝒳*	Meant to emulate engravings and are still used today in casual and formal typographic messages
Transitional 1750	X	Revision of Oldstyle to further define the contrast between thick and thin strokes
Modern 1775	**X**	Extreme contrast is achieved in Modern typefaces such as Bodoni and Didot
Square Serif 1825	**X**	Includes a new modification specifically to the serif, which appears blockish and heavy (sometimes referred to as *Egyptian* or *slab*)
Sans Serif Developed in 1816 by William Caslon but not used widely until the 1900s	X	The serif was eliminated completely so the letterforms appear even more geometric. Variations on the sans serif form include humanist, geometric, and calligraphic forms.

TABLE 7.1

SERIF VS. SANS SERIF

It's important for digital artists and designers to be able to distinguish the difference between a serif and sans serif typeface (FIGURE S4.6). Legibility is one of a typographer's key concerns, and the differences between these two typeface styles can greatly influence the legibility of the text in particular situations. A serif typeface is easier to read in the body copy (paragraph text, for instance) of printed documents, such as newspapers, magazines, pamphlets, and brochures. The serifs offer contrast between the paper and ink that aids reading in this situation, where light is reflected from the paper to the reader's eye.

Help!	**Help!**
Help!	**Help!**
Help!	Help!
Help!	**Help!**
Help!	**Help!**

FIGURE S4.6 In the left column, the word "help!" is set in several **SERIF** typefaces: Adobe Caslon Bold, Adobe Garamond Bold, FF Scala Bold, Goudy Old Style Bold, and Didot Bold. On the right side, the **SANS SERIF** typefaces used are Helvetica Black, Akzidenz Grotesk Extra Bold, Franklin Gothic Medium, News Gothic Bold, and Univers 65 Bold.

EXAMPLES OF SERIF AND SANS SERIF TYPEFACES

Serif typefaces include Caslon, Sabon, Garamond, Palatino, Baskerville, Bodoni, and more. On the web, you might commonly see Georgia or Times New Roman, among others.

Sans serif typefaces include Akzidenz Grotesk, Helvetica, Gill Sans, Franklin Gothic, Futura, Univers, and more. On the web, you might commonly see Verdana or Arial, among others.

Sans serif typefaces are easier to read in body copy that appears on a screen, such as websites, mobile apps, and videos. Since light is being projected from the screen to the reader's eye, the tiny serifs at the edges of the letterform become an annoyance that hinder legibility while the crisp edges of the sans serif form are simpler to perceive.

REFERENCE [2] You can see clips from the movie on the Helvetica website, www.helveticafilm.com/clips.html.

The 2007 movie *Helvetica* includes interviews with an international group of typographers and graphic artists who, for the most part, have strong opinions about the typeface Helvetica [2]. This ubiquitous font, designed by Max Miedinger in 1957, has been used in commercial advertising, corporate logos, information graphics, and so on for more than 50 years. Some designers view this modern, geometric typeface as a stifling indicator of a homogenous corporate culture. Others find beauty in the letterform's chameleon-like flexibility. This particular font and Gary Hustwit's movie provide an opportunity for reflection on the physical and symbolic differences between Roman typefaces (old style, transitional, and modern) and sans serif letterforms.

TYPE AND IMAGE

REFERENCE [3] Philip B. Meggs, *Type and Image: The Language of Graphic Design* (New York: Van Nostrand Reinhold, 1989). pg. 41.

REFERENCE [4] Ibid., pg. 45.

In Chapter 10, you'll add type to the collage you created by completing the Chapter 8 exercises for Luis Buñuel and Salvador Dalí's film *Un Chien Andalou.*

Google Doodles are short animations that transform the Google type-based logoform into a themed motion graphic. View the whole collection at www.google.com/doodles/finder/2013/All%20doodles.

Philip Meggs's 1989 book *Type and Image* remains one of my favorite resources for articulating the relationship between two visual elements that could be read as graphic and abstract, dominant and symbolic, or signs and pictures. Meggs quotes French critic and philosopher Roland Barthes in an observation of the way in which the word became subservient to the image as society's pace quickened in the 20th century, "Formerly, the image illustrated the text (made it clearer); today the text loads the image, burdening it with a culture, a moral, an imagination" [3]. Typography can be rendered as an image form (see the Google Doodle note in this section). Text can alter the meaning of an image or direct the viewer toward an interpretation. As type and image are juxtaposed, their relationship dictates a layer of meaning to the viewer. Conventionally, type is isolated from images (for instance, in the way this book is designed). Juxtaposing text and image in surprising ways can result in a powerful message. Meggs suggests, "Frequent use is made of type that surprints or overprints an image and type that reverses or drops out from the image...to create strong visual hierarchy and effective communication" [4]. In the exercises in this chapter, you'll overprint big, bold text on the collage you created in Chapter 8. The type will become a new graphic element in the composition, and its vector format will contrast with the photographic texture of the collage.

CONTRAST AND HIERARCHY ON THE GRID

Typefaces are designed in sets known as *families*, which include a variety of styles and point sizes. A display font may have a limited family (or none at all), while a typeface revised and redesigned for different type factories will include a lush set of varieties (FIGURE S4.7). While you may need only one version of a typeface for a headline (where you might use a display font), it's important to choose a large family for variations made in body copy. Using a single type family for the body copy in a layout will help keep the composition unified. However, using multiple varieties of that family will let you create typographic contrast. These two elements, unity and contrast, are used to direct the reader's gaze as she scans a layout. To organize the layout, a simple (invisible) grid is established, and type is limited to alignment along its horizontal or vertical guides. Contrast is introduced through the usage of multiple guides. Hierachy is established through contrast and the perception of isolation or a shift in the ratio between negative and positive space. Different parts of the text (headings, body copy, image captions, and so on) play different roles in the composition—each corresponds to a different level of hierarchy and should be treated visually as such.

In Chapter 11, *The Grid*, you'll use a grid to organize a typographic layout. You'll create contrast and hierarchy through space, size, and typographic varieties.

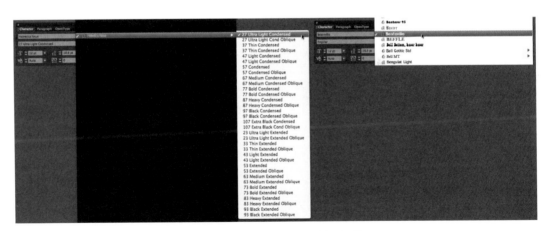

FIGURE S4.7 The lengthy list on the left shows variations for the typeface Helvetica Neue. The display typefaces listed on the right include few or no variations.

WHICH APPLICATION SHOULD I USE?

In Chapter 12, *Continuity*, you'll develop a multipage PDF portfolio using InDesign. Since the PDF is meant to be viewed on the screen, you'll use a sans serif typeface throughout the document.

REFERENCE [5] xtine burrough, *Create A PDF Portfolio Using Adobe Illustrator*, October, 2010, www.peachpit.com/articles/article.aspx?p=1636981.

While you're already familiar with Adobe Illustrator, there are good reasons to use Illustrator and equally good reasons for using Adobe InDesign. Illustrator has all the tools you need to produce posters, identity materials (business cards, letterhead, logo designs), and other one-page items. InDesign has additional tools and panels useful for controlling the design of multipage layouts, not to mention its recent additions for the development of electronic books and mobile applications.

I recommend that students create a straightforward PDF of their portfolios for email correspondence with human resources staff or internship supervisors. This can be accomplished using multiple artboards in Illustrator. I've documented the process in an article on Peachpit.com [5], for anyone who doesn't want (or have the time) to learn a new application.

CHAPTER 10
TYPE AND IMAGE

THE EXERCISES IN this chapter will provide technical and aesthetic lessons in the juxtaposition of type and image. In these exercises, you'll finalize the *Un Chien Andalou* poster that you started as a collage in Chapter 8, *Select, Copy, Paste, Collage.* You'll also place your Adobe Photoshop collage file into Adobe Illustrator in order to set the type and create a PDF document for viewing or printing.

CONTRAST AND RHYTHM

Contrast and rhythm are essential principles to keep in mind when designing with type. In Gestalten TV's interview with Erik Spiekermann, the Berlin-based typographer compared type design to musical composition. The silence between notes in music is equivalent to the positive and negative spatial relationships in typographic design (**FIGURE 10.1**). Spiekermann says,

REFERENCE [1] See the complete interview with Erik Spiekermann, "Putting Back the Face into Typeface" on Vimeo at https://vimeo.com/19429698

> Type is all about rhythm and space. It's actually not about form very much. You look at the rhythm and the contrast of the word...Every word has a rhythm. It's like looking at a park or a building. You don't see the details, you see all of it...What we read is the contrast between thick and thin, light and dark, square and round. And the rhythm is the rhythm of words, of spaces between words, spaces between characters. Just as in music, that makes it exciting. If it was just the notes without any meter or timing, every tune would sound the same. So my role is to put rhythm into [the layout] [1].

REFERENCE [2] See video documentation of Jürg Lehni and Alex Rich's 2008 *Empty Words* on Vimeo at https://vimeo.com/16379809 or play with the interactive simulation of this project at http://thingstosay.org/empty-words/.

Jürg Lehni and Alex Rich's *Empty Words* (**FIGURE 10.2**) is an installation of mechanized typography using a standard CNC plotter, a rotated LCD display, an Apple TV, and a software interface [2]. The resulting drilled posters display text written by participants. Letters are formed of repetitive circles, drilled at a uniform speed. Drilled holes in the paper create contrast between presence and absence (of the paper or the letterform, depending on how you think of it). The effect is reminiscent of os and 1s or the on and off nature of digital technologies. The similarity of the letterforms and the speed with which they're created contribute to the rhythm of the work.

When an image is introduced into the graphic equation, it's important to establish contrast and rhythm between the image and the type. But when text is overprinted or superimposed on an image, contrast must be extreme.

FIGURE 10.1 Screenshot of the Gestalten TV interview with Erik Spiekermann.

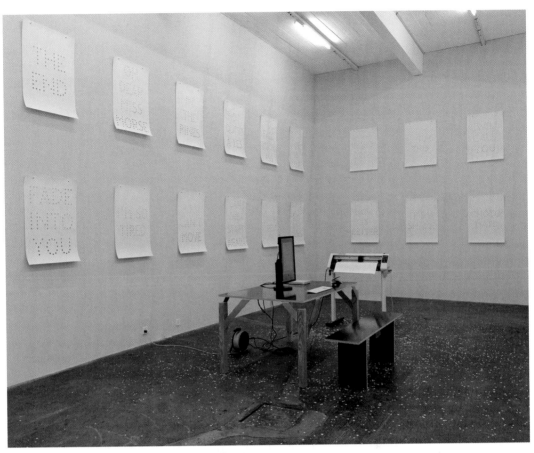

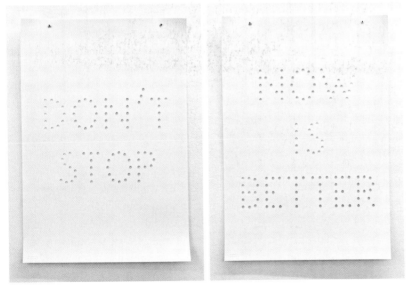

FIGURE 10.2 Top: Jürg Lehni and Alex Rich, *Things to Say*, Kunst Halle Sankt Gallen, 2009. Furniture by Martino Gamper. Bottom: Jürg Lehni and Alex Rich, *Empty Words*, 2008.

SAGMEISTER TEAM FOR AIZONE Creative Director: Stefan Sagmeister; Art Director/Designer: Jessica Walsh; Photographer: Henry Hargreaves; Body Painter: Anastasia Durasova; Creative Retoucher: Erik Johansson; Hair Stylist: Gregory Alan; Producer: Ben Nabors, Group Therapy; Production Designers: John Furgason, Andy Eklund.

FIGURE 10.3 Sagmeister & Walsh for Aizone: an advertising campaign for a luxury department store in the Middle East. The legibility of this composition relies on the stark contrast between the typography and the body in value (black and white) and movement (horizontal type across a vertical body). Rhythm unifies the message because the size of the type is nearly as large as the body on the page. The organic flow of the hand-drawn letterforms feels as personal and intimate as the naked form.

Legibility relies on contrast, which can be adjusted as a relationship between two or more elements in terms of size, hue, value, shape/form, amount of negative space, and so on (**FIGURE 10.3**). In the following exercises, you'll mesh typography with the collage created in Chapter 8. Philip Meggs writes, "*Simultaneity* means fusing unlike forms so that they exist or occur at the same time. Borrowing a visual technique from their contemporaries, the cubist painters in Paris, futurist artists also used it to mean fusing more than one view of an object into one image" [3]. The following exercise relies on this notion of simultaneity for the viewer to understand the fusion of the type and image in the visual communication. Specifically, you'll create a single block of large type, left aligned on a single margin, and superimposed over the organic composition defined by the collage. The rectangular shape of the type and its crisp, vector shapes contrast with the photographic, irregular shapes in the image. You'll repeat the image of the moon (covering Dalí's eye) as a substitution for the letter *o* in the word *Andalou*.

REFERENCE [3] Philip Meggs, *Type and Image: The Language of Graphic Design* (New York: Van Nostrand Reinhold, 1989). pg. 56.

TEXT BOXES

In Adobe applications such as Illustrator and Photoshop, you can use the Type tool in two main ways to set type on the page. You can click with it one time anywhere on the page and create a single, long line of type. This is a great way to add a headline or display type to the page. Alternatively, you can click with it and drag to create a text box. (In Adobe InDesign, this action creates a text frame.) This establishes the width of a column of text. The type you add conforms to the size of the box (which can always be modified). When you know you're setting body copy, columns of text, or text that should appear on multiple lines to fit a certain space, plan to create a text box or text frame with the Type tool. In the following exercises, you'll create a single text box. In the next chapters, you'll explore both methods of working with the Type tool.

TEXT ADJUSTMENTS: KERNING AND LEADING

Once you place copy in a text box, you'll likely need to modify its formatting. You can set character elements such as the typeface, size, variation or style, and more, as well as paragraph elements such as alignment, indents, and hyphenation. These are all decisions you'll make based on an informed view of the typography with which you're working. The *informed nature* of your view is what you'll be crafting throughout all the exercises in this section. There are many pieces of the typographic puzzle to keep in mind at once, so you'll learn small, central elements of typographic design in each chapter.

Three typographic spacing issues specific to a block of text include *kerning*, or the horizontal space between the letters in a single word; *tracking* (sometimes called *letter spacing*), or the evenly distributed horizontal space between letters in a line of type; and *leading*, or the vertical space (or distance) between each line of text. You will explore all of these throughout Chapters 10, 11, and 12. In the following exercises, you will modify the kerning of the large text in order to adjust the contrast and repetition of the typeface as it relates to the image beneath it.

The key commands to adjust kerning, tracking, and leading are easier to use than the Adobe panels, and they're simple to remember: press the Option key in combination with the Left, Right, Up, or Down Arrow key. If you're adjusting kerning, as you will in the following exercises, place your Type tool cursor between two letters (that is, nothing is selected) and then Option-← (to tighten the space between the letters) or Option-→ (to separate the letters).

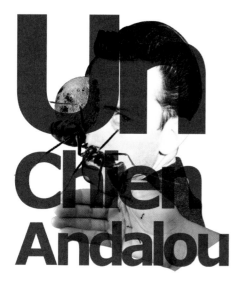

FIGURE 10.4 In the composition on the left, the overprinted type is kerned too tightly. Letters nearly run into each other, resulting in poor legibility. The composition on the right displays equally poor legibility for the opposite reason: the kerning is too loose. The gaps between the letters draw too much attention.

You can adjust tracking by selecting a line of type and using the same key commands, and you can adjust leading by selecting one or more lines of type and using the same key commands (substituting the ↑ and ↓).

In the following exercise, you'll pay particular attention to contrast and the repetition of space between letters. When there's too much space between letters, the reader will notice the negative space (likely the white space) and lose focus on the letterforms (the positive space). If there's not enough space between letters, the shapes seem to run together, and the viewer has a hard time differentiating letters, resulting in poor legibility (**FIGURE 10.4**). Since the type will be on top of the image in the following exercises, tight kerning between letterforms will help the viewer see and read the block of type as one, legible, unavoidable visual group. However, you'll be sensitive to creating large enough rhythmic gaps between the letters for the viewer to be able to discern the words *Un Chien Andalou.*

Finally, to make this even more difficult, true, even spacing between the letters (that is, if you literally measure the space between the letters and make them all exactly the same) will not result in an optically harmonic typographic layout (**FIGURE 10.5**). There are some situations where you'll pull two letters closer together (for instance, watch for this between slim and round letters such as the letters *l* and *o* or *o* and *u*) or push them farther apart (such as an *A* and *n* where the uppercase *A* requires more space, even though the overall amount of white space between the letters seems full).

FIGURE 10.5 The type on the left is kerned with precisely the same amount of space between each letterform. Notice the uneven spacing between the resulting text block, especially between, for instance, the *A* and *n* or *l* and *O* in *Andalou*. The type on the right is kerned to create optical harmony.

Un
Chien
Andalou

Un
Chien
Andalou

Un
Chien
Andalou

Un
Chien
Andalou

If you're using a Macintosh computer, you can press ⌘-**Tab** to scroll (keep pressing Tab) through open applications.

WHAT YOU'LL NEED

Download the following source materials to complete the exercises in this chapter:

✔ The **chapter10-start** folder from the Chapter 10 downloads area on the companion website includes my resulting file from the Chapter 8 exercises. Alternatively, you may use your own Chapter 8 results file.

Place or copy this file into a folder on your hard drive named **chapter10**. You'll save a new Illustrator file there in the first exercise.

You'll benefit from the ability to see the relationship between positive and negative space in letterforms.

WHAT YOU'LL MAKE

In the exercises in this chapter, you'll finalize a type and image collage based on the Surrealist film *Un Chien Andalou* by juxtaposing its name on top of the collage you created in the Chapter 8 exercises where the *o* in Andalou is replaced with the photo of the moon (**FIGURE 10.6**). You'll be working with both Photoshop and Illustrator, toggling between the applications to separate

parts of the image for the final layout composition. Overprinted, extra-large, sans serif typography is a modern treatment traced to Swiss International typographic styles, which you will explore further in the next chapter.

FIGURE 10.6 The resulting file after completing Chapter 10 exercises.

DEFINE A COLOR MODE

Commercial printing machines commonly utilize four colors, CMYK (or cyan, magenta, yellow, and black), which are based on the inks used on four separate screens in a traditional four-color printing press. Your intent is to print this document on a consumer inkjet printer, which is typically a device designed to be compatible with files made for the screen in RGB color mode. This will present an immediate conflict, as you'll set the document to the print profile only to have to alter the color mode once the new document is created. Setting the file to match the color mode of your printer is one of the many ways you can attempt to synchronize the colors on the screen and those in the resulting prints.

1. Since the end goal is to print this document, create a new file in Adobe Illustrator, by pressing **Command(⌘)-N** or choosing File > New, and choose Print from the Profile pull-down menu. Modify the new document settings to a create a 7 by 9-inch document showing units as inches (**FIGURE 10.7**). Notice that the print profile automatically assumes that you'll be creating a document in CMYK color mode. In some situations, Illustrator would be making a good guess that you want to set the document to the CMYK color space. In the next step, you'll correct this false assumption.

2. Choose the File menu > Document Color Mode > RGB (**FIGURE 10.8**) to correct the errant color mode.

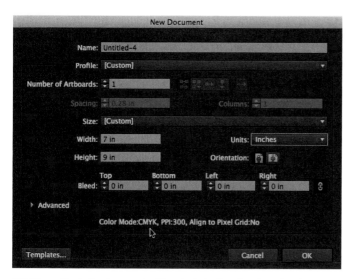

FIGURE 10.7 Illustrator document settings include changing the units of measurement to inches.

FIGURE 10.8 You can modify the color mode at any time from the File menu.

EXERCISE 2 PLACE AND RELINK AN IMAGE

1. Choose File > Place and select the file **chapter08.psd.** Do not check the Link box because you want to embed the image in the Illustrator document. Press the Place button. In the second screen, you can press either the Convert Layers to Objects or Flatten Layers to a Single Image radio button. Since there's no type in the collage, both options will lead to the same result. I typically choose to flatten the layers, but unless I'll be editing my Photoshop layers in Illustrator, my native .psd file is not affected by this decision.

2. Notice that in the final file (Figure 10.6), the large ant on a diagonal baseline appears in front of the type. You're about to add typography on top of this image. However, the ant will appear beneath the type if you leave it *flattened* into the collage. Save a new ant-less version of the file now and replace the **chapter08.psd** file embedded in the Illustrator document. Open **chapter08.psd** in Photoshop.

3. In the Layers panel, press the Eyeball icon on the **ant** layer to hide the ant.

4. Choose File > Save As and name the file **chapter08-no-ant.psd.** Save the file to the **chapter10** folder or wherever you're saving your Chapter 10 work files.

5. Toggle back to Illustrator. Click once on the placed image with the Selection tool. Choose Window > Links to show the Links panel. From the pull-down menu in the top-right corner of the Links panel, choose Relink (**FIGURE 10.9**).

In Step 4, you could have saved on top of the **chapter08.psd** file because you didn't delete the ant, you simply hid it. I've found that new students are easily confused when the file name doesn't indicate a change, so I made an extra/duplicate file.

FIGURE 10.9 Relinking image files simplifies the design process, as the newly linked file is substituted for the current image, while maintaining the same position.

FIGURE 10.10 The collage of Dalí, the moon, and the hand now appears without the ant.

6. Select the **chapter08-no-ant.psd** file and choose one of the methods in the follow-up dialog. (Again, I selected Flatten Layers to a Single Image.) The new version of the file has replaced the file displaying the ant (**FIGURE 10.10**).

 **ADD A TEXT BOX**

In this exercise, you'll superimpose a text box on the collage image. Letters are typically designed to be well-spaced for small sizes (between 8 and 16 points). However, once the type is enlarged, you'll notice that the spacing between the letterforms becomes disharmonious. You'll kern the large letters in this exercise. When you add other graphic elements to the design, you may end up repositioning or modifying the type. Remember to keep an eye on the spacing between all design elements in the document (including kerning) during the entire design process. You may need to revisit your kerning efforts toward the end of these exercises.

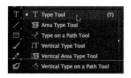

FIGURE 10.11 The Type tool in the Tools panel.

SELECTING WITH THE TYPE TOOL You can select just parts of the text with the Type tool by clicking and dragging to highlight the desired type elements.

1. In the Illustrator Layers panel, rename Layer 1 to **collage** and then lock the collage layer. Add a new layer named **type**.

2. Choose the Type tool (**FIGURE 10.11**) and draw a large box on top of the collage image. Enter the following text: Un Chien Andalou.

3. While the text box is still active, press ⌘-**A** to select all of the type in the text box. Click on Character in the Type tool control panel to expand the Character panel. Set the typeface properties for the active text (**FIGURE 10.12**). I used Verdana Bold because I can trust that most, as not all readers will have Verdana installed on their computers. If you use a different typeface, your settings will likely be different than mine. If I were to create this in a lab where I knew which typefaces were installed, I might select a geometric typeface such as Futura or a grotesque typeface such as Franklin Gothic instead.

4. Use the Selection tool to modify the size of the text box by clicking and dragging on any of the anchor points surrounding the box (**FIGURE 10.13**). Notice that the type inside the box remains aligned on its baseline while conforming to fit the shape of the box by pushing letters that no longer fit down to new lines or by fitting more letters on a longer line-length. In other words, the integrity of the letterform is upheld while the space within which the type is set changes. Resize the text box so it fits the 100-point word *Andalou* on a single line.

FIGURE 10.12 Click on the Character link in the Control panel to expand the typographic options.

FIGURE 10.13 The type should be set to 100 points. Expand or collapse the type box to fit the words on the number of lines you desire.

EXERCISE 4 RESIZE AND KERN DISPLAY TYPE

In these exercises, the only type that exists in the final document is large display type (that is, any type that's larger than body copy). All of the type is set in one text box. However, you'll modify each of the three words separately using the Type tool.

1. It's very easy to accidentally make a new text box or line of text with the Type tool when you're trying to select preexisting type. So be attentive to your document in this step. Place the cursor near enough to the letter *U* in *Un* that you will see the Type tool change from the Make New Type icon (**FIGURE 10.14**) to the Select Type icon (**FIGURE 10.15**). Then click and drag over the first word (**FIGURE 10.16**).

FONT SIZE KEY COMMANDS
You can use ⇧-↑ or ⇧-↓ to increase or reduce the Font Size value by 10 points. Use just ↑ or ↓ (no Shift key) to increase or reduce the Font Size value by a single point.

2. I want this first word to be so large that it covers most of the collage image beneath it. Since it's only two letters long, it will be the largest word in the three lines of type. With the first word selected, any changes I make in the Character panel will affect only that word. You can type in a new size (which would likely be a guessing game to repeat until you see the size you like), or you can use the keyboard (my personal preference). Highlight the Font Size field and press **Shift(⇧)-↑** until the size covers the collage—mine is 280 points (**FIGURE 10.17**). ⇧-↑ increases the Font Size value by 10 points. I find it easier to watch my design while pressing keys, which lets me evaluate the results while modifying the settings simultaneously. Did you notice how these two letters crept far apart as they increased in size? You'll have to adjust the kerning next (see **FIGURES 10.18 AND 10.19**)!

FIGURE 10.14 A view of the Type tool icon when you're about to create new type.

FIGURE 10.15 A view of the Type tool icon when you are about to edit preexisting type.

FIGURE 10.16 Highlight first word, *Un*.

FIGURE 10.17 Increase type size in the Control panel.

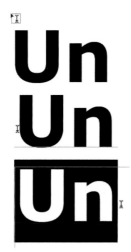

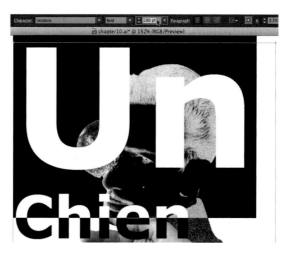

FIGURE 10.18 Position the Type tool between the *U* and *n;* then click once to modify the kerning.

FIGURE 10.19 Tighten the space between the letters *U* and *n*.

FIGURE 10.20 Display the Character panel from the Type submenu in the Window menu.

3. Modify the space between the letters by adjusting the kerning. Place the Type tool cursor between the letters *U* and *n*. You'll see a flashing Type cursor (Figure 10.18). Press **Option-←**. Each time you press this key command, the kerning tightens. Repeat the key command until the letters are close enough together to read as though they relate to one another, but not so close that they're overlapping or difficult to read (Figure 10.19). I pressed **Option-←** seven times.

4. Repeat Steps 2 and 3 for the next line of type *chien*. I ended up with a Font Size value of 130 points, and I kerned the letters *h* and *I* (**FIGURE 10.21**), as well as *i* and *e*, a bit tighter than the letters *C* and *h* (**FIGURE 10.22**) and *e* and *n*.

FIGURE 10.21 The kerning is modified between the letters *h* and *i*.

FIGURE 10.22 Tighten the space between the letters *C* and *h* by holding the Option key while pressing the Left Arrow key.

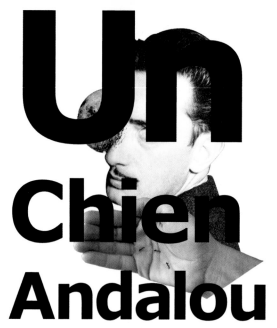

FIGURE 10.23 View the work at 100% or actual size to review the spacing between letters.

5. Leave the word *Andalou* at a size of 100 points but adjust the kerning so that the space appears optically even between the letterforms. Remember that this means some letters will in fact be closer to one another while some will have more distance between them—optical harmony is not equivalent to mechanical sameness.

6. View your work at 100% to see how the positive and negative spaces between the letterforms read (**FIGURE 10.23**).

For additional practice and help with kerning letters, play Mark MacKay's interactive game, *KERNTYPE* (**FIGURE 10.24**), at http://type.method.ac.

FIGURE 10.24 Warning: This game is highly addictive. I was relieved to score 100%, although you can see that my adjustments deviated slightly from the answer.

7. I'm about to rotate the text box, but before I do something like this I always create a copy of the text box and leave it positioned off the artboard. Use the Selection tool with the Option key to click and drag a duplicate of the text box to any position outside the artboard. Leave it there and pay no attention to it for the rest of the exercises. Consider this step a good habit rather than an action necessary to complete the exercise.

8. Choose the Rotate tool from the Tools panel. You'll have to use this tool to rotate a text box. Select the text box on the artboard by using the key command to access the Selection tool: press the Command key and click on the text box to select it. Release the Command key, and you're back to a loaded Rotate tool. Click on one of the anchor points surrounding the text box and drag to the left, slightly, to rotate the type (**FIGURE 10.25**).

9. Open the Transparency panel by choosing the Window Menu > Transparency. Select the rotated text box and set the Opacity value to 60% (**FIGURE 10.26**). The black type on top of the collage made the type more dominant than necessary for a simultaneous reading of the type

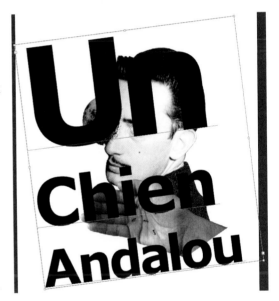

FIGURE 10.25 The text is rotated counter to the image elements in the collage to create contrast.

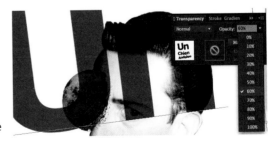

FIGURE 10.26 The type is 60% transparent.

FIGURE 10.27 When there's too much leading, you'll notice the white spaces between the lines of type and legibility suffers.

FIGURE 10.28 The type is more legible when the leading is adjusted.

and image juxtaposition. Reducing the transparency doesn't hinder legibility because this type is so large, and it aids the visibility of the underlying collage image.

10. The amount of vertical space between the lines of type is preventing the block of text from being easily read as one unit of text. I notice the spaces between the lines of text more so than the lines of text themselves (FIGURE 10.27). Decrease the leading to fix this typographic issue. Select all the text and press **Option-↑** to tighten the leading. You can start by repeating that key command a bunch of times. (I think I pressed **Option-↑** 15 times to begin.) Eventually, you'll have to adjust the single line for *Chien* and the single line for *Andalou* separately (FIGURE 10.28). You can see the results of your leading adjustments in the Paragraph panel.

You'll learn about the Gestalt Law of Continuation in the next chapter.

11. Finally, tweak the left alignment of the first letters in each of the three words. You can't draw a diagonal guide (yes, this is frustrating), so I drew a thin blue line extending down the layout at the edge of the letter *U* (FIGURE 10.29) to show the misalignment with the other two words. To kern the first letter of each word, *Chien* and *Andalou,* you'll have to set them to be the first word on the line (press the Return key just before the word) and then add a space (press the space bar). Finally, use **Option-←** to bring the letter back into alignment with the implied line of continuation suggested by the letter *U* (FIGURE 10.30).

FIGURE 10.29 Draw a line to use as a temporary diagonal guide. FIGURE 10.30 Each word begins with a letter aligned with the *U*.

 EXERCISE 5

REPLACE TYPE WITH AN IMAGE

Adding typography to the composition has created contrast between the sharp vector contours of the type and the photographic texture of the collage. In this exercise, you'll add the large ant on top of the type, creating yet another spatial relationship between the type and the image. You'll also replace the *o* in *Andalou* with the photograph of the moon. For these two additions, you'll want to isolate the two images (the ant and the moon) in their own Photoshop documents.

1. Open **chaptero8.psd** in Photoshop and make the **ant** layer visible. Click once on the layer thumbnail icon of the **ant** layer to activate it; then press ⌘-A to select all, ⌘-C to copy the layer, ⌘-N to make a new Photoshop document, and the Return key to accept the new document settings.

2. Did you press ⌘-V to paste the ant into the new document? If so, you'll find that the ant photograph is pasted, but the paste command didn't attach the layer mask to the pasted photograph. Instead, return to the **chaptero8.psd** file, deselect the selection of the ant (⌘-D), and move the layer from this document to the new one using the Move tool.

3. Option-click on the mask icon on the *ant* layer to clean it—all parts of the background should be black. Use the Brush tool with black paint to fill in any white gaps. Option-click the mask icon to return to the normal view.

MOVING LAYERS
Use the Move tool to move the ant layer from the application window to the open tab for the new document; then bring the tool into the application window of the new document before releasing the mouse. (See Chapter 8, Exercise 6, Step 2 for more details and images documenting this process.)

4. Choose the File Menu > Save As (⌘-Option-S) to save the new document as **ant.psd** in your **chapter10** folder. It's a native Photoshop file that you'll place in Illustrator.

CROP If you want to go the extra mile, you can also crop the transparent space from the **moon. psd** document before saving it.

5. Repeat Steps 1 through 4 to create a document with the **moon** layer group (be sure to paste the layer and its adjustment and then clean the mask) and save the new document as **moon.psd** in your **chapter10** folder.

6. Return to Adobe Illustrator. Create a new layer named **top images** in the Layers panel. Choose File > Place and select **ant.psd**. Move the ant onto the image. I liked the relationship between its two back right legs as a V-shape surrounding Dalí's eye (which also placed its front left feeler into a position that points to a smaller ant) (**FIGURE 10.31**).

7. Place **moon.psd** onto the image and position it over the *o* in *Andalou*. Add a drop shadow to the moon image by choosing Effect > Stylize > Drop Shadow. I left most of the default settings in place, but changed the opacity to 55%. Press the Preview check box to see your results before committing to the shadow effect (**FIGURE 10.32**).

FIGURE 10.31 The ant is placed over the text. A view of the Layers panel shows the stacking order.

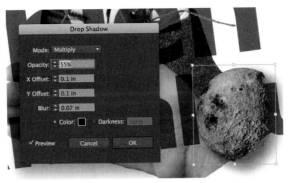

FIGURE 10.32 Choose Effect > Stylize > Drop Shadow to add this effect.

FIGURE 10.33 Remove the letter *o* beneath the image of the moon.

8. Although the moon will print over the letter *o*, it's a good idea to remove the letter. This means that you need to delete the letter from the text box and then kern the *u* into position. I clicked with the Type tool on the line of type away from the moon (positioning my cursor between the letters *d* and *a*). Once the cursor was on the line of type, I used the Right Arrow key to move the cursor so it was just after the *o*. I pressed the Delete (or Backspace) key to remove the *o*. Naturally, the *u* moved to take its place, behind the moon. I then pressed the space bar key twice. Finally, I pressed **Option-←** twice to tighten the kerning between the *u* and the spaces after the letter *l* (**FIGURE 10.33**).

EXERCISE 6 · ADD VECTOR SHAPES TO FRAME THE COMPOSITION

Now that you've added more graphics on top of the typography, you'll continue to make contrast between the bitmap and vector images. The frames you'll create in this exercise are simple rectangles with a slight shape modification using the Direct Selection tool.

1. To begin making the frame, choose the Rectangle tool and set black as the fill color with no assigned stroke. Click and drag a simple rectangle that roughly matches the width of the top part of the letter *U* in the word *Un*. Use the size of the width in this part of the letter as the approximate size of the height of the frame to make a relationship between the frame and the typography. Once you've determined the width, rotate the shape 90 degrees. Stretch it to build the top part of the frame (**FIGURE 10.34**).

2. Select the bottom-left anchor point with the Direct Selection tool and press ⇧-↑ about four times to move this anchor point toward the left-top anchor (**FIGURE 10.35**). The static rectangular shape is transformed into a dynamic form, mimicking the dynamic structure of the composition.

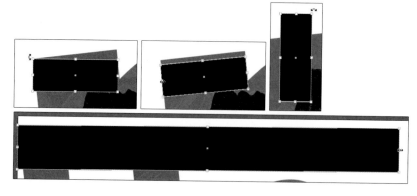

FIGURE 10.34 Determine the width of the top frame by fitting it to a letterform. Rotate and stretch it to create the top part of the frame.

FIGURE 10.35 Use the Direct Selection tool to move an anchor point and modify the shape of the frame.

3. Move the top portion of the frame into position over the top of the letter *U* in *Un*. Copy and paste the shape to create the left edge of the frame. Rotate the new shape to the left while pressing the Shift key to limit the degrees of rotation to 45-degree increments. Position the new shape and lengthen it to fit the left side (FIGURE 10.36).

4. Select the top part of the frame with the Selection tool. Choose the Eyedropper tool (FIGURE 10.37). Make sure the Fill color chip is in the foreground of the Tools panel. Click on the ant's head to fill the top portion of the frame with a red hue (FIGURE 10.38) to create a repetition of hue in the layout.

5. Group the two frame edges together. While the group is selected, double-click on the Reflect tool. (It hides beneath the Rotate tool in the Tools panel.) In the Reflect dialog, press the Vertical radio button and press the Copy (not the OK) button (FIGURE 10.39).

FIGURE 10.36 The left part of the frame.

FIGURE 10.37 The Eyedropper tool in the Tools panel.

FIGURE 10.38 The red hue in the top frame shape is based on a color sampled from the ant.

FIGURE 10.39 Press the Copy button in the Reflect dialog to save an additional step before reflecting the shape over a vertical axis.

FIGURE 10.40 A view of the composition with the frame moved into position.

6. While the new frame edges are still selected, double-click the Reflect tool again. This time press the Horizontal radio button and the OK (not Copy) button. Nudge the frame into position with the Move tool (FIGURE 10.40).

FINAL DESIGN ADJUSTMENTS

This exercise is a simple series of final adjustments. The frame is a bit off-center, and the type could better fit the alignment of the frame edge now that it's in place. The composition feels a bit cramped, so you'll loosen some of the spacing by adjusting the red parts of the frame. Finally, the composition ended up being a square rather than a rectangle, so you'll crop the artboard using the Artboard tool.

1. Nudge the left- and top-grouped frame shapes to the left edge of the composition so the tiny white margins are the same on the left and right sides of the layout (FIGURE 10.41).

2. Choose the Direct Select tool and click on the two anchor points on the right side of the top red frame shape to modify them simultaneously. While they're selected, nudge the two anchors to the right until they just barely touch the black frame with the Right Arrow key. When they touch, press ⇧-← twice to create negative space on this part of the frame. Repeat the same process with the two anchor points on the left side of the bottom red frame, reversing the arrow key directions (FIGURE 10.42).

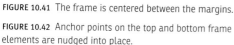
FIGURE 10.41 The frame is centered between the margins.

FIGURE 10.42 Anchor points on the top and bottom frame elements are nudged into place.

FIGURE 10.43 The collage image is repositioned.

3. With the Selection tool, select the type text box and press the Shift key to add the moon to your selection. Then move both the type and the moon image about 17 units to the left, while keeping an eye on the margin space on the left and right sides of the typographic layout.

4. Unlock the collage in the Layers panel and select and then move the collage image down and to the right (FIGURE 10.43). The arm should seem to grow out of the bottom red frame.

You can create clipping masks in Adobe Illustrator to hide or show design elements. In Exercise 6, you hid part of the hand that was showing beneath the red frame by cleverly placing a white shape to match the contour of the red shape in the space beneath it (atop the hand image). This technically works, but a better practice would be to apply a clipping mask on the hand. Clipping masks fall outside the scope of this chapter, so I've demonstrated this technique in this chapter's screencast.

All screencasts are available on the companion website, www.digitalart-design.com, or on the YouTube playlist, www.youtube.com/playlist?list=PLAy6P5IoEjy2v3kZKCt8spqJ50nLb2XQI.

5. Eliminate the view of the hand beneath the red frame by covering it with a white shape (matching the page). I'll explain this shortly; however, it's easier to understand by watching, so I'm including this exercise as part of this chapter's screencast:

   A. With the Direct Selection tool, select just the red bottom frame. (It's grouped with the black, right side of the frame so the Direct Selection tool will let you select just one member of the group.)

   B. Double-click the Reflect tool and press the Vertical radio button and then the Copy button.

   C. Double-click the Reflect tool again and press the Horizontal button and then the OK button.

   D. Move the new red shape so it's aligned precisely with the bottom of the red frame shape.

   E. Fill the shape with white, instead of red, to hide the parts of the hand image that extend beneath the frame (FIGURE 10.44).

6. Rearrange the stacking order in the Layers panel: drag the **frame** layer so it's beneath the **top images** layer. The moon's drop shadow now imprints on the frame.

> Instead of drawing a random white rectangle to cover the hand image, it's important that the covering extends the length of the red line—this ensures that the line will remain smooth if any areas accidentally overlap. (See a bumpy accident in the screencast.)

FIGURE 10.44 Hide the bottom parts of the hand with a white shape.

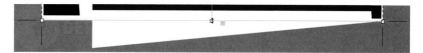

FIGURE 10.46 Crop the artboard using the Artboard tool; then check the Control panel.

FIGURE 10.45 The Artboard tool in the Tools panel.

FIGURE 10.47 Modify the artboard size in the Control panel while the Artboard tool is active.

7. Lastly, choose the Artboard tool (**FIGURE 10.45**) and crop the artboard. You can move the anchor points on the edges of the artboard to crop the empty white space on the top and bottom of the layout (**FIGURE 10.46**). If you pay attention to the Artboard Control panel, you'll likely find that your composition is close to square dimensions. Mine was awfully close to 7 by 7 inches, so I simply entered 7 *in.* into the W and H (width and height) fields in the Control panel (**FIGURE 10.47**). Press the Return key to commit your entries. If you use the Option panel, then click on any other tool (by default, I always return to the Selection tool) to exit the Artboard tool. If you need to, press ⌘-**A** to select everything on the page and nudge the composition into position. Save the file.

 LAB CHALLENGE

Create a type and image relationship where the image is used to replace a word or letterform or where the image extends the typographic letterform (**FIGURE 10.48**). Use Photoshop to edit the image or images and Illustrator to set the typography.

FIGURE 10.48 Oded Ezer, *Helvetica Live!* poster, 2004. The *Helvetica Live!* poster presents formal intersections between the famous Helvetica letters and various object silhouettes. Consciously ignoring logical context, Ezer was influenced by Dadaist methods and contemporary virtual hybridizations of animals and human beings.
© Oded Ezer

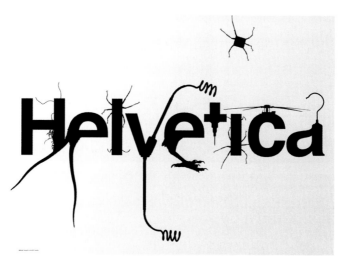

ext.

esent ac laoreet tortor. Integer
m nisl, condimentum et commodo
, ultricies sit CHAPTER 11 urabitur
aretium THE GRID
utam

THE EXERCISES IN this chapter will provide technical lessons and aesthetic exercises in using a grid to align a typographic layout. Following the Swiss International Style of typographic composition, the final layout includes hierarchies of type that readers can consume with an economy of eye movements. You'll continue to use tools learned throughout chapters in this section, with an emphasis on Adobe Illustrator's Type tools. In the next chapter, you'll create a typographic layout using Adobe InDesign, where your knowledge and familiarity with Illustrator tools will assist you in learning a new application.

The grid is essentially a tool that helps artists and designers organize and align a composition. As a utilitarian device, the grid has been used in urban planning since the Indus Valley civilization (present-day Pakistan) and ancient Rome. The simple organization of vertical and horizontal lines is also used in sketching electrical circuit diagrams. Engineering draftsman Harry Beck revitalized cartography with his grid-based 1931 redesign of the London Underground map, which used only 45- and 90-degree angles [1].

REFERENCE [1] The Real Underground Morphing Map (seen in Figure 11.1) is best demonstrated at www.fourthway.co.uk/ realunderground.

LINK You may also enjoy the articles "Mr. Vignelli's Map" at http://observatory.designobserver.com/ feature/mr-vignellis-map/2647and "The London Tube Map, Redesigned for a Multiscreen World" (featuring Mark Noad's redesign of Harry Beck's map for interactive screens) at www.fastcodesign.com/1664662/ the-london-tube-map-redesigned-for-a-multi-screen-world.

REFERENCE [2] Ellen Lupton and J. Abbott Miller, eds., *The ABCs of ▲■●, the Bauhaus and Design Theory* (Princeton Architectural Press, 1991). pg. 28.

Max Wertheimer, Kurt Koffka, and Wolfgang Köhler founded Gestalt psychology. Many students of art theory and visual communication today refer to writings by Wertheimer and his student, Rudolf Arnheim.

His version became a beloved work of design, although there was one major rivalry between form and function: because the map displayed equal space between stations, it in no way reflected the actual London landscape (**FIGURE 11.1**). This story of how the grid can abstract reality is a reminder of its cold and schematic nature. While the grid is an essential device for organization, it's also devoid of the complexities and nuances inherent in the human condition. So the grid and its emphasis in the Swiss International Style have come to connote design that is efficient, organized, and legible, but also unfeeling, nonemotive, and machine-oriented.

Ellen Lupton and J. Abbott Miller explain the grid as a "structural form pervading Bauhaus art and design, [that] articulates space according to a pattern of oppositions" [2]. The obvious oppositions are the vertical and horizontal structures inherent to a grid, which you'll create with guides. Positive and negative space, implied lines of never-ending continuity and abrupt spatial impositions, rhythms formed by repetition and then challenged by a lack of repetition, and geometric and organic forms are all possible dyads when placed in a relationship on a grid.

GESTALT

The Bauhaus school was in operation from 1919 to 1933. Coincidentally, new Gestalt (the German word for "shape") psychological studies in perception were developed in Berlin from the 1920s to the 1940s. The primary concept of Gestalt is the commonly stated truism, "The whole is greater than the sum of its parts." Indeed, readers, viewers, and users will classify and organize whole structures (layouts, grids, symbols, forms, and so on) before recognizing the minor parts used to compose them. This regular, simple, symmetric, and orderly way of perceiving is known as the *Law of Prägnanz*, one of the eight Gestalt laws.

Understanding as many of the Gestalt properties and laws as you can will help you anticipate how your viewer will experience the visual works you create. Since these properties and laws relate to the split between the whole and its parts, understanding Gestalt will fine-tune your ability to create visual unity. When relating design elements to one another (and the page or viewing space) on the grid, you should be purposefully orchestrating visual unity and its opposite, discontinuity.

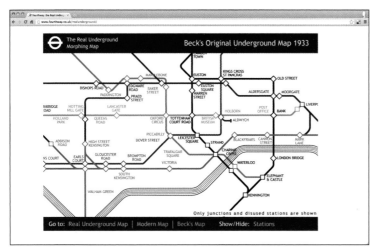

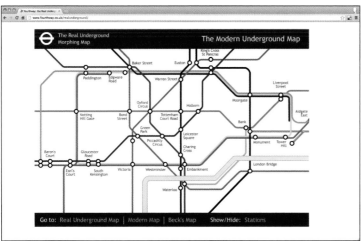

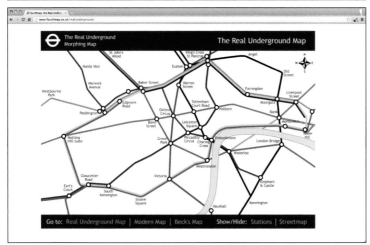

FIGURE 11.1 The map of London's Underground, based on Harry Beck's electrical grid-inspired design, contrasts with London's actual landscape.

EIGHT GESTALT LAWS YOU CAN'T LIVE WITHOUT

The Wikipedia page for Gestalt Psychology is an excellent resource as it has brief descriptions and images for each law and property (http://en.wikipedia.org/wiki/Gestalt_psychology). Here's a quick list of laws you can draw on when creating visual unity:

1. Proximity: Elements near one another are united.

2. Similarity: Elements like one another (in shape, color, or value, or so on) are united.

3. Closure: Elements missing minor visual details will be united into a functioning form in the mind of the viewer. (For example, even if you never see a cartoon character's toenail, you still assume the character has feet and toes.)

4. Symmetry: Elements balanced on or around a center point are united.

5. Common Fate: Elements moving in the same direction are united.

6. Continuity: Elements aligned on an implied guide are united.

7. Good Gestalt: Elements that are repetitive, simple, and orderly are united. This is sometimes referred to as the *Law of Prägnanz*.

8. Past Experience: Elements encountered in the past will affect how new, similar elements are perceived and united.

REFERENCE [3] Ellen Lupton, *Thinking with Type* (Princeton, NJ: Princeton Architectural Press, 2004). pg. 115.

Ellen Lupton reiterates the importance of negative space in *Thinking with Type*, writing, "Designers focus much of their energy on margins, edges, and empty spaces, elements that oscillate between present and absent, visible and invisible" [3]. As mentioned in Chapter 1, *The Dot, the Path, and the Pixel*, the Gestalt property of multistability indicates that the relationship between the visible and invisible is unpredictable. While developing the grid for exercises in this chapter, be attentive to margins, edges, and empty spaces.

SWISS INTERNATIONAL STYLE

REFERENCE [4] Ibid., pg. 8.

In *Thinking with Type*, Lupton writes, "Swiss designers in the 1940s and 1950s created design's first total methodology by rationalizing the grid. Their work, which introduced programmatic thinking to a field governed by taste and convention, remains profoundly relevant to the systematic thinking required when designing for multimedia" [4]. This emphasis on systematic logic directly correlates the motives of mid-20th century Swiss designers with those of today's digital artists. As this is a foundational text, it focuses on the language and tools common to typography with the grid-based Swiss International Style as a guide. The style that has become associated with Swiss designers emerged in Russia, Germany, and the Netherlands in the

1920s. It was made famous by works and texts that urged a novel approach to typography, such as Jan Tschichold's *The New Typography* (1928) and Josef Müller-Brockmann's *Grid Systems in Graphic Design* (1961). As Diogo Terror writes for *Smashing Magazine*, "Keen attention to detail, precision, craft skills, system of education and technical training, a high standard of printing as well as a clear refined and inventive lettering and typography laid out a foundation for a new movement that has been exported worldwide in [the] 1960s to become an international style" [5].

Lessons from the Swiss International Style include seemingly simple tenets that are much more difficult to execute on your first try than they are to memorize. (I've noticed many students who can memorize and produce this list on a quiz, but struggle to demonstrate the aesthetic principles in their homework.) What follows is a modified version of Tschichold's principles, outlined in *The New Typography*. A typographic layout should contain:

- Imbalanced asymmetry

- Active negative space

- Minimal use of illustrations or decorations

- Color for the purpose of navigation

- Extreme groupings of contrasting elements

In this chapter, the typographic layout will be simple. You'll work with just two guides that you'll understand as implied lines demonstrating the Gestalt Law of Continuity. Then, in Chapter 12, *Continuity,* you'll design a more complicated (or flexible) grid and revisit lessons associated with the Swiss International Style and the Gestalt laws.

SENTENCES AND PARAGRAPHS

When assembling type into sentences and paragraphs, there are a number of design issues to consider, including alignment, line length, and spacing. Each of these relate to legibility in as much as they relate to the overall composition. There are basic principles of legibility, of which most people are unaware. So if you show your work to others and it includes typography, you may have to educate your audience.

LINE LENGTH AND SACCADIC MOVEMENTS

English readers move their eyes from left to right across the page or screen, following the length of the line. This is a simple truth. New to you might be the saccadic movements that the eyes follow when reading or seeing in

REFERENCE [5] See www.smashingmagazine.com/2009/07/17/lessons-from-swiss-style-graphic-design.

LINK Explore the exhibition *The New Typography* (December 23, 2009–July 25, 2010) at the Museum of Modern Art at www.moma.org/visit/calendar/exhibitions/1015 and be sure to click the "View the exhibition checklist" link to see examples from this time period.

LINK Explore the Swiss Poster Collection in the Carnegie Mellon University Libraries at http://luna.library.cmu.edu/luna/servlet/CMUccm~3~3.

Lorem ipsum dolor sit amet, consectetur adipiscing elit. Phasellus blandit, dui ut vehicula lacinia, diam dolor accumsan dolor, id auctor nulla libero et risus. In ut eros ut nibh ultricies rhoncus. Proin iaculis venenatis justo sed eleifend. In hac habitasse platea dictumst. Ut ut nunc sed odio lacinia consequat. Morbi ipsum justo, suscipit non consectetur eu, varius in nisi. Mauris interdum bibendum congue. Pellentesque euismod, eros sed auctor porta, eros sem elementum ipsum, vel semper tellus purus in lorem. Duis ac nulla nec neque tristique tincidunt id quis leo. Cras bibendum mattis orci at rhoncus. Nulla magna mauris, ornare eget convallis eget, commodo vel urna. Vestibulum in facilisis lorem. Integer sollicitudin, eros non adipiscing posuere, orci velit dignissim dui, id tempus ligula risus non augue.

Nulla facilisi. Cras id nisl lectus, at pretium odio. Nulla ornare enim non velit ornare ultrices. Integer vel arcu eros. Morbi fermentum dictum augue et ultrices. Cum sociis natoque penatibus et magnis dis parturient montes, nascetur ridiculus mus. Maecenas id porta urna. Donec porta mi congue tortor pellentesque vel condimentum purus suscipit.

Lorem ipsum dolor sit amet, consectetur adipiscing elit. Phasellus blandit, dui ut vehicula lacinia, diam dolor accumsan dolor, id auctor nulla libero et risus. In ut eros ut nibh ultricies rhoncus. Proin iaculis venenatis justo sed eleifend. In hac habitasse platea dictumst. Ut ut nunc sed odio lacinia consequat. Morbi ipsum justo, suscipit non consectetur eu, varius in nisi. Mauris interdum bibendum congue. Pellentesque euismod, eros sed auctor porta, eros sem elementum ipsum, vel semper tellus purus in lorem. Duis ac nulla nec neque tristique tincidunt id quis leo. Cras bibendum mattis orci at rhoncus. Nulla magna mauris, ornare eget convallis eget, commodo vel urna. Vestibulum in facilisis lorem. Integer sollicitudin, eros non adipiscing posuere, orci velit dignissim dui, id tempus ligula risus non augue.

Nulla facilisi. Cras id nisl lectus, at pretium odio. Nulla ornare enim non velit ornare ultrices. Integer vel arcu eros. Morbi fermentum dictum augue et ultrices. Cum sociis natoque penatibus et magnis dis parturient montes, nascetur ridiculus mus. Maecenas id porta urna. Donec porta mi congue tortor pellentesque vel condimentum purus suscipit.

FIGURE 11.2 These two views of Lorem Ipsum text show the contrast between the easy reading of a suitable line length (right) and the difficulty in staying with a long line length (above).

LINK For more on saccadic movements, see "Computer Text Line Lengths Affect Reading and Learning" by Peter Orton, PhD, of the IBM Center for Advanced Learning at http://edlab.tc.columbia.edu/files/eye-tracking%20article.pdf.

general. The eyes don't focus in one location. Instead, they move back and forth rapidly. When reading, the eyes move "in little hops—called 'saccades'— and come to brief stops, about 250 milliseconds each—called 'fixations.'" (Follow the link provided to Peter Orton's article.) It's during this fixation time that the eyes see and read multiple words. Then the gaze regresses into a backward movement before hopping forward again. At the end of the line, the eyes sweep back to the beginning of the next line of type and proceed again.

Once you know how the eye moves during reading, you can design typography for the best possible reading conditions (**FIGURE 11.2**). Most readers will be able to read a line length of nearly five inches before having to cycle through a regressive phase. In *The Elements of Typographic Style*, Robert Bringhurst suggests that the line length for body copy be limited to 45–75 characters or three to five inches. This is a wide range that's meant to allow for multiple columns on a page (where you would use a shorter length). In *Typographie*, Emil Ruder suggests an optimal length of 50 to 60 characters (including spaces). Others offer an equation of 1.5 to 2.5 times the size of a lowercase alphabet set in whichever typeface and size you're using.

ALIGNMENT: LEFT, RIGHT, CENTERED, JUSTIFIED

Alignment is not just the button you press to align a paragraph to the left, center, right, or in a justified block (**FIGURE 11.3**). Alignment can also be used within a typographic design to signify hierarchy. Indentations or negative spaces can be combined with an invisible line of continuation to help readers make associations between blocks of text through their alignment. You'll see how to arrange for this in the following exercises.

FIGURE 11.3 In this seven-column layout of a 1902 edition of the *Washington Times*, several varieties of alignment are used to create contrast and hierarchy in a unified grid.

SPACING: KERNING AND LEADING

Contrast and rhythm are essential design principles that affect how the viewer understands a typographic layout. Rhythm is understood through regular repetitions and interruptions. Contrast is understood through differences once similarities have been established. The rhythm of text can be controlled by two types of spacing:

- The space between letters: *kerning* between individual letters or *tracking (letter spacing)* across whole sentences, paragraphs, or documents

- The space between lines of type: *leading* (line spacing)

You'll learn more about how to adjust these basic typographic elements throughout the exercises in this section (**FIGURES 11.4 AND 11.5**). Squint your eyes and view all three paragraphs in Figures 11.4 and 11.5. The gray value that you see in your squinted view of the text block is created by the combination of text and whiteness on the page. The top paragraph reads as a dark gray, the middle paragraph translates to a medium gray, and the bottom paragraph is light gray. The text is easiest to read when the gray is close to a medium or medium-dark value.

Lorem ipsum dolor sit amet, consectetur adipiscing elit. Phasellus blandit, dui ut vehicula lacinia, diam dolor accumsan dolor, id auctor nulla libero et risus. In ut eros ut nibh ultricies rhoncus.

Lorem ipsum dolor sit amet, consectetur adipiscing elit. Phasellus blandit, dui ut vehicula lacinia, diam dolor accumsan dolor, id auctor nulla libero et risus. In ut eros ut nibh ultricies rhoncus.

Lorem ipsum dolor sit amet, consectetur adipiscing elit. Phasellus blandit, dui ut vehicula lacinia, diam dolor accumsan dolor, id auctor nulla libero et risus. In ut eros ut nibh ultricies rhoncus.

Lorem ipsum dolor sit amet, consectetur adipiscing elit. Phasellus blandit, dui ut vehicula lacinia, diam dolor accumsan dolor, id auctor nulla libero et risus. In ut eros ut nibh ultricies rhoncus.

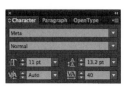

Lorem ipsum dolor sit amet, consectetur adipiscing elit. Phasellus blandit, dui ut vehicula lacinia, diam dolor accumsan dolor, id auctor nulla libero et risus. In ut eros ut nibh ultricies rhoncus.

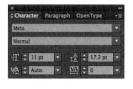

Lorem ipsum dolor sit amet, consectetur adipiscing elit. Phasellus blandit, dui ut vehicula lacinia, diam dolor accumsan dolor, id auctor nulla libero et risus. In ut eros ut nibh ultricies rhoncus.

FIGURE 11.4 The tracking in the top paragraph is tight—notice the setting of -40 in the Character panel. The middle paragraph is unadjusted. The bottom paragraph tracking is set to +40 in the Character panel. The type is set loosely, with too much space between the letters.

FIGURE 11.5 The leading in the top paragraph is tight—notice the setting of 11.2 in the Character panel. Also notice that the type size is 11 points. This combination of point size and leading is articulated as 11/11.2. The middle paragraph is unaltered at 11/13.2. The bottom paragraph is light because of the increased leading of 11/17.2.

WIDOWS AND ORPHANS

Typographically speaking, widows and orphans break the rhythm of a block of text (FIGURE 11.6). The *Chicago Manual of Style* defines an orphan as a dangling word or sentence fragment that appears at the end of a paragraph or column. A widow is a dangling word or sentence fragment (the last sentence or word in a paragraph) that appears at the start of a new column. There's no universal agreement about these definitions (and which is which), but both are to be avoided. If you notice dangling text, adjust the leading, type box (or line length), margins, or letter spacing (for the whole block), or force a paragraph break.

Lorem ipsum dolor sit amet, consectetur adipiscing elit. Morbi est est, posuere sit amet congue sit amet, eleifend sit amet nunc. Cum sociis natoque penatibus et magnis dis parturient montes, nascetur ridiculus mus. Fusce dolor justo, vulputate eu fermentum nec, bibendum ut mauris. Sed feugiat lobortis mauris, ut porttitor tortor egestas a. Vestibulum ante ipsum primis in faucibus orci luctus et ultrices posuere cubilia Curae: Donec ac justo sit amet enim egestas tristique vitae sollicitudin elit. Mauris sit amet sem at lacus lacinia sollicitudin. Sed sit amet fringilla arcu. Lorem ipsum dolor sit amet, consectetur adipiscing elit. Etiam eu orci sit amet dolor pellentesque dictum vel sit amet lorem. In hac habitasse platea dictumst. Nam dolor massa, pretium nec vehicula at, sodales non erat. Mauris magna arcu, ultrices at pharetra et, rhoncus vel nisi. Praesent ultricies sodales sem vel mollis. Curabitur turpis sapien, pretium at luctus sit amet, fermentum et

lorem.

Vestibulum ut sollicitudin dui. Donec porta est odio. Aliquam neque libero, adipiscing eget eleifend vitae, sagittis id libero. Suspendisse potenti. Mauris tristique dapibus nibh ac pretium. Curabitur vestibulum vestibulum massa, imperdiet pulvinar quam scelerisque in. Maecenas ac magna lacus, vitae molestie quam. Aliquam erat volutpat. Quisque sodales dictum erat ac mattis. Vivamus a ante egestas leo laoreet ornare eu nec turpis. Nam hendrerit magna quis lectus pharetra sit amet sollicitudin nulla porta. In dolor tortor, pellentesque a rhoncus vitae, ultrices vel enim. Phasellus tempor posuere laoreet. Aenean ultricies elit vel quam bibendum ut sodales felis placerat. Vestibulum ante ipsum primis in faucibus orci luctus et ultrices posuere cubilia Curae.

Lorem ipsum dolor sit amet, consectetur adipiscing elit. Morbi est est, posuere sit amet congue sit amet, eleifend sit amet nunc. Cum sociis natoque penatibus et magnis dis parturient montes, nascetur ridiculus mus. Fusce dolor justo, vulputate eu fermentum nec, bibendum ut mauris. Sed feugiat lobortis mauris, ut porttitor tortor egestas a. Vestibulum ante ipsum primis in faucibus orci luctus et ultrices posuere cubilia Curae; Donec ac justo sit amet enim egestas tristique vitae sollicitudin elit. Mauris sit amet sem at lacus lacinia sollicitudin. Sed sit amet fringilla arcu. Lorem ipsum dolor sit amet, consectetur adipiscing elit. Etiam eu orci sit amet dolor pellentesque dictum vel sit amet lorem. In hac habitasse platea dictumst. Nam dolor massa, pretium nec vehicula at, sodales non erat. Mauris magna arcu, ultrices at pharetra et, rhoncus vel nisi. Praesent ultricies sodales sem vel mollis. Curabitur turpis sapien, pretium at luctus sit amet, fermentum et lorem.

Vestibulum ut sollicitudin dui. Donec porta est odio. Aliquam neque libero, adipiscing eget eleifend vitae, sagittis id libero. Suspendisse potenti. Mauris tristique dapibus nibh ac pretium. Curabitur vestibulum vestibulum massa, imperdiet pulvinar quam scelerisque in. Maecenas ac magna lacus, vitae molestie quam. Aliquam erat volutpat. Quisque sodales dictum erat ac mattis. Vivamus a ante egestas leo laoreet ornare eu nec turpis. Nam hendrerit magna quis lectus pharetra sit amet sollicitudin nulla porta. In dolor tortor, pellentesque a rhoncus vitae, ultrices vel enim. Phasellus tempor posuere laoreet. Aenean ultricies elit vel quam bibendum ut sodales felis placerat. Vestibulum ante ipsum primis in faucibus orci luctus et ultrices posuere cubilia Curae.

FIGURE 11.6 The word *lorem* is both a widow and an orphan in this example: it dangles at the top of the first paragraph in the right column (left) and at the bottom of the last paragraph in the left column (right).

WHAT YOU'LL NEED

It's not necessary to download files to complete the exercises in this chapter.

✔ I used the Helvetica type family, which is installed on most computers, so you should be able to follow my steps without installing new fonts on your system. If you don't have Helvetica, use another sans serif type family.

You'll benefit from seeing how the grid aids alignment in a typographic layout design. The law of continuity will be evident even when the guides are invisible.

WHAT YOU'LL MAKE

In the exercises in this chapter, you'll create a PDF document with trim marks for a typographic design to be printed on tabloid (11 by 17 inch) paper (**FIGURE 11.7**).

FIGURE 11.7 The resulting file created in this chapter's exercises.

ALTERNATIVE PAPER SIZES

Begin by creating a new file in Illustrator. In many situations, the paper size you'll be printing on is not the same as the size of the document you're designing. Create a 10- by 16-inch document in preparation for printing on tabloid paper with trim marks in place. To do this, set the document at the alternative size. You'll select the paper size later during the printing process. Trim marks (which you'll add in Exercise 7) will help you cut the paper to the specified working size.

1. Open Illustrator and choose File > New or press **Command(⌘)-N.** Choose Print from the Profile menu and Inches from the Units menu. Enter a Width value of 10 inches and a Height value of 16 inches.

2. It's not time to print yet, but if you would print this document it would likely be on a standard paper size of 10 by 16 inches or larger. Since 10 by 16 inches is not a standard U.S. paper size, you would print this document on tabloid-size (11 by 17 inches) paper. Check your printer to see if this is possible. If it isn't, you may need to visit a consumer-level printing house, such as FedEx Office or AlphaGraphics, or a lab or service through a school or university.

GUIDES AND THE GRID

While you may sometimes know exactly where to place guides, most of the time you'll set guides intuitively, based on relationships among other design elements on the page. I'll demonstrate my intuitive working process for establishing guides on the page in this exercise. Then you'll sort out the relationship between the measurements of the black rectangle and the page.

REMINDER When you're creating just one line of type, like a headline, click once with the Type tool and enter the text. Reserve clicking and dragging with the Type tool to create a text box for longer lines of copy. See Chapter 10, Exercise 4, Step 3 for a demonstration of kerning.

1. In this exercise, you'll create hierarchy on the page by contrast through scale and an active use of negative space. The largest element on the page is the negative space, but the largest *foreground* element is the black rectangle overlaid with the white words *Lorem Ipsum*. View the final image file for a visual reference and then use your eye to judge approximately where these two items should be placed on the page you created in Exercise 1. You'll fix their placement in a moment, but try this step intuitively. The black rectangle should have no stroke value, and the white text should be set in 60-point Helvetica Black (Regular). Don't forget to adjust the kerning on such a large block of type (**FIGURE 11.8**).

FIGURE 11.8 A single line of white text set on a black rectangle.

FIGURE 11.9 Use the Control panel to adjust the Height value of the rectangle.

FIGURE 11.10 Guides set at the intersection of the bottom-right corner of the rectangle.

2. Select the black rectangle and view its Height value in the Control panel (**FIGURE 11.9**). Mine was close enough to one inch that I modified the value by entering "1 in" into the Height box so my rectangle is an even one-inch tall.

3. Turn the rulers on if they're not already showing (press ⌘-**R**) and then drag a vertical guide from the left ruler to the edge of the black rectangle— don't release the mouse. When I did this, I could see that my rectangle landed just a tad past two inches on the horizontal ruler. Place the guide at two inches to make the numeric relationships between elements conform to simple numbers or fractions. Do the same with a horizontal guide at the bottom of the black rectangle. Mine landed at 13.5 inches. I find that working in whole numbers or easy fractions (eighths, fourths, thirds, or halves) makes transforming and scaling elements a bit easier when I want them to relate to one another and the page geometrically. Finally, group the type and rectangle (select both; then press ⌘-**G**) and move the block so it aligns with the new guides (**FIGURE 11.10**).

CREATE YOUR OWN "VIRTUAL LEADING" PLACEHOLDERS

This simple, first element on the page will relate to every other item in the composition. To make this point clear, you'll create a series of rectangles in cyan (heights) and magenta (widths) to show how the final elements on the page will stack up. This may seem abstract right now, but you'll see in Exercise 5 how you can use these shapes as placeholders for chunks of negative space in your composition. This is a digital analogy to the concept of "leading" in analog typesetting—blocks of lead were literally inserted into the layout to preserve negative space.

1. Zoom in and create a rectangle that's exactly the height from the bottom of the page to the bottom edge of the black rectangle. (*Hint:* you already know this will be 2.5 inches based on where you placed the guides in Exercise 2, Step 3; however, a guide can easily be just a hair off so this way you'll have an accurate visual aide.) The width of the new rectangle is insignificant. After you've drawn it, set the Stroke value to none and fill the rectangle with 100% cyan and 0% each of magenta, yellow, and black (**FIGURE 11.11**).

2. Move the cyan rectangle off the artboard and align its top with the guide at 13.5 inches to remind yourself that this is a height spaceholder. Double-click the Scale tool in the Tools panel and select the Non-Uniform Scale radio button. Enter 100% for the Width value and 50% for the Height value; then press the Copy button to make a copy that's half as tall as the original (**FIGURE 11.12**).

FIGURE 11.11 A cyan rectangle is used to measure vertical space.

FIGURE 11.12 Create a copy of the cyan rectangle at a reduced size all at once in the Scale dialog.

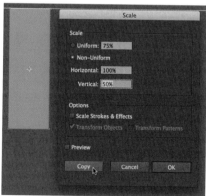

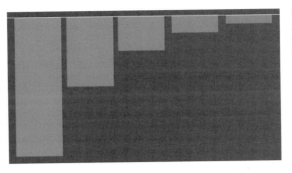

FIGURES 11.13 AND 11.14
Scaled copies of the cyan rectangles are positioned using the guide.

3. The copy will be placed atop the original. Use the Selection tool to move it to the left or right of the original and align it to the top guide (**FIGURE 11.13**). Select the second rectangle and repeat the scaling in Step 2 three more times (**FIGURE 11.14**), resulting in five boxes that are incrementally halved in height. (See the *Get Efficient with Key Commands* sidebar for a fast way to accomplish the three copies.) You'll make use of these shapes to measure height values in the negative space within the composition after you've added more elements to the positive space in the next exercises.

4. Repeat Steps 1, 2, and 3 to create magenta rectangles in a variety of related widths. Start with a magenta rectangle exactly the width from the left margin to the vertical guide (aligned with the black rectangle at approximately two inches on the page). Then create five additional rectangles at half of the previous widths (**FIGURE 11.15**).

GET EFFICIENT WITH KEY COMMANDS

You can complete the three additional copies using the key commands in Step 3 by staying with the Scale tool, rather than alternating between the Scale and Selection tools. Once you've made the copy, press the Command key to access the Selection tool and keep the Command key pressed as you move the rectangle into position. Release the key, and you're back to the Scale tool. Press the Enter key to enter the Scale dialog (without double-clicking the tool). Press the Copy button as the settings are already established from your prior use of the tool. Press and hold the Command key to move the next rectangle, release the key, press Enter, press the Copy button, and repeat.

FIGURE 11.15 Magenta rectangles demonstrate a variety of proportional widths.

EXERCISE 4 — LINKING TEXT BOXES

You created and modified text in a text box in Chapter 10, Exercise 3. However, in this chapter, there are two text boxes that will contain the same article. You'll use Lorem Ipsum dummy text to fill the boxes with nonrepetitive place-holder type. Of course, you'll also adjust the leading and set some of the type using a font variation. Kerning will not be an issue in this situation because the body copy is traditionally of a small enough size that the typeface remains well kerned.

1. To fill a text box with dummy text in Illustrator, you'll need some place-holder type. Don't use a repetitive copy and paste of a few words (such as "dummy text goes here"), as the repetition in the phrase will dominate the visual impression. Instead, copy and paste placeholder text from a website (such as lipsum.com or blindtextgenerator.com, or perhaps a news story from your favorite news site). For this exercise, I copied eight paragraphs of the classic Lorem Ipsum text from lipsum.com—more than enough to fill two text boxes (**FIGURES 11.16 AND 11.17**).

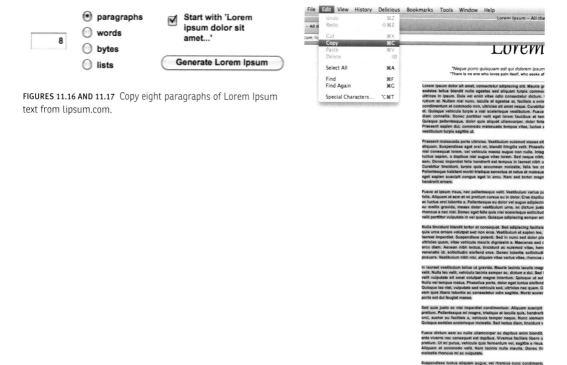

FIGURES 11.16 AND 11.17 Copy eight paragraphs of Lorem Ipsum text from lipsum.com.

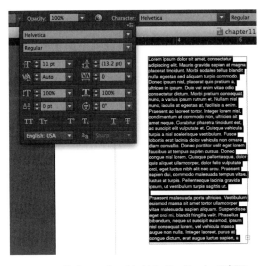

FIGURE 11.18 Lorem Ipsum type is pasted into a new text box.

FIGURE 11.19 Body copy is set to Helvetica Regular 11/13.2.

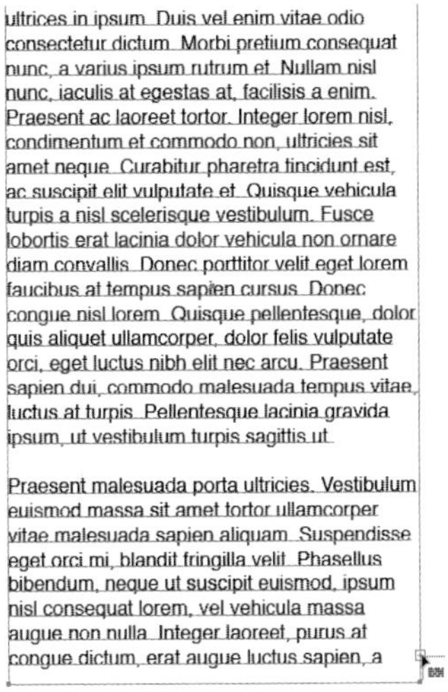

FIGURE 11.20 Overflow text is indicated by the red plus sign in the lower-left corner of the text box.

2. In Illustrator, create a new text box by clicking and dragging anywhere on the artboard with the Type tool. You'll correct the positioning of the box later. Once you've made the text box, press ⌘-V to paste the placeholder Lorem Ipsum text you just copied from the website (**FIGURE 11.18**).

3. The type settings from the last time you used the tool are active, so this body copy has been pasted in gigantic, bold type. While the Type tool is still active in the box (you should see a blinking cursor), press ⌘-A to select all of the text. Change the type settings to create a more reasonable reading experience. I used Helvetica Regular set at 11 points (**FIGURE 11.19**). I didn't alter the kerning or leading (so technically my type setting is 11/13.2 points, that is, the type size is 11 points, and the leading is automatically set at 13.2 points).

4. In the lower-right corner of the text box, you should notice a small red plus sign (+) with a square outline around it. This indicates that there is *overflow text*. In other words, there's more text pasted into the box than the text box is showing on the page, due to the limited size of the text box. You can change the dimensions of the text box to show all the text in it, delete the overflow text, or create another text box that the overflow text can flow into. You'll link this second text box to the first. Any time you make a typographic modification in the first text box that results in more or less space for characters in the box, the linked text box will also be affected. To link the overflow text to a new text box, start by zooming in and clicking with the Selection tool directly on the red plus sign (**FIGURE 11.20**).

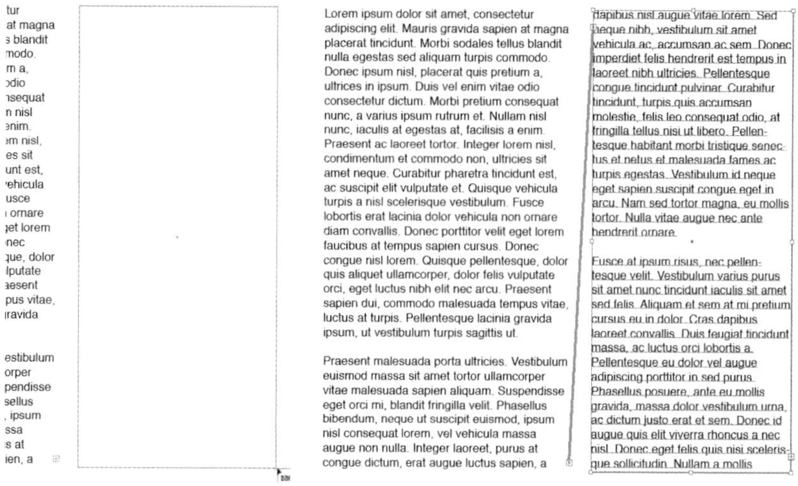

FIGURES 11.21 AND 11.22

The loaded text cursor is used to place text in a new box. The blue line between the two boxes indicates that they're linked.

5. The cursor changes from a type cursor to a *loaded text* cursor. This indicates that you've selected overflow text from one text box and now Illustrator is waiting for you to tell it what to do with the overflow text. Click and drag the loaded text cursor to create a new text box to the right of the first one (**FIGURE 11.21**). The two text boxes are now linked, and the text from the first box flows into the second text box (**FIGURE 11.22**).

6. I'll assume that in my final layout I'll have a short first paragraph that I can set in slightly larger type to create contrast between the two columns. Press the Return (or Enter) key after the sixth (or so) sentence to create a paragraph break. Then select the first six sentences with the Type tool cursor and change the size to 14 points. With the Selection tool, click and drag the bottom anchor of the text box to modify its height so only the larger text appears in the first text box (**FIGURE 11.23**). You'll see that the overflow text runs into the second linked text box.

7. I had a straggling word at the end of my paragraph, so I modified the shape of the text box by dragging the bottom-left anchor point inward with the Selection tool (**FIGURE 11.24**). The left text box will be slightly skinnier, again to create contrast between the two text boxes. Some may see this as a radical concept. In many publications, text boxes are always the same width to create repetition and unity on the page. Dare to explore contrast and hierarchy in this exercise by ignoring the typical layout paradigm of even, repetitive spacing.

8. Select just the first two words, *Lorem Ipsum*, and then click the Character link in the Control panel and select Small Caps from the top-right pulldown menu (**FIGURE 11.25**). The first two words will contrast with the rest of

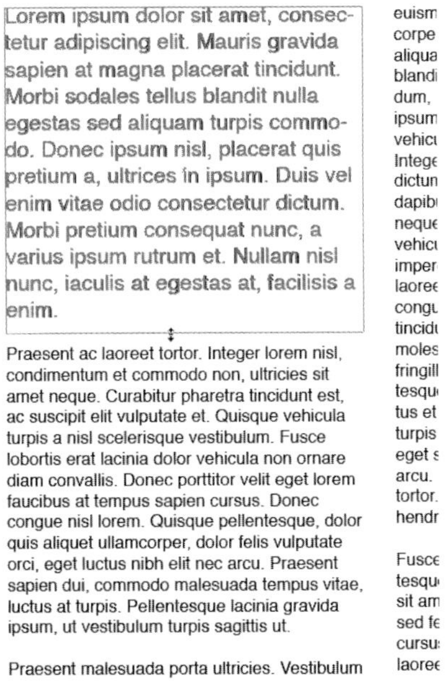

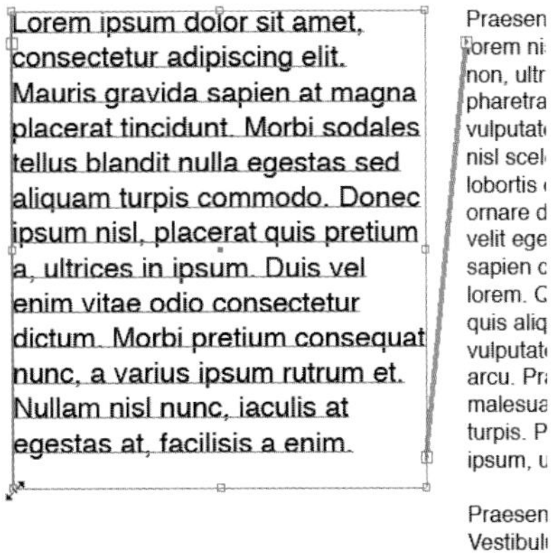

Lorem ipsum dolor sit amet, consectetur adipiscing elit. Mauris gravida sapien at magna placerat tincidunt. Morbi sodales tellus blandit nulla egestas sed aliquam turpis commodo. Donec ipsum nisl, placerat quis pretium a, ultrices in ipsum. Duis vel enim vitae odio consectetur dictum. Morbi pretium consequat nunc, a varius ipsum rutrum et. Nullam nisl nunc, iaculis at egestas at, facilisis a enim.

Praesent ac laoreet tortor. Integer lorem nisl, condimentum et commodo non, ultricies sit amet neque. Curabitur pharetra tincidunt est, ac suscipit elit vulputate et. Quisque vehicula turpis a nisl scelerisque vestibulum. Fusce lobortis erat lacinia dolor vehicula non ornare diam convallis. Donec porttitor velit eget lorem faucibus at tempus sapien cursus. Donec congue nisl lorem. Quisque pellentesque, dolor quis aliquet ullamcorper, dolor felis vulputate orci, eget luctus nibh elit nec arcu. Praesent sapien dui, commodo malesuada tempus vitae, luctus at turpis. Pellentesque lacinia gravida ipsum, ut vestibulum turpis sagittis ut.

Praesent malesuada porta ultricies. Vestibulum

euism
corpe
aliqua
blandi
dum,
ipsum
vehicu
Intege
dictun
dapib
neque
vehicu
imper
laoree
congu
tincid
moles
fringill
tesqu
tus et
turpis
eget s
arcu.
tortor.
hendr

Fusce
tesqu
sit am
sed fe
cursu
laoree

Lorem ipsum dolor sit amet, consectetur adipiscing elit. Mauris gravida sapien at magna placerat tincidunt. Morbi sodales tellus blandit nulla egestas sed aliquam turpis commodo. Donec ipsum nisl, placerat quis pretium a, ultrices in ipsum. Duis vel enim vitae odio consectetur dictum. Morbi pretium consequat nunc, a varius ipsum rutrum et. Nullam nisl nunc, iaculis at egestas at, facilisis a enim.

Praesen
orem ni
non, ultr
pharetra
vulputat
nisl scel
lobortis
ornare d
velit ege
sapien c
lorem. C
quis aliq
vulputat
arcu. Pr
malesua
turpis. P
ipsum, u

Praesen
Vestibul

FIGURE 11.23 Resizing a textbox creates more room for type to flow—it doesn't resize the type inside the box.

FIGURE 11.24 Reshape the text box in the left column.

LOREM IPSUM dolor sit amet, consectetur adipiscing elit. Mauris gravida sapien at magna

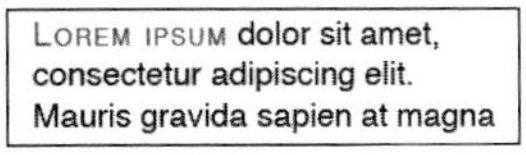

FIGURE 11.26 Small caps are set in dark red at the beginning of the first paragraph.

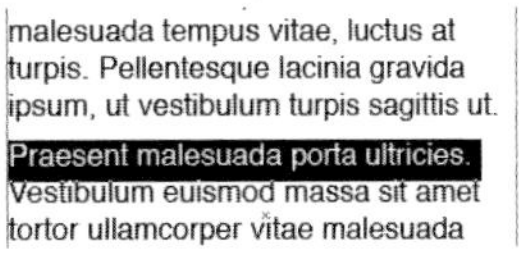

LOREM IP
sectetur
gravida
at tincidu
blandit n

malesuada tempus vitae, luctus at turpis. Pellentesque lacinia gravida ipsum, ut vestibulum turpis sagittis ut. Praesent malesuada porta ultricies. Vestibulum euismod massa sit amet tortor ullamcorper vitae malesuada

FIGURE 11.27 Adjust the leading by selecting a line of type and pressing **Option-↑** or **Option-↓**.

FIGURE 11.25 Small Caps are accessed from the pull-down menu in the Character panel.

the body copy by this elegant variation. Also change the color of the text using the Color panel to 0% cyan, 100% magenta, 100% yellow, and 50% black (**FIGURE 11.26**).

9. Alter the leading at the paragraph break in the second linked text box so the space between the two paragraphs is less noticeable. The space should be evident, but it shouldn't catch your eye as one of the more important spaces in the layout. Select only the first sentence in the second paragraph and then press **Option-↑** to tighten (or decrease) the leading. I pressed the **Option-↑** command three times (**FIGURE 11.27**).

10. You're not quite finished with these two text boxes: you still need to consider the relationship between them and the rest of the page. You'll begin to work on this in the next exercise.

EXERCISE 5 · PLACING ANOTHER GUIDE ON THE GRID

The second text box, the large copy, *Lorem Ipsum is my favorite text* and the website addresses are aligned on the page along a single guide. In fact, the italic text *Lorem Ipsum dummy text is not repetitive* is also aligned on this guide. (It's right aligned rather than left aligned.) This second guide is a major contributor to the information flow on the page. It establishes a line of continuation (referring to the *Gestalt Law of Continuation*) or an implied line within the compositional layout. By aligning these four items on the same guide, you're helping the reader to group those elements together. You'll also ensure that the word *Ipsum* in white on the black rectangle you created in Exercise 2, Step 1 is aligned with this guide. Since the guide is so essential to the layout, you'll want to ensure that its placement is logical within the system of your page. You'll use the measuring boxes created in Exercise 3 to accomplish this task.

1. Zoom in and drag a guide to the letter *I* in the word *Ipsum* on the black rectangle.

KEY COMMAND You can unlock locked guides by pressing ⌘-Option-; (semicolon).

2. Use the magenta measuring blocks to see if the width between the edge of the page and the start of the letter *I* just happen to be related. Place a copy of the largest block at the left margin; then duplicate it until its duplicate extends beyond the guide. Remove the overextended duplicate. Use the next smaller box and repeat until you reach the guide (**FIGURE 11.28**). The final measuring box will probably surpass or not quite meet the guide by a hair (**FIGURE 11.29**). You'll correct for that in the next step.

3. Move the guide so that it aligns with the edge of the magenta measuring box (**FIGURE 11.30**).

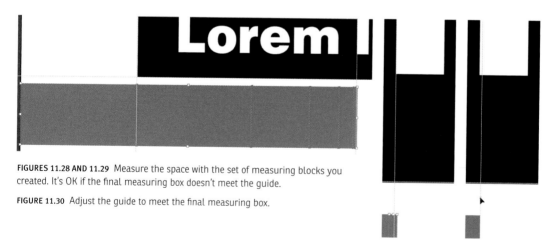

FIGURES 11.28 AND 11.29 Measure the space with the set of measuring blocks you created. It's OK if the final measuring box doesn't meet the guide.

FIGURE 11.30 Adjust the guide to meet the final measuring box.

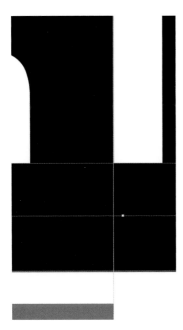

LOREM IPSUM dolor sit amet, consectetur adipiscing elit. Mauris gravida sapien at magna placerat tincidunt. Morbi sodales tellus blandit nulla egestas sed aliquam turpis commodo. Donec ipsum nisl, placerat quis pretium a, ultrices in ipsum. Duis vel enim vitae odio consectetur dictum. Morbi pretium consequat nunc, a varius ipsum rutrum et. Nullam nisl nunc, iaculis at egestas at, facilisis a enim.

Praesent ac laoreet tortor. Integer lorem nisl, condimentum et commodo non, ultricies sit amet neque. Curabitur pharetra tincidunt est, ac suscipit elit vulputate et. Quisque vehicula turpis a nisl scelerisque vestibulum. Fusce lobortis erat lacinia dolor vehicula non ornare diam convallis. Donec porttitor velit eget lorem faucibus at tempus sapien cursus. Donec congue nisl lorem. Quisque pellentesque, dolor quis aliquet ullamcorper, dolor felis vulputate orci, eget luctus nibh elit nec arcu. Praesent sapien dui, commodo malesuada tempus vitae, luctus at turpis. Pellentesque lacinia gravida ipsum, ut vestibulum turpis sagittis ut.

Praesent malesuada porta ultricies. Vestibulum euismod massa sit amet tortor ullamcorper vitae malesuada sapien aliquam. Suspendisse eget orci mi, blandit fringilla velit. Phasellus bibendum, neque ut suscipit euismod, ipsum nisl consequat lorem, vel vehicula massa augue non nulla. Integer laoreet, purus at congue dictum, erat augue luctus sapien, a dapibus nisl augue vitae lorem. Sed neque nibh, vestibulum sit amet vehicula ac, accumsan ac sem. Donec imperdiet felis hendrerit est tempus in

FIGURE 11.31 Kern or nudge the letter *l* to meet the guide.

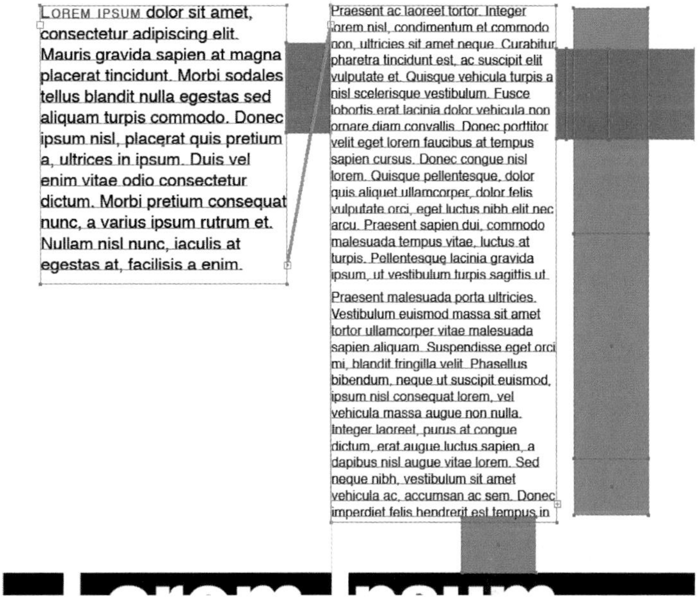

FIGURE 11.32 Adjust the linked text box for the guides using the magenta boxes to measure widths and cyan boxes to measure heights.

4. Adjust the kerning before the letter *I* to see if you can nudge the letter into alignment. If it's still slightly off, use the Selection tool to drag the type so the letter meets the guide (**FIGURE 11.31**).

5. Delete the magenta measuring blocks. (You should still have your original copy to the left or right of the artboard.)

6. Position the linked text boxes so that the second is aligned on the new guide. Pay attention to the space between the two boxes and the vertical distance between the text at the end of the second box and the black rectangle (**FIGURE 11.32**).

SCREENCAST 11-1 USING THE GRID

Exercise 6 is explained only briefly: you'll complete it mostly on your own. However, I've captured my process in this chapter's screencast to demonstrate how to use measuring boxes to see the relationships between elements on the grid.

All screencasts are available on the companion website, www.digitalart-design.com, or on the YouTube playlist, www.youtube.com/playlist?list=PLAy6P5IoEjy2v3kZKCt8spqJ50nLb2XQI.

USE THE GRID

To finalize the layout, you simply need to add three new text boxes. These are not linked, but they're aligned on a line of continuation. Font variations will assign contrast and hierarchy in the layout.

1. Create a text box for each of the three remaining elements. My settings are as follows: *Lorem Ipsum dummy text is not repetitive* is set in Helvetica Light Oblique 10/12. The copy is set to right alignment. (Select the text and press the Align Right button in the Control panel.) *Lorem Ipsum is my favorite text* is set in Helvetica Black Regular 60/60 with optically adjusted kerning. The two web addresses (http://www.blindtextgenerator.com/lorem-ipsum or lipsum.com) are set in Helvetica Light 10/12.

2. Aligning the boxes horizontally is a breeze: just use the guide you created in Exercise 5. Set the text box on the top so its right edge meets the guide, while the others meet the guide at their left edges.

3. Aligning the boxes vertically requires some thought. Use the cyan measuring boxes to create contrast while retaining a geometric relationship in the space. I left all of my measuring boxes (my "virtual leading") on a new layer named **positioning** so you can see my process (**FIGURE 11.33**).

FIGURE 11.33 A view of the resulting file after all items are placed on the grid. Negative spaces mathematically relate to one another as a result of using a set of "measuring tools." You can see my measuring tools (the magenta and cyan rectangles) throughout the document.

SAVE A PDF WITH TRIM MARKS

Since the size of the poster is 10 by 16 inches and the paper it will be printed on is tabloid size (11 by 17 inches), you'll have to cut the poster from the larger sheet of paper after it's printed. You could measure and mark the page with a pencil, but why add an extra step (and risk human error) when the Save Adobe PDF dialog will print trim marks for you?

1. Choose File > Save As to save the file in native (.ai) format as **chapter11.ai.**

2. Choose File > Save As, again, but this time select Adobe PDF as the file format.

3. In the Save Adobe PDF dialog, click on Marks and Bleeds from the left menu listing. Then check the box to apply Trim Marks in the Marks and Bleeds area of the dialog (**FIGURE 11.34**). Press the Save PDF button.

4. Open the PDF file in Preview, Adobe Acrobat, or another preview application. Notice the thin black crosshairs at the corners of the document (**FIGURE 11.35**). These trim marks will print on the page. Use them to align your ruler when trimming the page to its nonstandard size (10 by 16 inches).

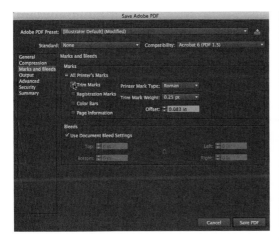

FIGURE 11.34 Turn Trim Marks on in the Save Adobe PDF dialog.

FIGURE 11.35 The final PDF includes trim marks to help you know where to trim the page after you've printed it.

LAB CHALLENGE

Redesign an event poster that you see in your neighborhood using a grid system. Search telephone or lighting poles, coffee shops, laundromat bulletin boards, and other public areas for amateur event posters. You'll notice before and after your redesign how much more organized and easier to read the content is when it's aligned on a systematic grid.

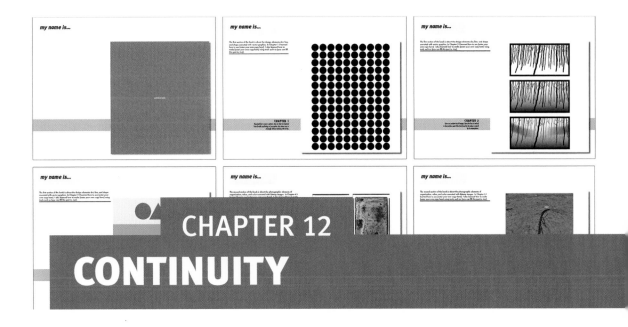

CHAPTER 12

CONTINUITY

THE EXERCISES IN this chapter provide technical and aesthetic lessons in using the Gestalt Laws of Similarity and Continuity to create stylistic consistency when sequencing layouts in a multipage document. Open the *New York Times* to any article in any section, and you'll always know that you're reading the *New York Times*. In the sixth edition of his *Visual Communication: Images with Messages,* Paul Martin Lester defines stylistic consistency as "a design concept in which multiple pages or frames of a piece appear to be unified" [1]. You'll create a multipage layout in Adobe InDesign in which you'll place 10 of your favorite exercise files from the previous chapters. This is essentially a practice activity for those who will ultimately design a multipage PDF portfolio using InDesign.

THE GESTALT LAWS OF SIMILARITY AND CONTINUITY

REFERENCE [1] Paul Martin Lester, *Visual Communication: Images with Messages*, 6th ed. (Boston: Cengage, 2013). pg. 195.

LINK See a Gestalt playlist I created on YouTube (apologies if some movies were removed by the time this book is published) at www. youtube.com/playlist?list=P L4809B9725FE6267B.

You learned about Gestalt laws in the sidebar in Chapter 11, *The Grid*. Study these laws carefully: understanding them will help you become deft at creating unity, balance, rhythm, and contrast in your designs. These essential, strategic design elements provide a way of developing a focal point or directing the viewer's eye toward or away from selected content. In the exercises in this chapter, you'll refer to the laws of similarity and continuity as you develop a multipage layout that can be viewed as one coherent work. (If this sounds familiar, it should—remember that the primary idea of Gestalt is that the whole is greater than the sum of its parts.)

To retain consistency in a multipage layout, commit to a small selection of typefaces, colors, and geometric relationships between the positive and negative spaces. Although every page should feel related, every page doesn't need to look the same. The Gestalt Law of Similarity holds that visual items with similar attributes (shape, color, value, texture, size, and so on) should be grouped together or considered to be part of a larger system. Logically, it follows that choosing a set of shapes, colors, values, textures, and sizes to use repeatedly within a designed system would encourage the viewer to recognize the whole as a work that's greater than the sum of its many parts (or in this case, pages). Nicholas Felton's *Feltron 2006 Annual Report* and *Feltron 2007 Annual Report* utilize different dominant fonts and colors, but the layouts are unified in their use of large typography and an overlay of graphic elements to suggest a timeline and various life activities (**FIGURE 12.1**). In the 2007 report, a four-column grid is used throughout the document (**FIGURE 12.2**). Sometimes a chart or graph spans all four columns (**FIGURE 12.3**). Given the consistency of the color palette, grid layout, and typeface choices, the viewer never forgets that she's reading a coherent document.

REFERENCE [2] See Richard Brautigan's work online to view the book as the pages are being flipped—and watch for continuity at www.farhadfozouni.com/ misc.php?t=22&id=92. While you're on Farhad Fozouni's website, also check out the video demonstrating the book *Lion under the Rainbow* for its clever representation of the text in multiple languages.

The Gestalt Law of Continuity accounts for the way that the viewer perceives elements aligned on a grid as part of a group. When a viewer notices an implied line, she'll read all the content on the line with the subtle understanding that those items belong together. In the exercises in Chapter 11, you created two implied lines (using guides) to establish the grid for the Lorem Ipsum poster. The Law of Continuity helps us see that the blocks of type are unified, even when their sizes, colors, and font variations change. In Richard Brautigan's *Please Plant This Book*, you'll notice implied and drawn lines that extend beyond the single page [2].

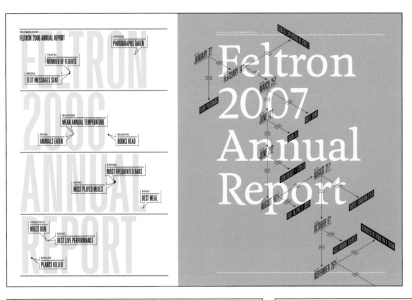

FIGURE 12.1 Nicholas Felton, *Feltron 2006 Annual Report.*

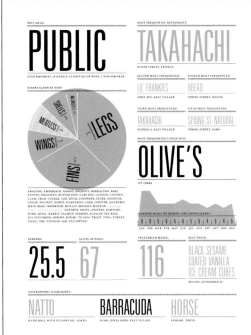

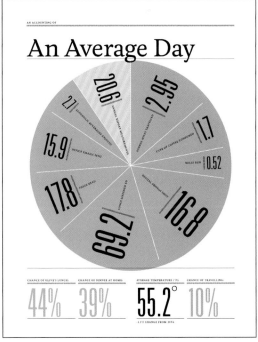

FIGURE 12.2 AND FIGURE 12.3 Nicholas Felton, *Feltron 2007 Annual Report.* This is the third iteration in Felton's continuing exploration of how to graphically encapsulate a year.

In Jody Zellen's *Trigger*, the type sits on the same baseline despite the juxtaposition of the video throughout the urban space (**FIGURE 12.4**). The contrast between the surfaces of the spaces where the video is projected and the consistency of the baseline of the typography helps the viewer understand the work as a cohesive piece. See www.jodyzellen.com/pace2.html for video documentation of the installation.

FIGURE 12.4 Jody Zellen, *Trigger*, 2005. Pace University Digital Gallery, New York.

MASTER PAGES

To apply all these grid possibilities with ease and agility to your designs, you'll use InDesign's Pages panel to access and apply a *master page*. A master page is simply a page that acts as a template on which guides and other items that you want to establish across a series of pages in your multipage document are saved. You can add typography, images, graphics, and guides to a master page. You can develop multiple master pages and then drag and drop them on top of any of the pages in your document—the content and guides from the master page of your choice will instantly appear on your document pages. This lets you visualize different layout designs by simply switching the master pages.

PARAGRAPH STYLES

Much like you would apply a master page throughout a document, you can use the Paragraph Styles panel to save specific typographic settings that apply to different hierarchies of type. InDesign's Paragraph and Character Styles panels behave similarly—one is used for paragraphs and the other for specific words or characters within a paragraph.

You'll use only the Paragraph Style panel in this chapter, but once you see how to create a new style and apply it, using the Character Styles panel will be intuitive.

READING ON THE SCREEN

Assume that the product of the exercises in this chapter will be a PDF intended to be read onscreen, so the typography should best fit the screen environment. The reader will likely be viewing the document on a personal computer (not sitting at a distance or watching a projected image), so you'll continue to work with body copy set at about 11 points. However, the typeface for body copy will be in a sans serif font. The serifs that are often used for body copy in printed documents can be difficult to read onscreen, because light is projected through such small graphic details. I used Futura throughout the exercises, which has a decent sized x-height (meaning that the font appears a little larger than others). If you don't have Futura installed on your computer, use any sans serif typeface to complete the exercises.

WHAT YOU'LL NEED

To complete the exercises in this chapter, you'll need the resulting files from the previous chapters, as well as a text file from which you'll paste the copy seen in the resulting PDF. Use your own work or download the archive of final files from the companion website.

✔ The **chapter12-start** folder from the Chapter 12 downloads area on the companion website.

(I included the Chapter 10 final poster file and omitted the Chapter 8 collage file to limit redundancy, and selected one example from chapters that resulted in multiple files.)

Expand or unstuff the archive (or create your own) and place the 10 files in a folder on your hard drive named **chapter12**. You will benefit from seeing how the Laws of Similarity and Continuity apply throughout a multipage document.

WHAT YOU'LL MAKE

In the exercises in this chapter, you'll create a layout for a multipage document that acts as a PDF portfolio of the exercises you've completed thus far (FIGURE 12.5). You'll be working with Adobe InDesign. If you're new to InDesign, you'll find that it's similar to Adobe Illustrator but with a more robust set of tools that support publication design.

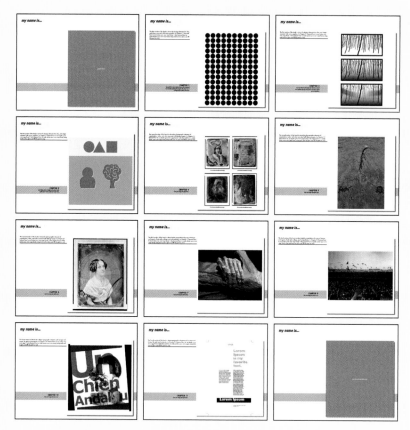

FIGURE 12.5 The resulting file for this chapter's exercises is a multipage PDF portfolio.

CREATE A NEW INDESIGN DOCUMENT FOR SHARING ON THE WEB

In this exercise, you'll use the File menu to create a new document, just as you've done in Illustrator. The InDesign presets, choices, and fields will seem familiar, although they're slightly different from what you've worked with before. Assume that the goal is to generate a PDF portfolio of images to be shared via email. You'll use a web preset to set your pages to a common set of screen dimensions.

You won't create spreads (pages that are side by side) in this chapter. You can revisit the concept of spreads in the online Chapter 17, *Pagination and Printing*.

1. Open InDesign. Choose File > New > Document or press **Command(⌘)-N**.

2. Choose Intent > Web. Enter 12 in the Number of Pages field and start at page 1. Select 1024 by 768 for the Page Size. Leave the rest of the choices in their default setting modes: no Facing Pages, no Primary Text Frame, 1 Column, 12 pixel Gutter, and 36 pixels for the Top, Left, Bottom, and Right margins (**FIGURE 12.6**).

3. Set the InDesign workspace to Typography using the pull-down list in the Application bar or by choosing Window > Workspace > Typography.

4. As in other Adobe applications, you'll notice a Tools panel on the left side of the application window, a Control panel (called the *Options panel* in Adobe Photoshop) beneath the menus across the top of the application, and a list of frequently accessed panels pertaining to the workspace you selected on the right side of the application window. If you're comfortable with Illustrator and Photoshop, most of the InDesign tools will be intuitive.

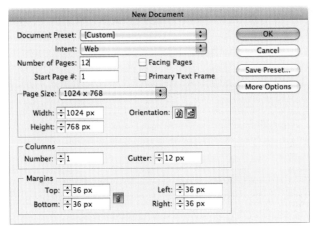

FIGURE 12.6 Since you have 10 images to showcase, you'll construct a document with a total of 12 pages: one for each image, plus one for your name and a closing page with copyright information.

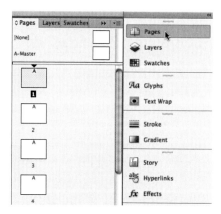

FIGURE 12.7 Use the Pages panel to navigate the document.

5. Open the Pages panel by clicking the Pages button from the list of panels on the right side of the application (FIGURE 12.7). The Pages panel lets you quickly navigate to each page in your document. Double-clicking on a page will put that page in the center of the application window. Notice the page icon for [None] and A-Master at the top of the Pages panel. InDesign assumes that you'll want to unify your multipage document by placing elements on a master page. For a unique page, such as a cover, you can clear the master settings. Notice that all of the pages in the Pages panel are identified with a small, uppercase A. By default, pages will be styled based on A-Master. Also by default, A-Master and [None] are both empty. In the next exercise, you'll set guides to use throughout the document on the A-Master page.

ESTABLISH GUIDES ON A-MASTER

Master pages are used to position guides and design elements on multiple pages within your document. When the document is printed, master elements will print, but the master page itself, like guides, will not be published. These pages are essentially a place for you to create a logical system that will rule the design of the multipage document, thus ensuring continuity and similarity. Your publication will appear unified because of the system you develop on the master pages. For this reason, master pages are an essential component in the multipage design process.

In this document, you'll want to showcase an image on almost every page, along with brief text to support each image. You essentially want to create a two-column layout. Asymmetry is more dynamic and can be read more quickly than symmetry, and it lets you direct more hierarchy to one part of the page. You might also decide that there should be more space allocated to the image than to the supporting text. Keep all of this in mind when setting guides on the A-Master page.

1. Double-click the A-Master page icon in the Pages panel. Since every page is blank, it can be difficult at first to know whether you're working on the master page or a page in the document. There are two ways to know that you're on the master page: the word A-Master will be highlighted in black in the Pages panel and A-Master will be selected at the bottom-left side of the application window (FIGURE 12.8).

2. Begin by positioning a common design element and then drawing guides based on it. Assume that you want to include a logo or your name on every page of the document. Choose the Rectangle tool from the Tools panel—be careful, there's a Rectangle Frame tool above the familiar Rectangle tool. Now draw a rectangle in the top-left corner of the A-Master page. Set the Stroke value to None and the Fill to black by using the pull-down menus in the Control panel (FIGURE 12.9). Turn on your rulers (⌘-R) and position the rectangle so it's aligned in the corner of the top and left margins, extending to 300 pixels wide and 100 pixels tall (FIGURE 12.10).

3. Notice that all of your pages now display a black rectangle in the top-left corner. Double-click any of the page icons in the Pages panel to see the repetition of the rectangle (FIGURE 12.11). Double-click on the A-Master page icon in the Pages panel to return to the master page you're developing.

KEY COMMAND REMINDER
As in Illustrator, the Command key will change a shape or drawing tool to the Selection tool. Adding the Option key indicates that you're making a copy, and the Shift key aligns mouse movements in 45-degree increments.

4. Use the black rectangle as a measuring device to help you imagine where guides might be placed on the page. Just as you would in Illustrator, press ⌘-Option-Shift(⇧) to create a copy of the black rectangle and position it precisely to the right of the first rectangle. While the second rectangle is selected, drag a vertical guide (from the vertical ruler) to its midpoint. The guide is now exactly one and a half rectangles across the page (FIGURE 12.12).

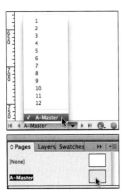

FIGURE 12.8 Select A-Master or any other page to work on from the bottom-left side of the application window.

FIGURE 12.9 Apply color from the Control panel.

FIGURE 12.10 Reposition and adjust shapes using the Selection tool.

FIGURE 12.11 Double-click a page in the Pages panel to see it in the application window.

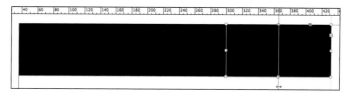

FIGURE 12.12 Use rectangles as measuring devices to help you set guides on the page.

FIGURE 12.13 Positioning a guide at what would have been one-quarter of the size of the original rectangle is made simple by halving the size of the original and then drawing a guide to the center anchor point.

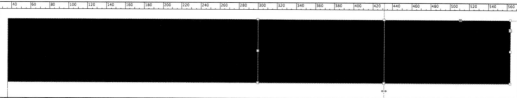

5. Drag the anchor point in the middle of the right side of the second rectangle to reduce its size. It's now the same height but half of its original width. Drag another guide to the midpoint of this reduced shape (**FIGURE 12.13**). The idea is that the right side of the page will be used to showcase images, and the left side will contain the text. The two guides that are close to each other will serve as a *gutter* between the text and the images.

6. Delete the second rectangle by clicking on it with the Selection tool and pressing the Delete key on your keypad. It's served its purpose.

7. Create some horizontal guides by dragging them from the top ruler. Copy the first black rectangle and position it directly below where the first one ends (beginning at 100 pixels). Add a guide at its center anchor point on the left and right sides (**FIGURE 12.14**). This guide will indicate the top alignment for the text and images on the page. It also creates negative space between the top name or logo and the rest of the page content.

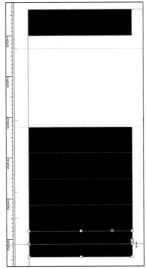

FIGURE 12.16 Set a guide at the anchor point in the middle of the last rectangle to measure four and a half boxes farther down the page.

FIGURE 12.14 Use shapes to determine where to add guides.

FIGURE 12.15 Drag a guide to the bottom edge of the last rectangle.

8. Move the copied rectangle so that it aligns with the new horizontal guide (where the start of a text box might be). Then copy and position the rectangle three more times and drag another horizontal guide along the bottom edge of the last rectangle (**FIGURE 12.15**). As in Step 4, the spaces created by these black rectangles are measuring devices, holding a place for the brief text in support of the image.

9. Now that you've defined the text area, delete two of the extra rectangles. Align one of the remaining ones at the intersection of the newest horizontal guide and the left margin. Create five copies of the rectangle going down the page and set another guide at the anchor point in the middle of the left and right sides of the last rectangle to measure four and a half boxes farther down the page (**FIGURE 12.16**).

FIGURE 12.17 The A-Master page with most of the black rectangles deleted and guides in place.

CAN'T TOUCH THIS (MASTER ELEMENTS)

At some point, you'll notice that any elements you add to master pages will be untouchable (unmovable, undeletable, uncontrollable, and so on) on regular pages in the InDesign document. If you need to move or modify an element, you'll have to return to the master page where it was placed. In *rare* circumstances, you may want to modify just one master element on your page. You can detach a master element by pressing ⌘-⇧ and clicking on the element to modify it. This action is *not* recommended.

10. Delete all of the black rectangles except for the original in the top-left corner of the page. You'll probably need another guide or two, but this will give you a good sense of where to position the text and image elements in the design. Save the file as **chapter12.indd**. Your A-Master page should be similar to mine (**FIGURE 12.17**).

 **PLACE IMAGES**

Now you'll place the final images from your work in the preceding chapters. If you're using my images, I prepared them by placing the .ai, .psd, and .pdf images in one folder for use in this layout. I also created a TIFF file for one of the images, as rasterizing was a better solution for that particular image. As a result, when placing all 10 images into the InDesign document, you'll be faced

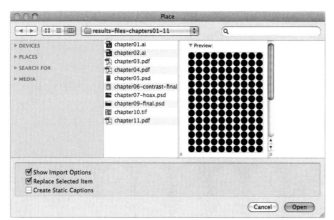

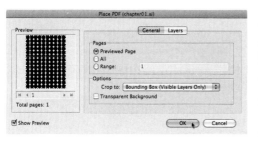

FIGURE 12.18 Click the Open button in the Place dialog to import images.

FIGURE 12.19 The Place PDF import dialog box allows you to choose which page or artboard to place, as well as other importing options.

FIGURE 12.20 Align the cursor using guides before placing image files. You can always move them after they're placed.

with questions via an Import Options dialog to tell InDesign how to handle the import. Most of the time, you can simply click the OK button. However, a short discussion of importing images is worthwhile. I'll weave that narration throughout the steps in this exercise.

1. Double-click the Page 2 icon in the Pages panel to begin placing images on the second page of the document. Choose File > Place or press ⌘-**D** to browse for files from the hard drive. You can place files in the document one at a time, or you can Shift-click to place several files at once. You'll place one file at a time in this exercise—you'll learn to place several files in Chapter 17 (available online for readers of the printed book). Click once on the first image, **chapter01.ai**, in your folder (**FIGURE 12.18**). Make sure that the Show Import Options box is checked and click the Open button.

2. In the Place PDF import options dialog, set the Crop to option to Bounding Box (Visible Layers Only) and press OK (**FIGURE 12.19**). The loaded cursor appears with a small icon of the graphic you selected. Place the cursor at the intersection of the guides where you want to position the image on page 2 (**FIGURE 12.20**) and click once.

3. Scaling the image to fit inside the guides requires an additional key command in InDesign. This is an Adobe anomaly: to scale the box in InDesign, you must press the Command key while dragging on one of the four anchor

IMAGE PREVIEWING

InDesign is essentially collecting your text and images for the printer, or in this case, for PDF export. Assuming that image file resolutions are large enough to generate a clear print on the printer you're using (or on the screen), you can trust that the layout you see on the screen will publish clearly, despite the low resolution of the screen preview. If trusting isn't something you like to do, print one of the pages to see that a low-resolution screen preview does not necessarily result in a low-resolution print.

FIGURE 12.21 Scale images in InDesign by pressing ⇧-⌘ while dragging an anchor point.

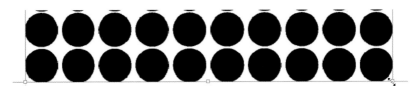

points at the edge of the frame of the image. As always, you should also press and hold the Shift key to constrain the proportions. Scale the first image (Shift-Command-drag anchor point) so it fits between the top and left image guides and the bottom and right margins (FIGURE 12.21). It's OK if the image doesn't fit the space perfectly—all the images have different proportions, so this is something you'll have to accommodate later.

4. Double-click the Page 3 icon in the Pages panel and repeat Steps 2 and 3 to place the second image on the page (FIGURE 12.22). You should start to notice that because the images are appearing in the same position on each page, there is continuity within the document.

5. Place the next image on page 4—if you're using my files, the next image is a PDF. Use the Forward button beneath a Preview window to tell InDesign which image you want to place (that is, which page of the PDF). You can choose to show any page from the file using this dialog. Leave the Preview Page radio button selected, and in the Options area, select Bounding Box (Visible Layers Only) from the pull-down menu. Don't check the Transparent Background button. Press the OK button to place the image and then scale it to fit the space while holding ⇧-⌘ (FIGURE 12.23).

6. Repeat Step 5 to place the next PDF on page 5.

7. On page 6, you'll place a PSD file. Once again, the Import Options dialog will change to accommodate your choices in regard to placing this file type. Double-click the Page 6 icon in the Pages panel, press ⌘-D to place an image, and select the next image (mine is **chapter05.psd**). The Image Options dialog for a Photoshop file lets you select which layers to show. Leave all the layers visible and press OK (FIGURE 12.24). Scale the image to fit the space.

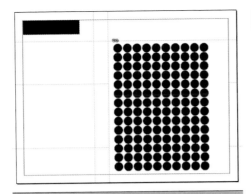

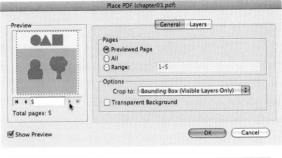

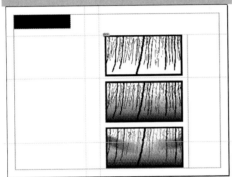

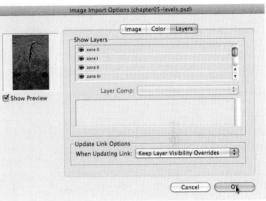

FIGURE 12.22 Multiple pages with images located in the same position.

FIGURE 12.23 Choose a page from a PDF to place in the InDesign file.

FIGURE 12.24 Leave all layers visible when importing the file.

SNAP TO GUIDES

When scaling an image in any Adobe application, you might find that the image or image frame snaps to guides. This is typically desirable, but in this exercise, the image is inside an image frame, so there's a little space between the frame (which is snapping to the guide) and the image. Snap to Guides is something you can turn on and off—turning it on prevents you from scaling the image with precision. If you're a Mac user, simply add the Control key while scaling to temporarily turn off snapping. In InDesign, this means that you'll press and hold ⌘-⇧ while initially scaling the image and frame together. However, you might end up pressing ⌘-⇧-**Control** to scale the image itself so that the image, not its frame, meets guides.

Now for the bad news: If you're working on a PC, the key commands to turn off snapping won't work. (Remember, the Command key on a Mac is the same as the Control key on the PC, which is already in use.) Instead, you'll have to select View > Grid & Guides > Snap to Guides to turn off snapping. Then press **Control-⇧** to scale the image without snapping interfering with your precise alignment.

8. Place and scale the rest of the files on pages 7–11. The file for Chapter 10 was saved as a TIFF image—it has limited options, and it's safe to leave the default settings in place.

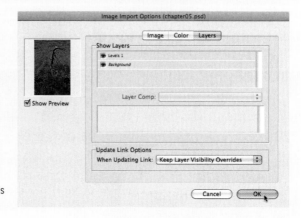

FIGURE 12.25
Chapter05.psd was created for use in this document.

ADD TEXT FRAMES

InDesign places images in Image Frames and text in Text Frames. These are similar to text boxes you've created in Illustrator, although InDesign gives you more control over frames. In this exercise, you'll add type to the layout. Create two text frames on each page—one for a short description of what you learned in the chapter (represented by the image to the right) and one to provide a one- or two-sentence description of the image. You'll be prompted to write some of your own copy during this exercise.

COPY AND PASTE Remember, the text you'll enter into each text frame is provided in a text document in the downloads section of the companion website. You can copy and paste from any text editing application to InDesign.

1. Choose the Type tool from the Tools panel. Click and drag the tool to create a text frame at the intersection of the guides beneath the logo placeholder in the top-left corner of page 2. Copy and paste from the downloaded .txt document or enter the following text in the frame:

   The first section of the book is about the design elements dot, line, and shape, executed with vector graphics. In Chapter 1, I learned how to see (enter your own copy here). I also learned how to make (enter your own copy here) using tools such as (you can fill this part in, too).

2. The second text frame should appear in a different position on the page, although it should still have a relationship to the grid. I aligned mine,

temporarily, with the left margin and on top of the bottom guide. Enter the text for the second text frame:

> Chapter 1 (line break) Repeated dots create a pattern. As I learned in my study of Gestalt psychology of perception, the viewer sees a rectangle before noticing 140 circles.

3. *Fix it!* Now you need to adjust the typography to create hierarchy and contrast. Before you do that in the next exercise, you can make a little contrast in the second text field by slightly altering its position. Return to the A-Master page by double-clicking its icon in the Pages panel. Click once on the logo/black rectangle to select it and drag a guide from the vertical ruler to its central anchor point. This will add another vertical guide to each page in the document (refer to Figure 12.5 for Steps 3, 4, and 5).

4. Return to page 2 and move the left edge of the text frame so it's aligned with the new guide, forcing the viewer's gaze to step down and to the right as she reads the text on the page.

5. Add one more guide to the A-Master page to set the height of the text frame. Copy the black rectangle/logo placeholder and use the height of that box to determine the height of the second text frame (add a guide from the horizontal ruler).

6. Adjust the text frame on page 2. The text frame may need to be larger than the width and height allow right now; that's OK. You'll modify the typography in the next exercise.

7. Add two text frames for pages 3–11 using the guides and copy from the .txt document.

 EXERCISE 5 ## PARAGRAPH STYLES

LINKING TEXT FRAMES
In Chapter 17, which is online and can be downloaded, you'll learn how to import text from a document, link text frames, and insert a frame break to accomplish Step 7 more efficiently.

You'll use the Paragraph Styles panel to create a set of styles that you can apply to all of the typography in the document. In a single-page document, styles aren't essential, but when you have many pages with the same type of content, at the same level of hierarchy on the page, it makes sense to create a style rule for the type and apply it with the click of a button. It's also convenient when you want to change a typographic style—one modification to the style rule makes the typography changes in all instances of its application. Using paragraph styles to govern type across the whole document helps you to achieve similarity in the typographic design.

Not surprisingly, styles are a common method of logically applying design elements to digital content. In the next section of this book, you'll learn about type on the web, where CSS is utilized to control styles for type and layout elements.

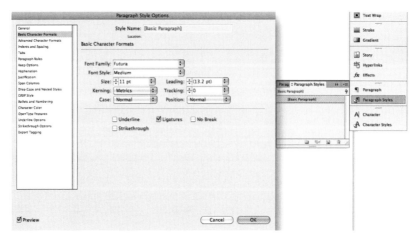

FIGURE 12.26 Use the Paragraph Style Options dialog to set basic character formats.

You can use any sans serif typeface for these exercises.

1. Expand the Paragraph Styles panel by clicking on Paragraph Styles in the right list of panels. Double-click the default [Basic Paragraph] because you'll modify this to set some typographic rules for the body copy in the first text frame (FIGURE 12.26). Click on the second button in the list on the left side to modify Basic Character Formats. Knowing that the PDF will primarily be viewed on the screen, I set the Font Family to a sans serif typeface (Futura, Style: Medium) and the Size to 11 points. Don't press the OK button yet.

2. In the same Paragraph Style Options dialog, click the Paragraph Rules button and add a Rule Below (click the Rule On button) with a Weight value of 2 points. Offset the rule (this will be a vertical offset) by 5 pixels (FIGURE 12.27). Don't press the OK button yet.

3. Click the Hyphenation button and uncheck the Hyphenate box (FIGURE 12.28). Alternatively, you could set hyphenation on for words with at least eight or nine letters to eliminate an abundance of hyphens in the copy. *Now* press the OK button.

4. Notice that since all the text on the page is ruled by the *Basic Paragraph* style, you've just changed all the text and added more line rules than you may have anticipated or wanted (FIGURE 12.29).

5. Create a new paragraph style by clicking the Create New Style button in the Paragraph Style panel (FIGURE 12.30).

6. Double-click *Paragraph Style 1* and rename it *Chapter Titles*. In the Basic Character Formats window, change the Font Style to Condensed ExtraBold (or something heavy if you're not using Futura), Size to 16 points, and Case to All Caps. Press the OK button. Nothing will change until you select some text and apply the style. Select Chapter 1 on page 2 and click once on the *Chapter Titles* paragraph style button.

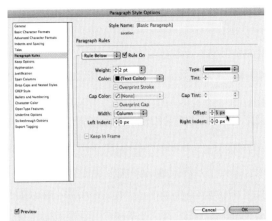

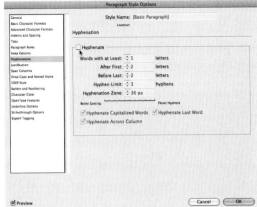

FIGURE 12.27 Use the Paragraph Style Options dialog to set typographic rules.

FIGURE 12.28 Set hyphenation options in the Paragraph Style Options dialog.

FIGURE 12.29 I temporarily expanded the text frame to show that a rule is applied throughout the page.

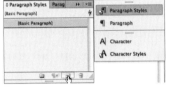

FIGURE 12.30 Create a new paragraph style from its panel.

FIGURE 12.31 Modify the tracking value and press the Preview button in the Paragraph Style Option dialog to see changes.

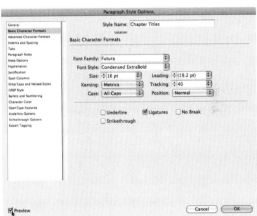

7. In this step, you'll right-align all the type in the smaller box, add a little tracking to the chapter title, and eliminate the line rule in the entire area. Double-click the *Chapter Titles* paragraph style button. Now that you've applied the style, you can see the results of additional tracking with the Preview button checked. I increased the Tracking value in the Basic Character Formats window to 40 points (**FIGURE 12.31**). Click the Indents and Spacing button and use the Alignment pull-down menu to right-align the

FIGURE 12.32 The *Image Descriptions* style is applied to the text that describes the image.

FIGURE 12.33 Set alignment in the Text Frame Options dialog.

text. Finally, click the Paragraph Rules button and uncheck the Rule On box. This will turn off the underline on the chapter title.

8. Create a new paragraph style named *Image Descriptions*. In the General area, choose [Basic Paragraph] from the Based On pull-down menu. Then modify the text so the Font Style is Condensed Medium, the copy is right aligned (Indents and Spacing menu), and there's no line rule (Paragraph Rules menu). Select the image description below the text, Chapter 1, and apply the *Image Descriptions* style (FIGURE 12.32). If you need to reset Chapter 1 to the *Chapter Titles* style, select the text and apply the style.

9. Click on the second text frame with the Selection tool and press ⌘-B or choose Object > Text Frame Options. Modify the alignment of content in the text frame so that it's vertically centered (FIGURE 12.33).

10. The type is in pretty good shape, but I wish the page had a little color on it (especially page 2), and having the text align on one guide is a bit boring. You'll make further modifications in the next exercise.

EXERCISE 6 COLOR AND A DROP SHADOW ON A-MASTER

The overall layout is in decent shape. However, you should give the composition a little more color and energy. This is a good place to be: the composition is organized, and you're ready to make some revisions.

1. Double-click the A-Master icon in the Pages panel as you'll add color, another guide, and a drop shadow on the master page.

2. Choose the Rectangle Tool and drag a new rectangle across the entire layout between the lower two horizontal guides. Fill the rectangle with a color of your choice and set the Stroke value to none. (I chose cyan as my color to keep it simple and modified the out-of-gamut color—I included this step in the screencast for this chapter.)

3. Set a vertical guide at the midpoint of the space where your images are positioned. (It should be approximately 710 pixels across the page.)

4. Fill the image area with a white rectangle—set the Fill to Paper and the Stroke value to none.

5. Right-click on the white rectangle (or Control-click on a Mac if you don't have a right-click mouse button). From the contextual menu, select Effects > Drop Shadow. I left the settings in their default mode, with the exception of the Opacity. I changed that to 50% (**FIGURE 12.34**). In Figure 12.34, you'll see the results of Steps 2 through 5 in this exercise.

SCREENCAST 12-1 PREPARING FILES FOR PLACEMENT IN INDESIGN—RELINKING IMAGES AND OUT-OF-GAMUT COLORS

A few parts of the final PDF produced in these exercises have been left out of the text to keep the word count and classroom time allocation consistent with other chapters. In the screencast, I demonstrate saving the resulting files for use in these exercises, relinking images in InDesign, choosing a color that's within printing gamut (in case the viewer wants to print the PDF), and setting up the first and last pages of the document.

All screencasts are available on the companion website, www.digitalart-design.com, or on the YouTube playlist, www.youtube.com/playlist?list=PLAy6P5IoEjy2v3kZKCt8spqJ5OnLb2XQI.

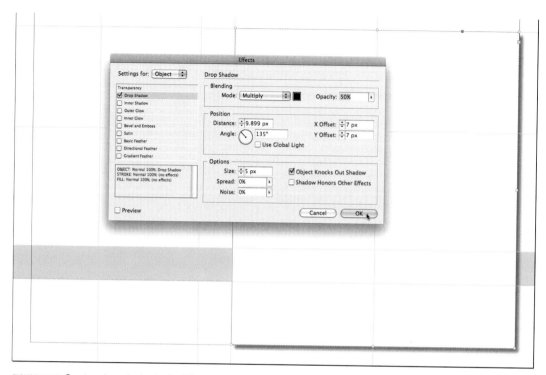

FIGURE 12.34 Create a drop shadow in the Effects dialog box.

FINAL ADJUSTMENTS AND EXPORT TO PDF

Double-click on the Page 2 icon in the Pages panel to see how these changes have affected the layout with content in your document. You'll make three additional changes to page 2, which you'll then repeat on pages 3–11.

PREVIEWING KEY COMMAND When nothing is selected on the page, if you press the W key on your keyboard, you can see the layout without guides or margins interrupting your view. Press W again to return to normal editing mode.

1. Reposition the first text frame so it extends to the next guide (where the image initially would have aligned left). This new position breaks the repeated line of continuation that's already well defined, allowing for a little contrast on the page. The same type treatment repeated throughout the document and the same positioning of these text frames contributes to unity through similarity.

2. Reposition the image so that its center anchor point is aligned on the new guide.

3. Click once on the image to activate it and then choose the Scale tool (**FIGURE 12.35**). Double-click the Scale tool and scale the image to 95% of its width and height to allow negative space near the edges of the drop shadow (**FIGURE 12.36**).

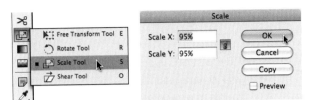

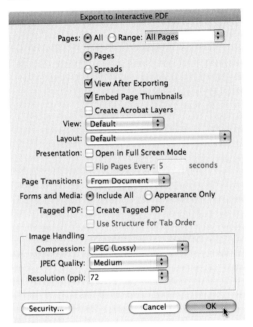

FIGURE 12.35 The Scale tool in the InDesign Tools panel.

FIGURE 12.36 Scale the width and height of a selected item.

FIGURE 12.37 Export the file to create a PDF. Click the Pages radio button for a document, like this one, made of single pages.

4. Repeat Steps 1 through 3 on Pages 3–11. Also fix the typography on the remaining pages by applying proper paragraph styles.

5. Create a cover and final page (Pages 1 and 12) on your own. I made a simple contrasting text frame in the image area with a background color and center-aligned, small type. Also swap the black placeholder on the A-Master page with your own logo or even just your name. Again, I made a simple text frame.

6. Save the native .indd document. Then choose the File menu > Export. Choose the format Adobe PDF (Interactive). In the PDF dialog, click the Pages radio button (not Spreads, as you didn't design the layout with spreads). Leave the rest of the defaults in place (FIGURE 12.37). View the PDF and return to the native InDesign file to make further adjustments before repeating the process of saving and exporting. When I first exported the PDF, I didn't like how the shorter images looked. I returned to the InDesign file and vertically center-aligned all the images before saving and exporting again.

LAB CHALLENGE

The obvious lab exercise would be to create a PDF portfolio of works for sharing. However, you just did that in this chapter, so a better challenge would be to express almost any other idea. Based on Nicholas Felton's work (see the introduction to this chapter and Figures 12.1 through 12.3), create a personal portfolio of visualized data. Choose any time frame (an hour, a day, a year) and create a unified PDF using InDesign to showcase one aspect of your life. You can track something that seems important or something ordinary. Charts, photographs, and text are all appropriate content elements. Try to achieve similarity and continuity in your multipage design.

CODA
REVISION PRACTICES

IN AN ADVANCED course that I teach, the latter half of the semester is used strictly for the revision of projects sketched as quick, weekly drafts during the first eight weeks. I begin the class with a reading and discussion of Bre Pettis and Kio Stark's *Cult of Done Manifesto* [1]. The manifesto speaks to procrastinators and finishers, though much is lost on the concept of revision. While some of the 13 lines espouse great advice (Line 8 comes to mind: "Laugh at perfection. It's boring and keeps you from being done."), others dismiss revision (or "editing") as a stage of development. Perhaps their point is that revision and editing are the sum total of the process of arriving at the "final" form. Like many manifestos, interpretation allows for different readings of the text and encourages the reader to consider her own process of revision, or at least, of getting things done.

What the *Cult of Done Manifesto* doesn't recognize is that for many, getting things done is not always the end goal. Revision is often a process of negotiation with clients or funders who want to meet specific brand and marketing goals. While aesthetics are important,

REFERENCE [1] Bre Pettis, *Cult of Done Manifesto*, 3/3/09, http://www.brepettis.com/blog/2009/3/3/the-cult-of-done-manifesto.html.

REFERENCE [2] Scott Simon, "A Thought That's Worth More Than a Penny (Or a Nickel)," NPR, 1/18/13, http://www.npr.org/2013/01/19/169723296/a-thought-thats-worth-more-than-a-penny-or-a-nickel.

REFERENCE [3] D. Wayne Johnson, "A Melted Penny for Your Thoughts," The Wall Street Journal, 1/14/13, http://online.wsj.com/article/SB10001424127887323374504578223484113806430.html.

FIGURE C.1 Christopher Doyle, *Identity Guidelines*, 2008. Designed by Christopher Doyle. Photography by Ian Haigh. © Christopher Doyle & Co.

some decisions are made for political reasons. In Scott Simon's review [2] of D. Wayne Johnson's proposal to eliminate the penny, nickel, and quarter [3] from U.S. currency, Simon makes the argument that the idea "sounds sensible every way but politically." Despite the fact that it costs more than the coins' actual value to make a penny or a nickel, ridding them from popular currency would create a new crisis—one that would pair Lincoln and JFK or Susan B. Anthony and Sacagawea in a face-off for honor. Although revising U.S. currency makes fiscal sense, Simon suggests that it would create more strife than perhaps the revision is worth. He also observes that the European Union chose details of architectural works to feature on their currency, rather than significant people.

Revision is often considered in reference to a product's identity or brand guidelines. While you may have a brilliant idea for presenting a product, if you fail to abide by the brand guidelines, your presentation will surely be rejected. As a comment on how carefully the presentation of a brand is outlined, designer and artist Christopher Doyle created *Christopher Doyle™ Identity Guidelines 2008* to showcase his personal set of "style guides" (**FIGURE C.1**).

CLEAR, OPEN COMMUNICATION AND ACCESSIBILITY

It's important to educate clients about how graphic design and visual communication can help create clear and open communication. In *Putting Back the Face into Typeface*, an interview with Erik Spiekermann on Gestalten TV, the typographer illustrates the strength of good design and the power of bad design. He says, "Bad government forms serve to separate us from the government because they make us stupid—because we don't understand—so we do what we're told. If things were designed to be more open or accessible, then we would be able to communicate more with each other" [4]. He advocates for designers to activate the system. "The system itself doesn't really want to communicate because then it becomes messy and dirty...We are supposed to shut up and make our little crosses and fill our forms and be quiet...and that's why I think designers should be in there trying to break things open."

Open communication is important not just for the end user, but also between the artist/designer and the client. The following interviews and contributions include a miscommunication that resulted in a remaking of a product (Pencilbox Studios) and a keen ear for communication that resulted in the repackaging of a popular toy (riCardo Crespo). Other revisions are based on surprise challenges that cropped up while executing a concept (Michael Demers) or revisions that met the demands of curators and funders (The League of Imaginary Scientists). Some even demonstrate a unique process for revision and editing during the brainstorming phase (Jovenville and Bill Thompson).

REFERENCE [4] Erik Spiekermann, "Putting Back the Face into Typeface," Gestalten TV, YEAR, https://vimeo.com/19429698.

PENCILBOX STUDIOS: MISSION HOSPITAL

Having completed assignments for other hospitals and healthcare organizations, Pencilbox Studios included Mission Hospital in its mailing list. So it was of little surprise when first-time client Mission called Pencilbox for a creative meeting.

PRINCIPAL PARTNERS
Kathleen Kaiser, Creative Director, and Bill Thompson, Photographer (www.pencilboxstudios.com).

12-PAGE BROCHURE WITH POCKET FOLDER

During initial meetings, Kathleen Kaiser, Creative Director of Pencilbox, spoke with the Mission Hospital team, including the head of imagery and a marketing specialist who was overseeing the marketing of the new imagery center. A new building with a state-of-the-art imaging wing was in the final stages of development. The hospital was eager to create literature for future patients of the advanced imaging center, while the marketing team was aware of a local challenge. Just miles from Mission Hospital, another hospital in a swanky part of town offered imaging services in a spa-like environment (marble floors, fresh floral arrangements, a limo ride to and from the center, and so on). While Mission's doctors and technicians were as qualified to perform imaging services as the local competition, many referrals went to the "nicer" location. Mission wanted to overcome this stigma and separate itself from its competition with a new, modern identity, specifically for the new location that showcased its new technology. The stakes of the design effort were high: the brochure not only needed to communicate to stressed patients, but it also had to create a public perception that could compete with the imaging spa down the street.

Any time a creative professional works with a large organization, one of the first requests is to review and understand the brand guidelines or specifications. Typically, there are strict rules about logo and color usage, among other design elements. There may be templates that should be used for certain types of visual materials. In this case, existing brand guidelines had been used for other areas of Mission's visual presence. However, the hospital team recognized that creating a new identity to promote the new building and equipment (and to compete with the nearby imaging center) took precedence. The guidelines were reviewed, but Pencilbox and the marketing team reached an understanding that they needn't be closely followed in order to create something unique for the new imaging wing.

As a result, Pencilbox developed a brochure that truly considered its audience. The unique size of the work was determined by the size of the physicians' lab coat pockets so doctors could keep brochures on hand. The colors were warm and relaxing. Topics were color-coded—would you rather have to remember that MRI information is filed under "Magnetic Resonance Imaging" or would you prefer to simply see the purple section? Real doctors and technicians were included in Bill Thompson's photographs, which accurately portrayed the machinery in use throughout the brochure. A custom die-cut pocket created harmony within the layout. Pencilbox team members felt that they were pushing the structure of their design beyond what would be allowed within the constraints of the brand guidelines. They talked about this approach with the client leading up to a final presentation of comps, and were pleased to be given approval to move forward with their strategy.

However, during the final round of proofing, the client delivered a message from someone who had not been directly involved in the process: the brochure would need to be redesigned in order to fit, precisely, the brand specifications.

This came as a surprise to Pencilbox, as they had included the brand guidelines in their communication with the hospital's marketing team. They had been transparent in regard to how much they needed to deviate from the guidelines in order to make a unique visual identity. However, what the marketing team hadn't realized was that the hospital was planning to rebrand the entire institution in the near future. In fact, shortly after this project was completed, Mission changed its marketing team. Kaiser recalls:

> As designers and creative directors, we need to know the bigger picture. Look what happened when we didn't—we didn't know they were facing a rebrand shortly after our project or that they would be hiring a new staff.

FIGURE C.2 In the original eight-page brochure design, a custom size was designed to fit easily inside a physician's coat pocket. The modern design and inclusion of negative space represented the new architecture and advanced, technological equipment. A slightly warmer color palette was chosen based on the hospital's brand colors. Curves and color organization systems were created, as well as a custom die-cut pocket. The goal of the piece was to be easy to follow and friendly for a reader who would soon be undergoing a diagnostic imaging procedure.

FIGURE C.3 In the revised design, the custom size was replaced by the traditional size specified by the brand guidelines. The consistent cover and format matches all of the hospital's literature, as does the limited color palette and template die-cut pocket. © Pencilbox Studios

BRAND GUIDELINES

Upon reflection, Kaiser offered the insight that a brand guide should consider its audience. Instead of being established to make visual content simply look the same, or to make a template for various departments, the brand guide should consider issues of flexibility and accessibility.

The hospital didn't want to publish something "between" the old brand guidelines and what would become the new identity. If Pencilbox had known this, they might have advised moving forward with a smaller project until the new brand guidelines were established.

The good news for Pencilbox was that the redesign was not too difficult to achieve, because the brand was so specifically designed, and the copy and photography easily fit into the brochure template. The client took responsibility for the miscommunication. In the end, Pencilbox was paid for the work twice over. The redesign matched the overall hospital brand, but lost the unique ideas that Pencilbox had brought to their version of the work. Even copy that Pencilbox authored, such as the front cover copy: "Excellence in Medicine Starts with Knowing and Knowing Starts Here" (which the team leaders appreciated) was changed to "Mission Advanced Imaging Center" to meet the guidelines (FIGURES C.2 and C.3).

Interestingly, photography was not included as part of the brand standards. Issues such as the colors of the clothing subjects wore or the direction that figures faced in images were unspecified. In Kaiser's and Thompson's working process, the photography was preplanned to fit the needs of the layout and design strategy. The photographs captured the essence of the client's needs. So even though the brand guidelines were not followed in the 12-page brochure, the photography did satisfy the needs of the clients. The imagery showcased the new, technological equipment and the new architecture, two pieces of the design challenge that the client was proud to communicate.

PERCEPTION OF THE PRINCESS: PHOTOGRAPH, SELF-PROMOTIONAL WORK

As a design photographer and partner in Pencilbox, everything Bill Thompson creates starts with a sketch. This series of image revisions shows part of Thompson's process. First, he photographs a model he will use as a figure (if required) in the work (FIGURE C.4). Then he gathers and photographs props. The visual message is built around the gestures and positioning of the figure, rather than the other way around (FIGURE C.5).

FIGURE C.4 Human figure photographed for the composite image, *Perception of the Princess* by Pencilbox Studios. In this series of images, you can see how the model changes position in collaboration with the photographer. © Pencilbox Studios

FIGURE C.5 Props photographed for the composite image, *Perception of the Princess,* by Pencilbox Studios. © Pencilbox Studios

In this image, based on his sketches, Thompson knew there would be rocks and a tilting structure. The woman would represent a princess reigning over her kingdom. With a strong concept in mind, Thompson started by keeping the composition of the photograph tightly related to his original sketch (often referred to as "tight to comp"). The composition loosened as the situation built, and the model was considered a collaborator. In this photo shoot, she would do something, and he would react. When asked to "be tall" or to "look over her kingdom," she stood on her tiptoes. He responded to that, asking her to put her heels together and noticing how her legs resembled a column. This induced the next photograph and repositioning, and so on. Everything Thompson saw in the frame was part of the design composition. In the end, he saw that the one-legged stance would give him more freedom in the final composite image and that the suggestion of dynamic movement made by her asymmetric stance would correspond to the stack of cards.

FIGURE C.6 *Perception of the Princess*, final composite photograph by Pencilbox Studios. © Pencilbox Studios

The final photograph consists of four composited images and includes the acrylic matte medium brushwork technique detailed in the sidebar (FIGURE C.6). Reflecting on Thompson's process, I just can't agree with the third line of the *Cult of Done Manifesto*. "There is no editing stage" might be revised to "every part of the process is an editing stage."

ADDING BRUSHWORK TEXTURE

Many artists and designers use analog techniques in combination with digital strategies. Bill Thompson often uses a coat of acrylic matte medium to create a painterly, atmospheric effect on the resulting digital image. He creates a preliminary composition in Adobe Photoshop and then makes an inkjet print on watercolor paper. He brushes clear matte medium directly on the print. Thompson advises that the amount of matte medium often depends on the amount of ink on the page. The clear coat dries in an evening before he re-photographs the work. It could be scanned, he notes, but it's important to control the lighting when photographing the new work. He again composites the newly digitized piece in Photoshop, paying special attention to areas of the image that will retain their original sharpness and ones left influenced by the matte medium.

RICARDO CRESPO: HOT WHEELS AND STANDING MEETINGS

RICARDO CRESPO

has held creative director positions at Mattel and 20th Century Fox. He is currently a CCO at Thirteen in Marina del Ray, California (www.th13teen.com).

While revision is part of any job, it was during riCardo Crespo's tenure at Mattel that he revised a product's packaging. One of my favorite revision stories is one that he delivered when he spoke on our campus at an AIGA event. He recounted how after being introduced as "riCardo from Mattel" at parties, he was often asked the same two questions: "Can you get me a deal on toys for my kids?" and, more important to the story, "Why is the packaging so difficult to open?" Tired parents posed a good question: Why must toy car packaging be so rigid?

Most designers and creative directors would roll their eyes in agreement and dismiss the design of the plastic packaging as a part of the product for which they weren't directly responsible. Crespo, however, invests himself in all that he does. After reflecting on this constant comment about the toy packaging, he decided to personally revise it to fit the needs of its second-level customers: parents (kids, of course, being the first). This would improve Mattel's reputation as well as his own. Ultimately, he wanted to make the packaging simple enough to open in 30 seconds or less. He achieved this by removing twist ties and plastic parts that contained the cars in the plastic packaging. He wanted to be introduced not as "riCardo from Mattel," but as "riCardo who finally made the Hot Wheels packaging easy to open."

Deciding to revise the packaging and actually making the change were two separate initiatives. The first resulted from brainstorming and reflection. The second required activity—a strategy for execution. As the Worldwide Group Creative Director, Crespo flew to China to work with the factory where the packaging was made. He convinced directors at Mattel to revise the packaging by (what else?) promising that the simplified package, with no twist-ties or additional parts, would be cheaper to produce (FIGURE C.7).

FIGURE C.7 YouTube user 10h41 demonstrates how he opens a Hot Wheels package. The packaging of this product is subject to much debate on YouTube and fan websites.

STAND UP

Another great story that Crespo recounted was how he changed meetings with his team. Meetings inevitably began with small talk as attendees waited around the table for everyone to trickle into the room. At Mattel, a company housed in a large structure, one meeting might take place 10 minutes away from the next. Crespo was tired of wasting time with chitchat at the start of meetings and then having to run from one side of the Mattel campus to the other. To eliminate chitchat and turn his peers' perception of "meeting" on its head, Crespo called his first standing meetings near plants, water coolers, and other landmarks. Asking someone to meet you in the boardroom at 10:15 (when the day is full of meetings in boardrooms) results in a casual approach to timeliness and the typical chitchat. Asking someone to meet you by a plant at 10:15 might actually result in a 10:15 meeting time. Standing, not seated, meeting participants provided the impetus to have an efficient dialogue and stay on task. The revision of the meeting ultimately affected the amount of time in the day for design and creative thinking.

Crespo's story of standing meetings can be extrapolated to summarize the last section of this text (available online for readers of the printed book). Effective work habits—whether they include using the Actions panel in Photoshop or rethinking your communication strategy with clients or team members—directly impact how much time you have for the creative process. Revision is salient in all aspects of your life. It's not just a way of rethinking your creative output, but a process in which you reflect on the past and make decisions for the future.

MICHAEL DEMERS: THE SKY IS FALLING (A DAY IN THE LIFE...)

In 2010, I received a "Terminal: Internet-Based Art" grant from Austin Peay State University for the production of a proposed online artwork that consisted of captured PlayStation 3 game footage from *Elder Scrolls IV: Oblivion*. The work would reflect the seamless passing of game time to contrast with the audience's external experience of real time. One minute of "real" time equaled approximately 30 minutes of game time, and the plan was to capture 24 two-minute videos representing the passing of one game day. These videos would be programmed to play on a web browser with the particular two-minute clip referencing the viewer's local time. (For instance, if a viewer opened the page at 3:40 pm local time, then video 15, containing game footage from 3:00 to 3:59 pm game time, would play in the browser.)

MICHAEL DEMERS contributed this story of The Sky Is Falling (A Day in the Life...). His complete portfolio is available at www.michaeldemers.com, and this project is at www.michaeldemers.com/theskyisfalling_terminal.

The full title is *The Sky Is Falling (A Day in the Life...) Elder Scrolls IV: Oblivion; 12:00am to 11:59pm, Heartfire 11, 3E433.*

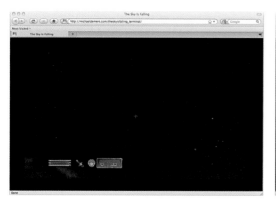

FIGURES C.8 AND C.9 Michael Demers, *The Sky Is Falling (A Day in the Life...)* Elder Scrolls IV: *Oblivion 12:00am to 11:59pm, Heartfire 11, 3E433*, Terminal: Internet Based Art, Austin Peay State University, 2010.

ONLINE DIGITAL VIDEO IN 24 TWO-MINUTE SEGMENTS, KEYED TO THE VIEWER'S TIME OF DAY

References to playable characters, AI characters, and accompanying sound effects would be edited from the video to focus on the notion of a virtual space with the possibility of nonvirtual habitation, defined in part by the passing of game time during the observer's "real" time. The health meter, magic meter, stamina meter, weapon and magic selections, and game compass would remain unedited as a digital referent in the hyper-real environment of the game engine.

The reason I chose *Elder Scrolls IV: Oblivion* as my source material was two-fold. First, the idea that game time consistently and uniformly progressed was an interesting one to me. As time was spent in the realm of the game, it passed more slowly in the real world. This was a radical departure from the kinds of games I had played when I was younger, where the idea of diversion from the real world was paramount and any relationship to external reality was suspect. The second reason for this choice related to the first, because *Elder Scrolls IV: Oblivion* presents the player with a robustly detailed environment (apart from the fantasy elements), where the sun rises and sets, clouds cross the sky, and rain falls. Switching from third-person to first-person view and commanding your playable character to look up, one is presented with a nuanced and boundless panorama of the sky and space that changes with each passing minute (**FIGURES C.8** and **C.9**).

THE PLAN AND THE PROBLEM

The actual recording of the game footage was easy: a Hauppauge HD PVR connected between my Mac and my PlayStation 3 copied footage on the television screen. Finding a location from which to command my character to view the sky for 24 hours, however, proved somewhat more complicated. All attempts to find a safe place where my character could stand while looking upward proved hopeless, as some creature or other would inevitably attack. It seemed the only safe option would be to stand on water, where neither the creatures on land nor under the sea could harm me. Doing that required me to locate a particular enchanted item, a ring that allowed walking on water.

Many hours later, with the ability to walk on water firmly under my control, I again set out to watch the sky for the next 24 hours of game time. While I was not harassed during this attempt, I found that after about 15 minutes of real time spent looking up, my character's health began to drain. I was dead three minutes later. Knowing that I was not being attacked (as I was unreachable on the surface of the water), and thinking my death to be a system bug, I reset both the game and the Hauppauge HD PVR and tried again. After another 15 minutes, I started dying once more. This continued for another three or four attempts before I found the consistent element: starting at game-time midnight, 15 minutes of real time brought me to approximately 6:00 a.m., or sunrise. At some point during my adventure to locate the magic ring, I had been afflicted with vampirism. The rising sun was my undoing.

I found a cure for my vampirism (a drawn-out period of collecting ingredients to give to a witch), and hence my demise at dawn, days later. Finally cured, I was able to stand still and gaze at the sky for the 24-hour game day duration. With my footage captured, all that was left for the completion of the project was the video splicing and HTML coding—and some vampire payback.

THE LEAGUE OF IMAGINARY SCIENTISTS: IN LEAGUE WITH AN INSTITUTION

For artists and collaborators, revision is essential to the working process. Art is arguably a revision of the world itself, certainly, a re-envisioning; and collaborations require endless negotiation and restatements. Revision accounts for creative evolutions, is the product of conceptual decision making, and results in more developed work. When one works with an institution, revision begins with the proposal, and it becomes the focus again with institutional deadlines for press and publicity. Proposals are rarely accepted as initially conceived and written, and publicity must serve the institution first and the art second. There are many institutional considerations—and these typically don't concern artists. Our experience demonstrates this paradoxical element of institutional programming.

LUCY HG SOLOMON
(Dr. L. Hernandez Gomez of the League of Imaginary Scientists) contributed this revision story. See the League's work at www.imaginaryscience.org.

We received an invitation—a great opportunity—to have a residency at the Museum of Contemporary Art, Los Angeles (MOCA) from December 2010 to March 2011. Each month was to culminate in a public event showcasing interactive artworks. The League was not new to artist residencies—to the slow and then suddenly fast-paced journey toward an art exhibition or event—often involving collaborators from the sciences.

Due to our frequent collaborations with scientists—waiting on research, discovering that the findings are not in conceptual alignment with the direction of a piece, or that the findings are not the anticipated results at all—the League is accustomed to improvisation and revision. These scientific redirections are meaningful bumps along the road that oftentimes change the course of the road altogether.

Collaborating with the exhibiting institution, however, was a new experience. A team of MOCA Think Tank members supported the residency and was privy to the major creative and budgetary considerations by our group. And with a larger institution came larger considerations—about the location, the rules of engagement with the public, and certainly about the relationship of newer works to the collection of Art (with a capital "A") contained within the museum.

We were transients, and our artwork would be impermanent yet interactive—a point for community involvement. The League of Imaginary Scientists proliferated ideas, most of which were tabled. We wanted, for instance, to perform the greatest museum heist in the history of heists, yet this was not a mission that could be condoned by security. We wanted to have rockets. (Who doesn't?) Budgetary constraints nixed that one. We envisioned a motorcyclist launching off the museum building and over the crowd—not sure why that didn't happen.

In constant communication with MOCA staff, the League of Imaginary Scientists along with MOCA's Think Tank, settled on three events that would emerge from a contraption—one that we would change over the course of the residency. We titled our residency and the project series, *The Evolving Contraption*. The name proved suitable for the residency, and indeed applies to most collaborative art projects, as they almost always evolve significantly from conception to completion.

The Evolving Contraption began with *Wormholes*, a warped take on airport security and travel (**FIGURE C.10**). *Wormholes* replicated individual travelers and sent them through a long wormhole security line and eventually placed their replicas into other space-time locations. This project had many permutations and went through a series of sketches—some of the early, discarded ones were considered too ambitious or costly. Ultimately, a long tent served as the conduit to becoming "replicated" and going on the wormhole journey. Small sculptures along the way allowed viewers to peer into other space-time locations, including into a biological engineering lab at MIT in the recent past as well as an artist's studio in the future.

The second exhibition, *The Automatoggler*, was to be the greatest invention ever made—a contraption to save humanity from, well, ourselves (FIGURE C.11). This project underwent numerous revisions over the course of its month of creation! Unlike many past collaborations by the League, the motto was "Divide and Conquer," as we were determined to create as much as possible so as to visually overwhelm a plaza with strange contraptions. *The Automatoggler* included the Evolve-You Machine (which evolved you to a new you + machine); The Universe Works, a stage for presenting the inner workings of the universe; interactive musical devices that generated images of war and harmony; and an Input-Output Machine that, when people input their arms, would output tattoos, along with real *and* digital toast, and drawings based on doodles inserted by viewers. The evolution of this project veered away from the more streamlined and unified *Wormholes* toward a more ambitious, multifaceted installation.

This ever-evolving (continually revised) project became something entirely different for its third iteration, *The Zephyr Experiment*. Not as singularly themed as *Wormholes* and its journey through space-time, or as multidirectional as *The Automatoggler's* myriad of interactive installations, *The Zephyr Experiment* was a playful exhibit that dabbled with flight in numerous ways (FIGURE C.12).

FIGURE C.10 The League of Imaginary Scientists, *Wormholes*, MOCA, Los Angeles, 2011. Participants' replicated selves were sent through a series of tubes into the wormhole. Photo credit: TRYHARDER.

FIGURE C.11 The League of Imaginary Scientists, *The Automatoggler*, MOCA, Los Angeles, 2011. Participants turn the cranks and pull the levers to evolve in The Evolve-You Machine (background); The Universe Works, a finely tuned contraption by which Dr. Stephan Schleidan kept the intricate workings of the universe in order (foreground). Photo credit: Brian Mettee.

Viewers could transform themselves with live puppetry into winged flyers, interact with a floating Dr. Stephan Schleidan, build and then test experimental flying objects through propulsion devices, and partake in the launching of the largest paper airplane ever to be launched at MOCA (by the League). While the rocket launching was intimate (not intergalactic), *The Zephyr Experiment* made for a satisfying culminating event.

FIGURE C.12 The League of Imaginary Scientists, *The Zephyr Experiment*, MOCA, Los Angeles, 2011. A MOCA visitor participates in the Learn to Fly station. One participant puppeteers miniature models of wings, while another "flies" through the clouds in an animated atmosphere. Photo credit: LOIS.

The entire three-month residency was a blur of starting and stopping, a constant negotiation with MOCA—mostly to stay on top of publicity. Artists are not always eager to articulate what their projects will be one month before completion, sometimes not even after completion. For this residency, many of the advantages of being the artist—such as the freedom to ignore institutional constraints—were forfeited. The project became an ever-shifting collaboration with a place, a space, and even the people who organized and supported the residency. Revision was a constant.

Continuous, fast revisions like those demanded by these one-month art exhibitions require a slow-down period of reflection upon completion. Extremely fast developments need to be mulled over and digested, as did the League's three-project series at MOCA. Our ruminations on the experience produced insights into the nature of revision and art: artists need to constantly revise in order to create, yet artists resist revisions imposed by an external entity; revising artworks in a series results in a diversity in style, often leading the artist in a new direction.

Thoughtful revision requires time, which is often a luxury when dealing with institutional deadlines. Fortunately, the fast pace of accelerated creative development can lead to the elements of surprise and delight—two happy results of a whirlwind revisioning!

JOVENVILLE: BOARDSTORMING

Joven Orozco has been the mayor of Jovenville, his graphic design company located in Newport Beach, California, for more than 17 years. About eight years ago, while working with creatives from other companies such as Disney Consumer Products, Orozco realized that the primary mission of the creative collaboration was to share ideas about solving communication challenges. Since other creatives could understand ideas and visual directions without the aid of a fully developed comp (or composition), the Jovenville team developed a new way to share their brainstorming efforts and named it "boardstorming."

Instead of meeting with the client to discuss the usual three comps showcasing a simple solution, a middle-of-the-road solution, and a wild version of a solution (neatly, the simple-middle-wild comps), boardstorming allows creatives from Jovenville to showcase 30 to 50 possibilities, including everything on the board from sketch drawings, paper samples, and internet downloads as visual references or conversation starters (**FIGURES C.13** and **C.14**). The brainstorm process always happens in the design studio—boardstorming simply allows the clients to peak behind the curtain. Orozco notes that with three comps you often find out that you're wrong about a client's needs, brand, or strategic plan.

JOVEN OROZCO,
Mayor of Jovenville,
www.jovenville.com.

FIGURE C.13 Jovenville, 2010. Sample boardstorming board. © Jovenville LLC

FIGURE C.14 Jovenville, 2010. Boardstorm for the OC Waste & Recycling Annual Report.
© Jovenville LLC

REVISING CLIENTS

On another topic that came up in an interview, Orozco shared his strategies for coping with difficult clients. Everyone has hard-to-manage clients at some point. Here are a few tips you can borrow as you enter the professional industry:

- Develop a prequalifying procedure. For instance, Jovenville will not work with clients who spend their own money or who have not worked with an outside firm before. While this limits the clientele and may exclude independent or start-up businesses, Orozco shared that people who spend their own money will pick at the design obsessively and ask for more revisions than were originally contracted. "A seasoned marketer or creative at another company," he said, "will understand deadlines and the process that a Mom-and-Pop wouldn't [know]."

- Diversify your clients. No single client at Jovenville ever defines more than 33% of the business's revenue. If a client becomes unprofitable, the team will finish the contracted work and move on.

- Allow the tough clients to "fire themselves." If a client was unprofitable, for instance due to extensive revisions, then the rate would be increased the next time the client called with a job. Clients will either pay for their former unprofitability after the fact or terminate the relationship.

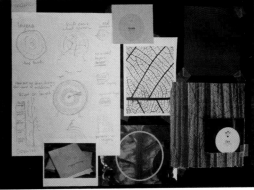

FIGURE C.15 Jovenville, 2010. One of the three creative directions chosen to move forward was to merge visuals suggesting "transparency" (left image) and "organic" (right image) in order to suggest the relevance of these themes in the OC Waste & Recycling Annual Report. © Jovenville LLC

"It's OK to be wrong," he said, "but it's easier to be wrong in an earlier process of discovery." Boardstorming, he emphasized, helps open a dialogue with the client about what you can't do. Knowing a client's limitations early in the design process is a crucial step in arriving at those final three comps.

After boardstorming with fellow creatives proved helpful, Jovenville took an experimental leap of faith by sharing this revision process with marketing clients. Marketing professionals are usually not trained visual communicators—your job as an artist or designer is in part to educate your viewers, collaborators, commissioners, and clients. When the boardstorm for the OC Waste & Recycling Annual Report was sent to the City of Irvine, for instance, Jovenville received a call asking, "What is *this*?" Of course, after meeting and reviewing each concept on the board, the team was better equipped to design the report. As proof of Jovenville's success, the final report was selected as one of *Graphis's* top 100 annual reports of 2010.

The boardstorming team at Jovenville might include up to three designers and two interns.

Boardstorming is not the end of the revision process (FIGURE C.15). Typically, the Jovenville team will review all ideas on the board with a client. Within that meeting, ideas that surpass the limits of the brand or simply don't meet the client's needs are removed. By the end of the meeting, there might be eight rough ideas left. From this, three comps (simple, middle, and wild revisions) are produced before a second round of revisions is created. After this, the final design is approved (FIGURES C.16 AND C.17). Boardstorming helps the design team learn about the client so that the initial round of comps is likely to fit the client's needs.

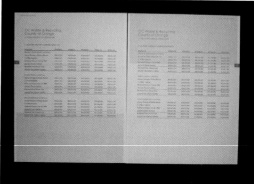

FIGURE C.16 Round 1 designs, clockwise from the top left: cover design, internal spread (A), financial spread, internal spread (B).
© Jovenville LLC

FIGURE C.17 Jovenville, 2010. Round 1 comps became the final design strategy for the OC Waste & Recycling Annual Report.
© Jovenville LLC

CONCLUSION

As mentioned in the introduction to this coda, the *Cult of Done Manifesto* makes no room for revision, while simultaneously alluding to the idea that all design work is a form of editing. The artists' and designers' stories in this coda suggest otherwise. Revision is a stage of development. However, it can be one that happens during any phase of the design process. While Jovenville's boardstorming demonstrates that revision is essential at the beginning of the design process, Michael Demers's revisions allowed the concept to guide the execution of the process in arriving at the final work of art. Revision is a personal process. As such, there are no rules or methods that will guarantee success. Unlike the binary nature of digital ones and zeros, revision is a subjective part of the design process. It may be led by intuition or feedback.

With this in mind, there are no exercises or directives that I could write for you in order to better revise one of your former projects. Instead, I'll simply state the obvious. Now that you've completed all of the chapters in this book, you'll notice that the design projects you created when you were in command of the content and skills presented in the first half of the book are not nearly as rich or complex as those you've developed in the latter half. It's probably time to revise!

INDEX

NUMBERS

2pxBorder, 41

A

Adams, Ansel, 61–62, 93, 100
Add Anchor Point tool, for modifying shapes, 49
additive processes, 109–111
Ades, Dawn, 128
adjustment layers
    for hue, saturation, and brightness, 116–117, 171, 177–178
    levels adjustment layer, 103–106, 172
    nondestructive editing and, 156
Adobe Bridge
    Batch Rename tool in, 82–84
    digital photography and, 67
    organizing digital photos, 80–81
    Output workspace, 85–88
Adobe Illustrator
    arranging stacking order of elements, 45
    creating circles, 10
    creating text boxes, 247
    file presets, 11–12
    Pathfinder panel, 188
    typographic treatment with, 208
Adobe InDesign
    creating document for sharing on web, 261
    placing text in text frames, 270–271
    preparing files for placement, 275
    scaling images, 268
    typographic treatment with, 208
Airey, David, 42
Albers, Josef, 112–113
alignment
    Align panel, 19
    of basic shapes, 46–47
    guides and, 264–265
    left, right, centered, justified, 238–239
    of rows of dots, 17–20

    on rule-of-thirds grid, 78–79
    of text boxes, 252
    typographic styles and, 273–274
alpha channels, 184. *See also* layer masks
analog, combining with digital techniques, 285
anchor points
    creating shapes, 44
    defining circle edges, 14
    modifying paths, 165–167
    modifying shapes, 48–50
    moving, 232
    Pen tool and, 154
    tracing an image with Pen tool, 162–164
    in vector graphics, 10, 43
aperture priority, 66, 77
aperture size, 72
appropriation practice, 133
apps, screen resolution for, 183
Arnheim, Rudolf, 39
artboard
    Artboard tool, 232
    creating shapes on, 43–45
    duplicating, 47–50
    features of, 12
artists/designers, communication with clients, 281
ascenders, of a letter, 203
Atkins, Anna, 128
augmented reality, 182
Azzarella, Josh, 137

B

background
    adding color to, 55–57
    creating background layers, 136, 140
    with repeated dots, 15–17
    shifting nature of, 7–8
backward compatibility, 37
Barthes, Roland, 42
baseline, of a letter, 203
Batch Rename tool, 82–84
Bauhaus school, of art and design, 113, 234
Bayard, Hippolyte, 128

Beck, Harry, 233, 235
Bézier handles
    controlling curves, 43
    creating curved paths, 154
    modifying paths, 165–167
    repositioning, 49–50
    tracing an image with Pen tool, 162–163
bitmap graphics
    digital photography and, 61
    pixels in, 10
    value/tonal range in, 91–92
bits, 4
black-and-white photo, applying color to, 125
Blank, Harrod, 65
blended images
    adding gradients and layer masks, 197–199
    adding vector mask, 192–193
    articulating the design challenge, 186
    combining vector shapes, 187–189
    creating basic button, 193–194
    creating layer groups, 195–196
    gradients, 184–185
    layer effects, 190–192
    networked technologies and, 180–182
    overview of, 179
    screen resolution, 183
    vector shapes, 183
blending modes, color, 120–121
blogjects, 180
boardstorming, at Jovenville, 293–296
Botanicalls project, 180–182
bracketing technique, 75–76
Brady, Mathew, 68, 80–81
branding, guidelines for design, 282–284
Braque, Georges, 133
Brautigan, Richard, 256
Breton, André, 131
Bringhurst, Robert, 238
brushes
    adding brushwork texture, 285
    adding details, 53–54